ALAN
RICKMAN
The Unauthorised Biography

Revised and Updated Edition

Maureen Paton

To Liam

This revised and updated edition first published
in Great Britain in 2003 by
Virgin Books Ltd
Thames Wharf Studios
Rainville Road
London W6 9HA

First published in 1996 by Virgin Publishing Ltd

First paperback edition published in 1997 by Virgin Publishing Ltd

A catalogue record for this book is available from the British Library.

ISBN 0 7535 0754 4

Typeset by TW Typesetting, Plymouth, Devon

Printed and bound by
Mackays of Chatham PLC

CONTENTS

ILLUSTRATIONS

ACKNOWLEDGEMENTS

In November 1994, I asked Alan Rickman via his agent whether he would be interested in co-operating with a biography to be published in the landmark year of his 50th birthday. In January 1995, Alan wrote me a scrupulously polite refusal in what the denizens of *Wayne's World* would call 'most excellent' handwriting; the influence of his art-school training is immediately apparent in the calligraphy.

Mal Peachey, my editor at Virgin, was so persuasive, however, that I decided to go ahead with the book. I informed Alan of my intentions, jokily begging him not to reach for the elephant-gun or the smelling-salts. He sent me another handwritten letter: 'Looking backwards is a strange thing to do – I will do it, but not now. It would take the smelling-salts, the elephant-gun and a large dose of hindsight to change my mind . . .' Looking back is, indeed, a strange thing to do; but in this case, it has been a fascinating and worthwhile exercise to study this unique actor and director. And when Virgin asked me to update the biography six years after the first edition, the case for a second edition seemed overwhelming in view of Rickman's output since 1996.

I am particularly indebted to the following people for their help: Peter Barnes, Stephen Davis, Jenny Topper, Thelma Holt, Blanche Marvin, Jonathan Powell, Catherine Bailey, Jules Wright, Jane Hackworth-Young, Stephanie Pennell, Gwenda Hughes, Michael Bogdanov, Clare Venables, Richard Wilson, Howard Davies, Ruby Wax, Christopher Hampton, Maggie Todd, Christopher Biggins, Dusty Hughes, Mike Newell, Peter James, Stephen Poliakoff, Harriet Walter, Adrian Noble, Emma Hardy, Nigel Hawthorne, Simon McBurney, Mary Whittingdale, Roger Spottiswoode, Clifford Williams, Stephen Crossley, Johnny Perkins, Trevor Nunn, William Burdett-Coutts, Saskia Reeves, James Shaw of the Shakespeare Birthplace Trust, Dave Granger, Paddy Wilson, Chris Taylor, David Rich of Channel 4, Nigel Orton and Chris Hammond of Latymer Upper School, Edward Stead, Matthew Bond, Barry Burnett, Wendy Dixon of West Acton Primary School, Charlotte Tudor, Charles Frater of Silverglade, Theresa Hickey, Ian Francis and Jonathan Donald of the *Kensington News*, John Prebble, Robert Cushman, Robert Holman, Ang Lee, Susanna Horng, Simon Langton, June Winters and Judy Arthur of Home Box Office, Iain Coleman, Peter Savage, Martin Reddin, Sheridan Fitzgerald, Susie Figgis, James Shirras of Film Finances Services Ltd, Ian Herbert of *Theatre Record*, Max Stafford-Clark, Snoo Wilson, Philip Hedley, John Byer and others who wished to remain anonymous.

Finally, I would like to thank my editors Mal Peachey and Kirstie Addis and my agent Judith Chilcote for their rigorous encouragement and advice, and my husband Liam Maguire for putting up with me.

PROLOGUE: VINEGAR IN THE SALAD

Call him a luvvie at your peril. According to one of his oldest female friends, he's the epitome of passive aggression. The passive-aggressive syndrome in psychology sounds impressive, but needs to be demystified. It used to be known as 'silent insubordination' in the Army: in other words, good old-fashioned bloody-mindedness. This syndrome says everything about the stubborn temperament of the internationally renowned British actor Alan Rickman. You can see just how this tall and scornful perfectionist, the nonpareil of nit-pickers, came to embody a formidable intelligence and reined-in power. He could never play a weakling.

At just over 6ft 1in and big-boned with it, he has the haughty bearing of a natural aristocrat. All his showiest roles point to a sense of innate superiority, from the terrorist Hans Gruber in *Die Hard* and the Sheriff of Nottingham in *Robin Hood: Prince Of Thieves* to the megalomaniacal Rasputin in the film of the same name and the disdainful Professor Severus Snape, scourge of the schoolboy wizard, in the *Harry Potter* films. It's a look that says he's a member of the theatrical master-race.

Which is a problem, since he's also a member of the Labour Party. Paradoxically, this enigmatic actor is a painter and decorator's son from working-class Irish and Welsh stock who was raised on a west London council estate. Given his high-profile support of socialism, he's oddly private about his humble background and doesn't do the cloth-cap-and-clogs routine. He has a rarity value, since he gives little away about himself. Alan Rickman, as all his many friends in the business testify, has a horror of anything that smacks of self-promotion. He backs shyly into the limelight. At the same time that he simultaneously opened in *Harry Potter and the Philosopher's Stone* and in the West End with an acclaimed revival of Noël Coward's *Private Lives*, Alan Rickman's sepulchral rasp could also be heard as the Genie of the Lamp for the Christmas pantomime *Aladdin* in one of the poorest boroughs in London. He recorded the performance for free on the condition that there was a publicity black-out.

Rickman has a strange aura around him that is extremely successful. However, he's also known to be socialistic and has avoided the honours trap. So he trails this remarkable integrity by being very Jesuitical about publicity; yet on the other hand he's a famous actor.

Indeed, on screen and stage, he can project everyone's idea of seigneurial decadence; an impression that gained hold when he played the first and best incarnation of the vicious Vicomte de Valmont in the acclaimed Royal Shakespeare Company production of *Les Liaisons Dangereuses*. Yet Alan Rickman longs to be thought of as a true man of the people. Inevitably, there is a conflict between his past and his present that he has never quite resolved.

Those narrow Grand Vizier eyes, the colour of pale amber, seem to look down his long nose. There is something of the Marquis de Sade in his anachronistic appeal to women as an arrogant, feline fop. His sudden gestures can be transfixing: Rickman has the most extraordinary way of laughing quietly with a sort of silent snicker, a grimace that contorts his face.

His personality is piquantly flavoured sweet-and-sour, Chinese style. The two phrases that crop up most about him are: 'He doesn't suffer fools gladly' and 'He's a guru.' They are by no means mutually exclusive; one has the feeling that, for many admiring acolytes, the rigorously principled Rickman has the elevated status of a jealous god who is just as likely to smite the sinful with a plague of boils as to reward the godly with his gracious approbation. They look up to him even though Rickman himself has admitted that his main vice is 'a wounding tongue. I'm working on it; perhaps it's the Celt in me.'

In a notoriously insecure industry, he is regularly paged for advice as if he were a Delphic oracle. 'He likes to be everyone's guru,' says the playwright Stephen Poliakoff. Rickman keenly feels the powerlessness of the actor's passive role, which is why he's a great organiser of support networks for fellow thespians. He espouses causes. In his heart, he's Don Quixote; in his head, he's Sancho Panza.

Yet he has his own raging insecurities, which may account for the public sulks when he can seem a spectacular misery-guts. There is the recurring stage fright that affects this most theatrical of animals: 'I get gremlins in my head, saying, "You're going to forget your lines",' he told *The Times* magazine in 1994. Film was a liberation in more ways than one. In June 2002, after a triumphant Broadway opening with an acclaimed, award-winning

London revival of Noel Coward's *Private Lives* that reunited the *Les Liaisons Dangereuses* team of Rickman, Lindsay Duncan and director Howard Davies, Rickman told the US TV interviewer Charlie Rose: 'I think I'm better at the stage work because of film work. The trouble in the theatre is that there's this huge fear. It's something that I guess is connected to adrenaline and focus and energy, but it's a useless thing – like some gremlin that sits on your shoulder and tries to make you fail. And often succeeds. At least on film if you screw up, you know there's another take. And it [the fear] doesn't get any better. I'm seriously thinking of trying to find some kind of hypnosis that will get rid of it.'

Sometimes there's a sense of simmering resentment underneath his surface calm; if he's the proverbial cold fish (given that there's no such thing as a warm fish), he is one that swims in hidden depths.

Occasionally, a bitterness breaks surface: 'Some actors have opportunities and shapes given to them,' he once said to John Lahr in *Woman's Journal*, January 1993. 'Not me. I've had to guide my career and seize any opportunity that came my way.' He made his first film, *Die Hard*, at the late age of 42 because he came cheap.

One publicist remembers with a shudder how rude Rickman was to her when he was still unknown. Perhaps it was simply her proximity to the Press, because he detests the snap judgements and pigeon-holing tendencies of the Fourth Estate. Yet scores of actors and writers testify to his warmth and kindness, even if he's not nearly so supportive of directors as a breed. 'All his roles have attitude,' as one former associate, the theatre director Jules Wright, puts it. 'Directors fear to take him on.'

'Alan has a lot of attitude . . . which is another aspect of control,' says his playwright friend Stephen Davis. 'I get the impression it's a bit arbitrary. He does have this awesome side to his character. Alan Rickman is the only person I know who will make me nervous about what I'll say next. He won't let you be self-pitying or gratuitous.'

In Hollywood, he has achieved the status of a brand-name: they now routinely refer to 'an Alan Rickman role' whenever they want someone with the gift of playful evil.

This multi-faceted man, who also created the comedienne Ruby Wax and discovered the award-winning playwright Sharman Macdonald, has walked away with film after film by turning his villains into warped tragic heroes with an anarchic sense of humour. Indeed, he's had such a spectacular career in grand larceny on screen that no one would guess he was born with a speech defect. It has made him so self-conscious about his voice that he still fears death by review as his frustration and despair at the critical mauling for his National Theatre debut in *Antony and Cleopatra* in 1998 showed only too clearly. After that disaster at the age of 52, he told one friend that he felt like never going back to the theatre again – even though he will say to people that he never reads reviews. Yet Rickman's bravura assurance and style has given him a greater following than Hugh Grant, fifteen years his junior.

'Alan has a quality which is attractive to both men and women. It's what makes star quality: it means that *everyone* is looking at you,' points out Jules Wright. 'Ian McKellen and Mick Jagger have it too; so do Alan Howard and Alec Guinness. There's an ambivalence: they're not macho, but they're not particularly feminine, either. There's an ambiguity there.'

The bizarre downside to the public fascination with this intriguing maverick comes in the form of sackloads of intrusive and obscene mail from otherwise respectable women, for whom he represents some kind of sexual release from repression. A typical letter to Alan Rickman goes: 'Dear Mr Rickman, I have always considered myself a staunch feminist, but you have a very disturbing effect on me . . .'

Even worse was the malicious correspondence from a (male) grudge-bearer who found out where he lived and made a point of sending him any bad reviews he could find.

For no one ever feels tepid about Alan Rickman. He inspires fierce loyalty, admiration and widespread affection, but some are highly critical of his apparent intractability.

'He's too intelligent to be an actor,' is the blunt opinion of one friend. That sets up a constant tension, partly because Alan is a frustrated director and partly because he entered the business at a relatively late age.

He has acquired a reputation for being difficult, culminating in damaging publicity on the litigation over the film *Mesmer*. The movie that was to provide him with his first lead role in the cinema became mired in law-suits. Rickman stood accused of intellectual arrogance; yet the real truth about *Mesmer* is more complex than mere tantrums. Alan himself, always his own fiercest critic, did concede in front of a packed audience for a question-and-answer session at the West Yorkshire Playhouse in 1995 that fame had probably corrupted him 'to some extent' by causing a mild outbreak of childish foot-stamping. Yet he had told Duncan Fallowell in the *Observer* a year earlier, 'There are plenty of people more "difficult" than me. Juliet Stevenson, for example. I would say that "difficult" means a highly intelligent human being who asks pertinent questions and tries to use her or himself to the fullest extent.' So there; trust Rickman to answer his carpers by turning the criticism into a compliment and throwing it back at them as a challenge. Even, it has to be said, at the risk of pomposity.

There is also an extraordinary allegation that, in the wake of the so-called Rivergate fiasco that lost him the chance to run his own London arts centre, Alan Rickman was seen handing out copies of a published letter of support from leading drama critics to a bemused queue at a fashionable London fringe venue. Not to mention a stand-up row in the foyer of another theatre with his rival to run Riverside, which had never – until this book – been reported. There's even talk of a confidential document that went missing.

Despite his languid image, there is clearly a lot of the street activist left in this former art editor of a radical 60s freesheet that was based in London's answer to San Francisco's Haight-Ashbury: Notting Hill Gate.

'Having done something else before acting made him a better actor,' says the writer Peter Barnes, a long-standing friend. 'It was a very deliberate U-turn.' The theatre director Michael Bogdanov, another mate, agrees: 'It's often an advantage in starting late as he did. Actors go to drama school far too young.' Alan has all the doubts of the late starter, with an understandable neurosis about his age: no one in his inner circle knew in advance about his landmark 50th birthday in February 1996. 'His age was a closely guarded secret,' says Stephen Poliakoff. 'Actors are much more secretive about their age than actresses.'

At the age of 38, a gloomy Rickman was in almost Gogolian despair about his long-term prospects in a wayward career that seemed to be going nowhere. Jules Wright remembers one outburst in Sloane Square at two in the morning after a meal. 'Alan suddenly said to me, "Nothing's ever going to happen for me. No one will ever notice me. My career isn't going to go anywhere." '

He also told *GQ* magazine: 'I lurch from indecision to indecision. All I ever seem to do is smash up against my own limitations. I have never felt anything but "Oops, failed again".'

As with all great actors, he takes a lot of calculated risks that have inevitably meant several brushes with failure. After learning his trade and paying his dues in provincial repertory theatre, he joined the Royal Shakespeare Company for a short and unhappy season in which he thought himself an unattractive misfit. He felt compelled to leave because, as he put it, he wanted 'to learn how to talk to other actors on stage rather than bark at them.'

As a television unknown in the early 80s, he went on to steal the BBC drama series *The Barchester Chronicles* as an ambitious young clergyman whose divine unctuousness upstaged such major players as Donald Pleasence, Geraldine McEwan and Nigel Hawthorne. Later he explained that, typically for Alan, he based Obadiah Slope on all the Tory politicians he detested, starting with Norman Tebbit and Margaret Thatcher. That was the first of many defiant challenges. Rickman rarely gives interviews; but when he does, they can be more like military skirmishes.

His shiftiness had become a star turn, yet he was still a recognisable face rather than a name. Only when he was invited back to the RSC in 1985 for a second chance did he reveal his true range in the leading part of the Vicomte de Valmont.

However, playing a professional seducer in *Les Liaisons Dangereuses* for almost two years nearly drove him mad: the political ideals that now make him feel guilty about his immense Hollywood bankability also make him yearn to be thought of as one of life's good guys. Yet there he is, playing a rapist or a murderer. It offends his puritanical streak.

'We had a harmonious relationship: affection is important to him,' insists the film director Mike Newell, who worked with him on *An Awfully Big Adventure*. 'He has private demons,' admits Peter Barnes.

One of them is his ambivalent attitude towards the sexual power that has played its part in making him a major star. 'Alan is incredibly aware of his professional sexual charisma,' says Stephen Davis. 'He has hordes of women writing to him. There is evidence that it gets in the way, and he wants to avoid being cast for it.

'He's not an exploitative person in his private life, not in the remotest a sexual predator. He's vexed by this image, this matinée-idol hold over the audience. In his personal life, he has enormous self-control . . . unnervingly so.' Alan was to remark tartly: 'I have never been remotely sexually voracious, whatever that is . . . but maybe I'll be sexually voracious next week.' In the grand old tradition of keeping them guessing, it was another example of his dry sense of humour.

For Rickman is a one-woman man who has known Rima Horton, his first and only girlfriend, for more than three decades. Their fidelity to each other is a legend. 'He's similar to John Malkovich, though not, perhaps, to Valmont in *Les Liaisons*, the character they both played, except in one important respect. Alan is quite unpromiscuous – which is very rare for actors,' says a friend, the playwright Dusty Hughes. Like Jean-Paul Sartre and Simone de Beauvoir or the late Peter Cook and his last wife, Alan and Rima keep separate establishments within a mile of each other. In 1989 they split up in order to stay together – but apart.

I interviewed Alan Rickman over the telephone in 1982 for a feature in the *Daily Express* on his performance as the oleaginous supercreep Obadiah Slope in *The Barchester Chronicles*. This breakthrough role introduced him to millions and made women, in particular, aware of his perverse sexiness. In that role, he sulked for Britain. He sounded suspicious to the point of hostility until I started inserting a few jokes about Slope into the conversation to lighten the atmosphere. I could almost hear the Titanic-sized iceberg slowly cracking up and defrosting at the other end of the line as the voice relaxed.

Given that he was playing a woman-chaser with such slithery conviction, questions about his own domestic set-up seemed justifiable, especially since he had managed to reach the age of 36 without the ritual march to the altar. In appropriately churlish Slope mode, Alan refused to discuss his private life. Later, someone told me that he had lived with the same woman for a long time. Just how long, not even their best friends knew.

I was subsequently to discover that Rima Horton and Alan Rickman have been together since the mid-60s, an impressive record by any standards whether in or out of wedlock. He met Rima, a labourer's daughter who became an economist and politician, at Chelsea College of Art in 1965. They appeared on stage in various amateur productions when he was nineteen and she was a year younger. That early shared interest plus his exact age – Alan is as vain as the next man – and his second name of Sidney were his most closely-guarded secrets. Not even Rima's friends knew that she was once an actress in the dreaded Ham Dram; perhaps she is too embarrassed to mention it in the same breath as Alan's career.

They are considered to have one of the strongest relationships in the business despite – or perhaps because of – the absence of children. It has survived the setting up of separate flats, when Alan decided he needed his own space and moved out of Rima's apartment to buy a maisonette.

Though the decision alarmed all their friends for quite a while, the arrangement seems to suit them both. So far they are as solid as ever. If he is a pessimist, she is an optimist. 'Rima has a very sunny nature, she's very pragmatic with her feet on the ground,' says Peter Barnes. 'It helps that she's not in the profession herself, a great help.' Espousing the easy-go attitudes of the 60s, they have never bothered to get married. Who needs a ring for commitment? Yet Peter Barnes, Alan's oldest friend after Rima, told me when I met up with him again over a plate of oysters in August 2002 that he had a gut feeling Alan and Rima would suddenly surprise everyone and tie the knot one day after all. 'I'm expecting their marriage to happen; it's the old romantic in me. And as he goes up the aisle, I shall be laughing madly,' Peter added fondly. Such steadfastness is remarkable in Rickman's peripatetic profession, since he necessarily spends much of his time abroad on location. 'Rima and Alan are like-minded people – it's a common-law marriage of true minds,' says the playwright Stephen Davis. 'They were once in CND together. They argue a lot about politics.' Indeed, a fervent political discussion is their idea of a good night in.

Alan has acknowledged that the reason for their relationship's longevity is that Rima is 'tolerant. She's incredibly, unbelievably tolerant. Possibly a candidate for sainthood.' And why, pray, does she need to be so tolerant? 'Because I'm an actor,' he added, only too aware of the self-obsession and insecurity that his profession breeds. 'I've never learned that trick of leaving business behind in the rehearsal room; I bring all problems home, I brood. But Rima just laughs and goes straight to the heart of the matter. No matter what problems she has, she puts her head on the pillow and goes straight to sleep.' Sounds like the perfect personality for politics, an arena where only the calm (or thick-skinned) survive. Actors, on the other hand, can, and certainly do, use their neuroses in their work. As the film director Mike Newell was later to say: 'Alan is neurotic but intense, incredibly focused and authoritative as an actor. All his insecurities as a person are completely healed by acting.'

Certainly it was impossible to imagine the mean-spirited, calculating Slope, forever in pursuit of rich widows and richer livings, as having a stable home life. Obadiah was anybody's, if they were wealthy enough. But Alan's remote air gives him an unattainable quality, which makes him a challenge; hence the intense female interest in him.

As the theatrical agent Sheridan Fitzgerald, his former leading lady at the RSC, remarks: 'Women are always falling in love with the unattainable.'

'Alan's too serious to be flirtatious,' says Jules Wright. 'He's not aware of his attractiveness, which of course is what makes him really sexy on stage. He's very grunge to look at in his private life, he doesn't run around flashily at the Ivy,' she adds, referring to the famous showbusiness restaurant in London's West End.

Rickman slops around in blue jeans and polytechnic-lecturer jackets in real life, looking deliberately downbeat. With his hair brushed forward over his forehead, he is almost unrecognisable. There are times when he looks as if he shops at Oxfam, although Peter Barnes, whose only sartorial concession to his own success has been to grow a beard, playfully points out that 'if he dresses down, he dresses down very expensively these days. But he's more or less the same Alan.'

'You won't find Alan guzzling champagne in some nightclub or driving a fast car,' says another friend, drama-school principal Peter James. 'He's like Bob Geldof – scruffy, yet asking serious questions.'

The forces of political correctness maketh the New Man, of course, and actor Christopher Biggins has the feeling that Alan is '. . . snobby. I often see him at dos and I think he looks like a maths teacher. He comes across as a sexual animal; you feel he's going to be brilliant in bed. But you wouldn't think he's an actor. There's no reaction. No sense of humour. Of course, he may be very, very nervous.'

(And with Mr Biggins – who has quite an edge to him under that jovial exterior – glowering at the apparent reincarnation of his least favourite teacher, who can blame him? But Biggins was right about the sexual aura, if a later remark by Rickman himself is anything to go by. 'Sitting around a table with good friends, some sympathy, nice wine, good talk, what could be better than that? Except sex? Or getting it right on stage,' he said, leaving us in little doubt how highly he placed sex as a priority. Because Rickman would never include any other leisure activity in the same order of importance as stage acting without meaning exactly what he said.)

'There is a chip on the shoulder. It doesn't surprise me that he was brought up on a council estate; so was I. But you either have a chip or you deal with it,' says Christopher, who makes no bones about being a true-blue Tory. 'These champagne socialists are very odd. I have a feeling that Alan surrounds himself with a close circle who are very protective. Some people don't want fame. They like it; but they don't want it,' he adds shrewdly.

Rickman's first property purchase back in 1989 was a spacious maisonette, part of an elegant Italianate terrace of Victorian houses in west London's fashionable Westbourne Grove. In 2001, he sold up and moved on to an even larger flat nearby. When he can, he pops over to France to a holiday cottage.

Until his mother's death in 1997, he lived just three tube stops away from her neat council house, only a few streets from Wormwood Scrubs prison with a bingo palace, DIY superstore and snooker hall nearby. His mother and younger brother Michael bought this trim semi-detached home together under the Right To Buy scheme introduced by the Tories and deplored by all Old Labourites. Alan visited her regularly; he has always had a good relationship with his family, even though he keeps those two worlds separate most of the time.

Though he would always see his mother, he seems to find it diffficult to come to terms with his background, to fit his family into his life as an actor.

His elder brother, David, works for a graphic design company and Michael is a professional tennis coach. They live quiet and modest lives far away from showbusiness circles, though they get on well with the famous member of the family.

'Class has been a bizarre accident that happened to Alan,' observes Stephen Davis. 'We were the post-Beatles generation: we invented ourselves. Alan's background is a major influence on him, though. He moves in a privileged world but refuses to forget his past. He wants to be sure that he's not confused in his own shaving mirror about who he is.'

Peter Barnes has a different perspective: 'My own feeling is that Alan has created himself. The persona has created him; the mask becomes the face. His family look very different. Actors have created themselves, they know exactly who they are. I haven't got the same confidence he's got on the phone, but then everyone recognises his voice because most actors have distinctive voices. Whereas I always feel I have to introduce myself by saying, "It's Peter, Peter Barnes."'

Another friend, Blanche Marvin, agrees: 'Alan likes to feel he's his own creation.' In other words, this fiercely independent man won't be beholden to anyone.

In some ways Rickman is a man born out of his time: there's a dark and disturbing retro glamour about this saturnine actor that really fires up an audience's imagination.

He's the antithesis of the bland boy-next-door with an Everyman persona, with whose unthreatening ordinariness millions of movie-goers will identify. And costume roles particularly suit Rickman because of that air of patrician superiority. It goes with the sometimes frightening looks that recall a well-known portrait of the writer, scholar and intriguer Francis Bacon whose unblinking gaze was once likened by a contemporary observer to the stare of a watchful viper.

In an age that lets it all hang out, Rickman is famous for giving audiences more fun with his clothes on. And this despite the fact that, back in 1983, he let it all hang out in a nude scene for Snoo Wilson's play The Grass Widow, later recalling, 'It was a very strange thing to do. You have to pretend that it's not happening to you.' Because of that very public early lesson in the vulnerability of standing on stage with no clothes on, he is a past-master at portraying the art of sensual anticipation and sexual control. In fact, Rickman's Valmont, a role for which he seemed to have been waiting all his life, was carefully based on a seventeenth-century rake he had played on stage with the disconcerting name of Gayman.

'He looks like a Russian Borzoi dog, one of those silent wolfhounds with a long neck and silky white coat. You always wonder whether you should speak to a Borzoi, as well . . .' says Peter James. 'It's his frame and physical look, a quality of stillness.

It reminds me of some astonishingly aristocratic faces I saw in Russia, who looked as if they came from a different race.' How appropriate, then, that he should later take on the role of Rasputin.

Yet, for all his air of seigneurial self-control, he has big vulnerabilities. Alan was born with a tight jaw, hence the slightly muffled drawl: it must be one of the sexiest speech defects in the business. 'He doesn't have an active up-and-down movement of his jaw,' says Blanche Marvin, a former drama teacher.

'It's the way that he's generally physically co-ordinated: he has a lazy physical movement and a lazy facial movement. He's big-boned, and it's hard for him to move in a sprightly way.' Hence his lifetime's obsession with trying to move with the fluidity of a Fred Astaire.

Despite the working-class upbringing, that honeyed-buzzsaw voice was perfected at private school: Latymer Upper in Hammersmith, also Hugh Grant's Alma Mater.

Rickman, a clever child, won a scholarship there at the age of eleven. The process of reinventing himself, of keeping his past at arm's length, began as English teacher Colin Turner became his mentor, much as the playwright Ben Jonson, stepson of a bricklayer, was 'adopted' by his teacher Camden. Alan was only eight when his father died of cancer, and Turner filled that gap in his life.

Latymer Upper has been almost as great an influence upon his life as Rima continues to be. He is emotionally attached to the place that gave him such a superior start.

In the autumn of 1995, this former star pupil had a minor falling-out with his old school when he refused to allow his photograph to be used in a recruitment drive. His political convictions simply wouldn't allow him to publicly endorse a private, fee-paying education. Rickman melodramatically asserts that he was born 'a card-carrying member of the Labour Party', but he only finally joined in 1987 after he and Rima had enjoyed a relatively frivolous youth in CND.

Rumours attach themselves like barnacles to Alan Rickman, who is famously economical with the facts about himself. There was once a wild story that this friend of former Cabinet Minister Mo Mowlam and millionaire Labour supporter Ken Follett was a member of Vanessa and Corin Redgrave's Workers' Revolutionary Party. Yet Rickman is far too straight and astute to get involved with the lunatic fringe. He is an idealist, but he's also startlingly pragmatic.

Rima, an economics lecturer at Kingston University (formerly Polytechnic) in Surrey, who took early retirement in 2002 at the age of 55, is a Labour councillor and former prospective parliamentary candidate for Chelsea, the safest Tory seat in the country . . . hence her defeat in the 1992 General Election.

She subsequently endured the indignity of losing another battle. Despite the fact she was selected as Labour's candidate for the Mayoral elections in Kensington and Chelsea in 2001, friends now believe she is no longer looking for a safe Labour seat in Parliament but has forced herself to be philosophical. She still looks young enough to stand for election; Rima and Alan are a striking couple who could pass for a decade younger than they are. Not having had any children probably helps; so, too, does Rickman's thick, dark-blond hair, which for years he wore slightly long.

It is Rima who dictates the political and intellectual agenda. This is borne out by Peter Barnes, who recalls Alan deferring to his girlfriend's greater judgement when the two men met up at the funeral of the director Stuart Burge. After the service, Peter started raging on about the 'iniquities' of Tony Blair's New Labour government, but Rickman refused to take the bait. 'I'm very Old Labour and I think Alan is. At least, I hope he is. But he got very defensive at that point,' remembers Peter, 'and said that it was more Rima's area.' Alan, who graduated from two art colleges with diplomas in art, design and graphic design, is the creative one; Rima is the academic one of the two.

Rickman is very far from being the humourless grouch that his famously cross-looking demeanour suggests. Always droll, he has mellowed a lot over the years as success has given him more confidence. His sense of humour alone would have kept him out of the paranoid ranks of the WRP, which seemed to expend most of its energies on slagging off other far-Left groups.

'He's a bit of a Wellington with his ironic bon mots and his raised eyebrows,' says Stephen Poliakoff. 'He's self-critical and he doesn't have a naturally sunny disposition. But he's very life-enhancing, despite the pessimism: it's a curious combination. People find his dangerous wit attractive. He's quite lugubrious, but he's also quite teasable. Some people find him intimidating, but he just has to be provoked out of a pessimistic view of the world.

'Acting is very serious for him, but he's more relaxed now. He loves to talk. He likes to feel things are controlled; he doesn't like to feel too exposed.'

In his fifth decade, at times Rickman resembles the late Frankie Howerd, especially when his large, crumpled face is split by a great pumpkin-head grin.

One of the more endearing aspects of Alan Rickman, who is not an immediately cuddly person, is that he has never bothered to get his crooked and discoloured bottom teeth fixed. When he became a Hollywood star at a relatively late age, it didn't go to his head (or his teeth).

'He was never one of the lads,' according to his old friend, the theatre producer Patrick (Paddy) Wilson. Alan has no interest in the stereotypical male pursuits of pubs and sports, hence his vast number of close female friends.

'New writing and politics are his life. He has no car, no interest in sport,' says Peter Barnes, although Alan watches Wimbledon out of loyalty to his tennis-coach brother Michael. 'He's interested in politics and the wider world,' says Stephen Poliakoff.

All this may make him sound like the career woman's ideal consort, yet he surprisingly admits that he had to have male feminism knocked into him; he was once a primitive model.

Now, surrounded by a seraglio that includes the actresses Juliet Stevenson and Harriet Walter, the comedienne Ruby Wax and the impresario Thelma Holt, he is everyone's theatrical agony uncle. 'He's got the widest circle of friends and acquaintants I have ever known,' says Peter Barnes. 'In the theatre, he unites opposites – because he knows so many people.'

'The only person I know who has more friends than him is Simon Callow,' says Jenny Topper, Artistic Director of London's Hampstead Theatre and a friend of Alan's since 1981.

'It feels nice to be around him. He has a very loyal group of female friends: not a harem, but very intense. Alan is very loyal, very protective and very kind. He has strong views. He listens: he has that concentration, hence the female friends. He's also very proper: he cares about fans at the stage door and those who seek his advice and support.

'That gliding movement of his is almost balletic,' adds Jenny of the man who would be Fred Astaire. 'He's a great comic actor: the secret is timing. But his humour is very dry: he doesn't suffer fools gladly.'

'I associate him with complete integrity,' says Harriet Walter. 'He is a central figure in a lot of people's lives. He's not a guru as such; I don't think of him as a saintly, priestly person. It's not all grovelling at the feet of the effigy. He just makes you laugh. He's like a good parent . . . there's a feeling that Alan won't let you get away with things.

'He can be intimidating, though he doesn't realise how much. But there are precious few people whose judgement you trust, and he is one of them. I do argue with him; we don't always agree. He has pretty tough standards, but he's a very good listener. He takes you seriously, you feel encouraged.'

'Actors are always being judged on their physical qualities, which makes them very vulnerable,' says Stephen Poliakoff. 'And Alan has big vulnerabilities.'

'This business gives you the impression you have to be a pretty boy and be successful before you're thirty in order to succeed,' says Royal Shakespeare Company head Adrian Noble. 'Alan Rickman was never a pretty boy and was not successful before he was thirty.

'He never courted success, but his success now gives people hope in a society that adores youth in a rather sickening and dangerous fashion. It's very good news for those who are not the prettiest people in the world. It gives people hope, that Alan was a play-reader at a tiny Fringe theatre like the Bush and all those other things, before he became famous.

'He has a good mug: that big nose. You need a big nose and big hands to be a good actor: look at Michael Gambon. And in the Green Room, Alan is always surrounded by women.'

Ah, yes. One can't get away from the women in the Alan Rickman Factor. When he played a licentious Caesar in Peter Barnes' 1983 radio play *Actors,* Rickman received more ardent letters from teenaged girls than for any of his other roles.

However, it was the Vicomte de Valmont that first made his name on both sides of the Atlantic, establishing that all-important, crowd-pleasing quality of sexual danger.

Lindsay Duncan, his co-conspirator in *Les Liaisons Dangereuses*, said wryly to Allison Pearson in the *Independent on Sunday* in 1992: 'A lot of people left the theatre wanting to have sex, and most of them wanted to have it with Alan Rickman.' Of all the original RSC cast in Howard Davies' famous, much-travelled production, Rickman is the only one to have made it on the world stage. He was nominated for a Tony award, as was Lindsay; and it rankled heavily with Rickman when he lost the role in the 1988 film version *Dangerous Liaisons* to the younger (and balder but heavily be-wigged) John Malkovich.

Instead, the real turning-point for Rickman came when he was offered the role of the German terrorist leader Hans Gruber in the Hollywood big-budget thriller, *Die Hard*. Alan's frightening degree of menace, allied to a fastidious humour, marked out a major stylist who outshone the film's star, Bruce Willis. Rickman became an international name overnight as a result of his first-ever movie, since when he has conducted a dangerous flirtation with screen villainy.

He could see himself falling into the trap of being typecast and deliberately changed pace with a performance of tremendous warmth and sensitivity as the mischievous returning spirit of Juliet Stevenson's dead lover in Anthony Minghella's 1991 low-budget hit, *Truly Madly Deeply*.

It became Britain's answer to *Ghost*. And Rickman's wry, doomed romanticism in the role eventually led to his casting as Colonel Brandon in the highly successful, Oscar-winning *Sense And Sensibility*.

Truly Madly Deeply offered the closest insights yet into the real Rickman, capturing that quality of benign bossiness which those who know him find both endearing and exasperating. Close friends confirm that he is indeed the character he plays in the movie. It established Rickman and Stevenson as one of the great screen partnerships, building on a friendship that began at the RSC in the company of Ruby Wax.

With her irregular but arresting looks, the *jolie-laide* Juliet could almost be Rickman's twin. They are brother and sister in socialism, yet brigadier's daughter Stevenson is a left-winger from the right side of the tracks. It says much for Rickman's panache, however, that he always seems just as classy as she.

Rickman's next feature film was *Close My Eyes*, the story of an incestuous affair between a brother and a sister in which Alan took an uncharacteristically passive role as the heroine's cuckolded husband. Nevertheless, he still stole the show with an unforgettable combination of silent rage and vulnerability.

He returned to Hollywood to add another rogue to his gallery, the Sheriff of Nottingham, in 1991's *Robin Hood: Prince Of Thieves*. Rickman says he tried to make him 'certifiable and funny', in which enterprise he wildly succeeded. So hilariously flamboyant was he that the film's star Kevin Costner reputedly played the villain in the editing-suite and chopped a number of Rickman's scenes to try to correct the inbalance between lead and support. This was the role that established Rickman's 'dark and dirty' attraction for millions of otherwise respectable females. Rickman's occasional flashes of camp only add to the intrigue of his personality.

Blanche Marvin, whose Hollywood producer daughter Niki acted in repertory theatre with Alan at Leicester back in 1975, describes Rickman as '. . . a very male man. So many men in the theatre are bisexual or homosexual, but Alan is intensely masculine'.

That feral charm and mesmeric hold over an audience marked him out for his role as Rasputin, an offer that had been hanging around in his life for a long time. His casting as the deranged monk with the malign influence over the last Tsarina of Russia once again attests to Alan Rickman's unique alchemy.

'He has very strange looks, not necessarily what you would cast as the romantic lead,' admits Carlton TV's Jonathan Powell, one of the first to spot his screen potential. He looks like a magus, which is why he has often been suggested for Shakespeare's capricious magician Prospero: a complex, tormented man whose nature is divided between the malign and the benign.

People talk of his so-called cold smoulder; his sharp features give him an alien look, despite the lush and passionate lips. At one stage, Steven Spielberg had him in mind to play the timelord Dr Who on American TV, but Rickman didn't want to be locked into a long-running series. He keeps his options wide open. Those spiky looks, however, plague him. He hates being judged on his appearance, arguing that an actor is a blank canvas on whom one ought to be able to paint a portrait of anyone. He himself is a living contradiction of that.

He is the most individual of performers, quite unique and inimitable. No one can clone Alan Rickman; no one approaches his qualities. He is instantly recognisable, and there is a piece of himself up there on the screen every time.

There is always an extra dimension to his characterisation that creates a mythic quality; like all the cinema greats, he has a very strong sense of self. Rickman has long fought an inferiority complex: once upon a time, he seemed like a misunderstood misfit from a classic fairy-tale, an ugly duckling who has been transformed into an attractive man by the flukes of an extraordinary career. He was not easily marketable; and he was in despair at ever achieving lasting success. It was twenty years a-coming.

As with all the best character actors, it took him time to grow into his face and learn his strengths. More than anything, maturity made a major star of Alan Rickman. The toy-boy syndrome among ladies of a certain age is much exaggerated. Grown women tend not to fall for pretty youths as a rule; they appreciate character and experience in a man.

'In many ways, he's a European actor,' observes director Jules Wright. And there is a French expression that sums up the paradoxical appeal of life's *jolies-laides*: 'I like a little vinegar in my salad.'

Most assuredly, Alan Rickman is the astringent vinegar in the salad.

1. THE FAUSTIAN GIFT

'He does have this power and charisma,' says playwright Stephen Davis, one of Rickman's oldest friends. Alan, Rima and sometimes their friend Ruby Wax spend weekends with Stephen's family in Gloucestershire, a county where, according to Davis, the British class system is in its death throes. 'In *Die Hard* and *Robin Hood: Prince Of Thieves*, he was acting the cosmos off the screen and Hollywood was opening a five-lane highway to him.

'The thing about actors is that they have a tremendous effect on people: Alan does in particular. He has an extra effect which he is aware of, but which he isn't always planning. He has a huge sexual charisma, but in real life he doesn't aim for that effect at all. This is what makes his personality so complex. It's a bit Faustian, cutting both ways.

'When you talk to him, you feel there are a lot of notional audiences in his mind. You never catch him off-guard. He always knows his lines. It's a very actorly quality. It's like being the friend of some of the characters he plays.

'He is enigmatic, not least with his friends. Really, I should write a play about him. He's an important figure in the lives of all his friends, but one could do without the stardom bit. It would do him good to be less written about. When close friends become stars . . . All of us are leveraged on the amount of attention we get. And Alan can be contradictory, moody.

'When he has problems, he broods. He was doing an extraordinary number of mundane tasks at the bottom of my garden once, digging and so on, while he brooded about something. If I had something on my mind, I would have told the entire village about it. But he internalises things while presenting this equanimity to the world. Ian Richardson shares that quality a little, too.

'Alan dominates rehearsal rooms and productions: he's very critical, and he thinks very hard. There's a stormy element in self-absorption that becomes very critical. It's hard working with successful people. Alan is not necessarily the kind of actor I ought to want to work with, because he defends the role of the actor. Actors have an illusory power in society, but they don't write their own lines. They are ventriloquists' dummies.

'I don't really understand the impulse to act. You are disappearing into another person, and yet you are exposing yourself. In a way, actors don't really exist.

'By that, I don't mean that Alan is artificial – far from it,' Davis adds hurriedly. 'He has one of the most positive and strong presences I've ever met. But he doesn't really empathise with people who are off-balance: it's as if he's working from a script.'

Alan Rickman's 'script' began in 1946 with a busy New Year in the modest London suburb of Acton, then in the county of Middlesex. On 12 February, the local newspaper carried the story that a woman had hanged herself with a ventilator cord. A weapons amnesty for wartime firearms had also been announced: unlicensed pistols brought home as souvenirs by Forces personnel were to be presented to Acton Police Station by 31 March to avoid prosecution. The only other direct reminder of the recent world-wide conflict was a chilling report in the 1 March issue of the *Ealing And Acton Gazette* on a talk that a girl survivor of a concentration camp had given to the Acton Business And Professional Women's Club. 'You do not know what a man is unless you see him with absolute power,' this pale, quietly-spoken wraith told the assorted good ladies in their tailored business suits, cut from wartime utility cloth. 'If he has absolute power and is kind, then he is a real man.'

Couples were dancing to the sound of the Carroll Gibbons Blue Room Orchestra at Ealing Town Hall, and those who stayed at home grumbled that coal was rationed to 34 hundredweight for twelve months. Thieves had broken into a solicitor's house and stolen three suits plus a copy of Archibald's Criminal Pleading; and two builders were charged with an armed robbery of two Maltese seamen.

In the weepie *Tomorrow Is Forever* at the East Acton Savoy Cinema, Orson Welles (of all people) was listed dead in the war but returned home with a new face to find his 'widow', Claudette Colbert, had married again. Not that the romantics among picture-goers were completely ignored by the programme for the week beginning 18 February. Roy Rogers and Trigger – the horse that could do everything except wear a cowboy costume – shared top billing and a capacious nosebag in *Don't Fence Me In*.

Prominent 'Keep Death Off The Roads' advertisements in the *Gazette* issued dire warnings about motorcar accidents, giving the impression that west London was full of road-hogs. And on 21

February, Alan Sidney Patrick Rickman was born at home at 24, Lynton Road, Acton . . . the second son for painter and decorator Bernard Rickman and his wife Margaret Doreen Rose, née Bartlett.

Their first boy, David Bernard John, had been born during the last year of the war while his father was working as an aircraft fitter.

The family had rented a flat in an imposing red-brick Edwardian semi-detached house in a central Acton backwater, just one street away from the railway line. Alan's Irish father and Welsh mother belonged to what was once proudly known as the respectable working classes, steady workers with lower middle-class aspirations. Number 24 was a multi-occupied house: other rooms on the premises were rented by an elderly lady, Hester Messenbird, and by a married couple, Rupert and Violet Oliver. The Rickmans were always staunch Labour voters who put the red posters up in the window as soon as an election was announced.

Alan has always felt influenced by a prominent radical Rickman from an earlier age: Thomas Paine's friend and biographer Thomas 'Clio' Rickman (1761–1834) who was a bookseller and reformer. He was the son of Quakers and was apprenticed with a doctor uncle to study the medical profession. At seventeen, he met the freethinker Thomas Paine who worked as an exciseman in Rickman's birthplace of Lewes, Sussex. They both joined the Headstrong Club, which met at the White Hart Inn. Rickman's precocious taste for poetry and history earned him the sobriquet 'Clio', which became one of his pen names. Disowned by the Sussex Friends because of his friendship with Paine and his early marriage to a non-Quaker, he left Lewes and became a bookseller in London: first in Leadenhall Street and, later, at Upper Marylebone Street.

Paine completed the second part of *The Rights Of Man* while lodging at Rickman's house. The two friends formed a circle of reformers with such eminent names as Mary Wollstonecraft and Horne Tooke; Rickman sketched them all in his biography *The Life Of Paine*, published in 1819. Frequently in hiding as a result of selling Paine's seditious books, he fled to Paris several times. The friends finally parted at Le Havre on 1 September 1802, when Paine sailed to America.

A satirist from the age of fifteen and a composer of republican songs, Rickman's pieces often appeared in such weekly journals as

The Black Dwarf whose title was revived by the counter-culture of the 60s. He died on 15 February 1834, and received a Quaker burial at Bunhill Fields. There is no evidence that Alan's family are direct descendants, but Thomas Rickman's reputation 'resonated' (to use a favourite expression of Alan's) down the years and made Alan a searching, well-read child acutely aware of a radical world elsewhere. No one would ever be able to claim 'Forever Acton' as *his* epitaph.

The working classes made him, but it was *The Ruling Class* that revolutionised Alan Rickman. He melodramatically told his old friend Peter Barnes that the latter's first hit play, later filmed in 1972 with Peter O'Toole as a mad aristocrat, had 'changed his life'.

The Ruling Class was premièred in Nottingham in 1968 and quickly transferred to the West End, opening at London's Piccadilly Theatre. It was one of those rotten-state-of-the-nation plays that proved uncannily prophetic, with a peer of the realm accidentally killing himself by auto-erotic strangulation in the first scene. With its great leaps of logic, this flamboyant attack upon the British class system was also hugely, and ambitiously, entertaining. Peter aimed to create 'a comic theatre . . . of opposites, where everything is simultaneously tragic and ridiculous'. Since he and Tom Stoppard both began writing plays around the same time, it is debatable who influenced whom. Both are great showmen, vaudevillians with serious things to say.

Nearly three decades later, the Tory MP Stephen Milligan was found dead in similar circumstances; only then was the pleasurable purpose of this bizarre and dangerous practice duly explained to a bemused general public by the sexperts of the popular Press. But Barnes' anti-Establishment audacity, at a time when few dared acknowledge the fact that hanged men get hard-ons, had deeply impressed the young Rickman in 1968. After all, it was only three years since capital punishment for murder had been abolished; although death by hanging has remained on the statute-books for piracy and, as critics of the late Princess Diana's former lover, James Hewitt, love to keep pointing out, for treason.

Bernard and Margaret Rickman were to have two more children. Alan's younger brother, Michael Keith, arrived 21 months after Alan on 21 November 1947. The only daughter, Sheila, was born on 15 February 1950.

Alan was later to describe himself as a 'dreamy' child, wrapped up in his own little world as he scribbled and doodled. David and

Michael, too, had artistic leanings, with the same beautiful handwriting. 'Alan is a very talented water-colourist. He has this elegant, flowing, effortless calligraphy,' says Stephen Davis.

He was the clever, petted one of the family, the future scholarship child, although Alan the egalitarian took pains to emphasise in a *Guardian* interview with Susie Mackenzie in 1998 that his parents had no favourites and treated them all equally. His slow way of speaking meant that he received more attention: his parents had to listen carefully to his every word. Alan was particularly fond of his father Bernard. Ignatius Loyola, founder of the Jesuits, famously said: 'Give me the boy at the age of seven and I will give you the man.' Alan's confident masculinity and self-contained air of assurance were shaped by that early closeness with the saintly-sounding Bernard.

When Alan was only eight and the youngest, Sheila, was just four, their father died of cancer. Alan subsequently talked of 'the devastating sense of grief' in the household; they were rehoused by the council and moved to an Acton estate to the west of Wormwood Scrubs Prison, where his mother struggled to bring up four children on her own by working for the Post Office.

She married again briefly, but it lasted only three years. Clearly Bernard had been the love of her life, although Alan recalled the relationship between his Methodist Welsh mother and his Irish Catholic father had often been volatile: the clash of cultures would sometimes end in sounds of banging doors and weeping behind them. But, despite their lack of money and their cramped surroundings, the little family of six were happy.

Everything changed with his father's death. 'His death was a huge thing to happen to four kids under ten,' he said, remembering how his headmaster had come into his class and spoken in an undertone to the teacher as they both turned to look at Alan – who already knew what they were going to say. He was being summoned home, where he was to be told that his terminally ill father had died. It was thought best that the children should not go to the funeral, but they were shocked afterwards by the sight of their mother, who loved colourful clothes, dressed all in black for the first time.

In 2001, with the benefit of much hindsight into that ghastly time, he told interviewer Tim Sebastian on BBC News 24 that he had long since reached the conclusion that 'my mother was so distraught that she couldn't have coped with having her children there as well. But it was a strange thing not to be there. It's not explained to you,' he said, adding that, in those days, everyone unquestioningly believed in the 'ethic' that 'children should be seen and not heard'.

Alan has never forgotten the sense of loss that bereaved people have, of being 'deserted' by a dying parent. It is a mixture of sorrow and resentment on the part of the person left behind to mourn; a child, in particular, cannot grasp the dread inevitability of a terminal illness and feels bewildered by its outcome. By never marrying Rima, despite their long-term relationship, Alan instinctively protects himself against the possibility of loss or betrayal. The same goes for his position as a 'guru' to his many friends. It empowers him to be seen as someone who doesn't need conventional props, who generously gives but rarely requires anything in return. It was a power, a privilege that he never had as a poor child. He rarely lets people get too close; otherwise panic sets in.

Bernard's untimely death also thrust the family into an alien environment. Alan hated the stigma of growing up in what he perceived to be a working-class ghetto, particularly when he won his scholarship; homogeneous local-authority architecture was instantly recognisable as cheap mass public housing.

There was far more anonymity, and therefore more scope for an aspiring child's imagination, in a privately rented flat in Lynton Road, where you could always pretend you owned the entire house. Years later, Alan shuddered to his friends about the awfulness of growing up on – whisper who dares – a council estate. It is a strange kind of snobbery, perhaps peculiar to Britain because of its obsession with home-ownership. I remember feeling the same way when my mother and I were finally assigned a chilly but functional flat on a spartan council estate after we had lived happily for twelve years in my aunt and uncle's bathroomless, terraced Victorian house, a cosy slum by any other name. There was far more character in the latter, despite the lack of mod cons, but council estates seemed to mark you out in some way as a loser. They were not designed for the enrichment of the working classes; it was thought sufficient that their lives were enhanced by having a bathroom and an inside lavatory.

Alan's mother, Margaret, had always been a strong character, spiritually connected to those indomitable matriarchs that feature in Sean O'Casey's slum-life plays. Working-class families tend to be verbally and physically undemonstrative; you get on with life, you don't agonise about it. What's the use of talk? It doesn't get you anywhere. She carried on grimly.

The passive-aggressive type is one who digs his heels in, who wants things his own way, but not in a loud way. Very often there has been an early battle in childhood, but he rebels quietly. He smiles on the surface but won't comply. His mother is always a matriarchal figure. There is also an inherent narcissism, which is certainly true of Alan. It's not just in the way he always wears his enviably thick, lustrous hair slightly long, but also in wanting to be the wise man at the centre of a group. Alan was very influenced by Margaret's will to survive at all costs. His later role as an adviser to a wide circle of friends is based upon holding the balance of power, just as he saw his mother do. In effect, he became both parent and teacher following the example of his mother and his influential Latymer Upper teacher and mentor, Colin Turner.

Until her death in 1997, Margaret Rickman lived in the same modest house that she had made her own with replacement windows and a smart new fence around the front garden. Under the Tories' 'Right To Buy' policy, she and her youngest son, Michael, jointly purchased the council property after years of renting. The novelist, Peter Ackroyd, was brought up not far away in a street with the Anglo-Saxon name of Wulfstan and proudly claims that Wormwood Scrubs cast a longer shadow over his beloved childhood home. But then Ackroyd always did revel in the macabre. In one of those cheek-by-jowl arrangements between very different neighbourhoods in which London specialises, Alan was based only a few miles away from his mother.

Alan visited his mother regularly until the very end, particularly when her health first began to decline in 1995; he once turned up at an RSC Christmas party at the then Artistic Director Adrian Noble's house in north London, with some of Margaret's mince pies in Tupperware boxes. She had pressed them upon him at the end of his visit, not letting him go until he had taken something home with him 'to keep him going'. It's a very working-class thing: providing hospitality even for passing guests who stay five minutes, let alone your own grown-up children, is a huge matter of pride with working-class matriarchs.

Rickman himself told Mackenzie that his mother was as fiercely protective of her children as a tigress; similarly, his brothers and sister have had nothing but 'the fiercest pride' for the famous member of the family – 'and I for them'. His mother, he said, 'was incredibly talented herself; she would have had a career as a singer in another world.' Which is why he took her to see the Andrew Lloyd Webber musical *Phantom of the Opera* for her 80th birthday, with a party afterwards that Margaret entered 'like the star she was. I've never seen anyone enter a room like that,' he added.

'He doesn't hide his family,' Stephen Davis told me a few years before Margaret Rickman's death. 'His mother is a real matriarch, and he takes a lot of care with her. Strength of character is genetic; Alan tells funny stories about her sometimes.' Yet another friend says that Rima feels Alan has never quite come to terms with his working-class background. Way over to the east of the 'Scrubs', Rima's outside interests – her work as a grass-roots local politician enables her to keep close to the people in the way that an actor can do only through his fans – have included the governorship of Barlby School and North Kensington Community Centre.

Alan's younger brother, Michael, is also a west Londoner; and his older brother David lives in nearby Hertfordshire. The vast majority of actors come from comfortable, impeccably bourgeois backgrounds, and Alan is all too aware that he came from tougher roots. When he goes back to them, he takes care not to flaunt his lifestyle.

Peter Barnes says he saw a lot of his own mother (who died in 1981) in Margaret Rickman. 'Alan and I came from the same background; both of us weren't in a position to buy property until quite late. Writing is as precarious as acting, and I had been struggling for twenty years until I made my name in Hollywood.

'I was born at Bow, so I'm an authentic Cockney. I recognised my mother in Alan's mother. My mother remarked at the first night of *The Ruling Class*, my first big success, that I could have gone into the Civil Service instead . . .

'It was a struggle for Alan and me to go off at a tangent and be artistic. In fact, I had even passed the local government exams for the Civil Service, just to please my mother.

'She was widowed too, and I was so taken with the comparison with Alan's mother. I met Mrs Rickman at the *Die Hard* première: when I said how marvellous Alan was in the role, she just said, "Yes, yes, he's very good". It was as if something was niggling her; she wasn't quite comfortable with it.

'They are terrified of boasting about their children's achievements, as if people might accuse them of showing off and aiming above their station in life. So they go to the other extreme. Alan sent his mother on a winter cruise: her comments mirrored my mother's when I sent her to Gibraltar. Never grateful – grudging comments, finding fault with the food. But still proud of her son in a reserved sort of way. She wouldn't like to make a show of things.'

It reminds me, too, of my own mother's reaction when I told her that I wanted to go to university. 'You're aiming above your station,' she said, automatically reaching for the hand-me-down phrase. And she was very uneasy with the cruise I sent her on, too! The working classes take years to shake off the serf mentality, the hopeless feeling that some things are just not for the likes of them. Alan Rickman's mother knew he was remarkable in many ways: he was her Alan, but he was also his own person to an almost aloof degree. He had to cultivate that sense of separateness and be quite ruthless about going his own way, or he would never have succeeded.

He certainly schooled her from the beginning of his acting career in how to talk to the Press; Alan, nervous about coming from the 'wrong' background to such a middle-class environment, was very concerned about saying the correct thing. An early cutting from the *Acton Gazette* of 26 May 1977 features a studio portrait of a fresh-faced Rickman and a careful quote from his mother. 'He was always keen on acting and even at school achieved recognition,' she told the *Gazette* almost primly. Clearly not one to gush about her boy, who was on tour at the time.

'Mr Rickman has not been lured into television yet, preferring to tread the boards in repertory where he gets an immediate audience response to his performances,' concluded the anonymous reporter, having been fobbed off with a standard response by both Alan and his mother. It was the kind of routine guff they teach you in your final term at drama school.

'My mother would come out with all sorts of bigotry against unions and strikes and foreigners on the TV, and then go out and vote Labour. She wouldn't think twice about it. She wouldn't see any contradiction in that,' says Peter Barnes.

'I do think that Alan still has a working-class view of life in a way,' he adds. 'He was round to dinner one night, and my wife was nagging me at the dinner-table about my eating and my weight. Alan said, "I would never let Rima speak to me like that." He said it in front of my wife, which I thought was a bit reactionary. It's very working-class.

'He said that his mother was like mine, would sit in front of the TV set and say that British workers never do any work, it's the unions . . . and then she would go out and vote Labour after all this bigoted, reactionary, right-wing nonsense. Working-class prejudices linger on.

'I would just say to mine, "Shut up, mother . . ." ' adds Peter fondly, finding it all rather amusing and touching.

It took Alan years before he sheepishly admitted to *The Times* magazine on 12 March 1994: 'I've had feminism knocked into me, and a jolly good thing too . . .' Margaret was a very strong role-model for the female sex; and he became very close to her. As a result, he has always been relaxed around women.

Alan also had another lucky start in life that money couldn't buy, since his local state infants' school just happened to be the only purpose-built Montessori school in Britain.

Officially opened in 1937, the building was designed on open-air lines with each classroom leading to a glass-roofed verandah. It followed the pioneering principles of the Italian educationalist, Dr Maria Montessori, in encouraging each child to learn and develop at its own individual rate with 'instructive play'.

To the traditional curriculum of the three Rs were added such social skills as self-expression – vital for a future actor – charity work and consideration for others plus classes in music, movement and dance, singing, craft, art, cookery, gardening, nature study and basic science, poetry and physical education.

At the age of four and a half, on 13 September 1950, Alan enrolled at what is now West Acton First School in nearby Noel Road. Play areas were dotted with flower gardens on a five-acre site.

The school served the new residential roads near Western Avenue plus the adjacent garden estate that had been built between the wars by the then Great Western Railway Company to house its workers.

In 1995 I went to meet the headmistress Wendy Dixon, who called the first school '. . . the seed-bed, which biographers so often ignore.

'Alan had a big advantage at the very beginning in going to a Montessori school, because visitors came from all over the world to monitor its progress. So children would always be presenting themselves in front of an audience,' she explained. 'They were making history all the time: they would have become quite sophisticated. You can always recognise a Montessori-educated adult: they have inquiring minds and a sense of wonder. They're not just chalked and talked like the rest.'

'The Montessori method gives a precociousness,' agrees the playwright Robert Holman, another of Rickman's long-standing friends. And Alan was a very precocious child.

His first acting experience came with *The Story of Christmas* on 12 December 1951, a short Nativity play and carol service 'for the mothers' as the school diary notes. Fathers were not invited; this was an afternoon performance when the men were deemed to be at work. Two years later, he first felt what he was to describe as the acting 'sensation' when he starred in the school play *King Grizzly Bear* (eat your heart out, Sheriff of Nottingham). At the age of seven, Alan Rickman had already made the crucial discovery that he could dominate an audience.

With low-ceilinged classrooms giving an inspirational view of the sky, plenty of fresh air in outdoor activities and the beginning of what is now known as 'child-centred education', this was a creative hothouse far removed from the high-ceilinged, daunting Victorian schoolhouse tradition that was still the norm across the country.

One very large window that reached to the floor enabled Alan and his classmates to step over the sill and straight into one of several playgrounds. There were no barriers to the outside world in this enlightened child-friendly environment that encouraged pupils to feel in control of their lives. Or, as Dr Montessori wrote: 'Education must be a help to life . . . and at this period of growth (3–5 years) should be based on the principle of freely chosen activity in a specially prepared environment.'

Rickman's future partner, Rima Horton, was to be equally fortunate in the early years. She went to an old-fashioned dame school, St Vincent's in Holland Park Avenue, which was run by an enlightened mother and daughter team, Mrs Reid and Mrs Bromley. Despite its name – St Vincent de Paul was the revered 'people's priest' who founded the charitable Orders of the Dazarists and the Sisters of Charity – it was not a Catholic school.

An old classmate remembers Rima as 'a very bright kid, a clever girl. She was the elfin type, petite but feisty. My mother said, "What a pretty little girl she is." There were only 40 in the school. It was very strict, with very good teaching – we would parse sentences and read Shakespeare from an early age, or there would be a rap over the knuckles.

'Mrs Reid and Mrs Bromley were incredibly intellectual women. We were all protected from the outside world in that school; it was a haven. It was co-educational, but they cared a lot about girls being educated to the same level as boys.

'It was fee-paying, but not terribly expensive. A lot of the parents were struggling actors or musicians. I wouldn't be at all surprised if Mrs Bromley had allowed some of them to postpone payment if they got into difficulties.

'They took on children they liked; and they liked real characters. Rima was always a character. We did a lot of theatre; I remember a production of *Dick Whittington* at the Mercury Theatre in Notting Hill Gate.

'Children were allowed to speak for themselves, and Rima always did that. We were brought up to be clever. The school really stood us in good stead. We were encouraged to be independent. Rima and I and a small pack would roam the streets at lunch-time; we had one fight with a posh primary school in Holland Park when the kids were making fun of our red blazers. We punched them in the playground; I remember it was snowing in the park.

'I was delighted to hear about Alan years later; they make a good couple. He's got to be the ultimate grown-up crumpet. I don't mind that his teeth aren't perfect, there's something so magnetic about him. He's just a fascinating man, he seems so warm and clever. You feel he's going to be fun. He's divine with children, they adore him.'

In 1953, at the age of seven, the future grown-up crumpet automatically transferred from West Acton to Derwentwater Junior School. There he won a scholarship in 1957 to the boys' independent day school Latymer Upper, the Alma Mater of fellow actors Hugh Grant, Mel Smith, Christopher and Dominic Guard and breakfast TV doctor, Hillary Jones, exposed as a two-timer by the tabloids. Old Latymerians are never dull.

Alan was born with the distinctive 'Syrup of Figs' drawl, as one friend calls it, but the emollient private-school accent was created at Latymer Upper in Hammersmith's King Street. The process of detachment from his past had begun.

The first school established by the Latymer Foundation of 1624 was in Fulham churchyard. In 1648 it moved to Hammersmith, but a new school was built in 1863. On the present site, the warm red nineteenth-century brick and the gables give Latymer a cloistered, rarefied atmosphere that comes as a welcome relief from the traffic of the highly commercial King Street.

Concerts take place in a long vaulted hall with stained-glass windows. Tranquil lawns lead via the adjacent prep school to the River Thames: in 1957, a child from a council estate must have felt as if he were entering the rarefied realms of the Hanging Gardens of Babylon.

The school has its own boathouse on the tideway, giving direct river access. In the summer months, outdoor life revolves around cricket, athletics, rowing and tennis.

The public floggings that one pre-war pupil, John Prebble, remembers had long been abolished. Each boy was assigned a personal tutor, responsible for his development and general welfare. With someone watching over him, Latymer Upper was to be an academic and dramatic Arcadia for the young Alan Rickman.

Here was a chance to put into practice – and how – the latent exhibitionism that was a vital component in the makeup of every passive-aggressive personality. The word 'latent' is the key to Alan's equivocal attitude towards the Press.

A perfectionist such as Rickman still resents the way in which, because of the ephemeral nature of live theatre, stage performances are immortalised only in reviews. The actor may be refining his technique night after night, but the notices have already set the show in aspic. He has always been touchy about critics because of their markedly mixed reactions to his voice; his hostility to the Press can be traced back to the paranoia of those early years when he was reinventing himself in the image of the silky-sounding matinée idol of his childhood. He was always anxious not to seem common; instead he became famously uncommon.

Laurence Olivier once said that all actors are masochistic exhibitionists. More masochistic than exhibitionist, Kenneth Branagh once mumbled humorously to me; but the oxymoron applies to Alan Rickman in particular.

Although he grew tall in his teens, he was to prove particularly good at female roles in Latymer productions because of his vocal musicality, a certain gracefulness and a chameleonic quality. Such transformations gave him the chance to escape completely into another world where he was no longer a poor kid who had to apply for a grant to buy his school uniform. The dressing-up box was his new kingdom. He could be whoever he wanted to be.

He was highly intelligent and academic enough to have earned his place at the school; but it was his supreme acting ability that was to give him the edge at Latymer Upper.

2. THE SURROGATE FATHER

On the last Saturday in January, 1990, a 55-year-old schoolmaster called Colin Turner was killed in a freak accident on a visit to friends. Colin had been hoping to retire to Stratford-upon-Avon five years later in 1995, looking forward to indulging his passion for Shakespearean research. He was walking down a flight of stairs in a block of flats in Stamford Court, Hammersmith, when he suddenly tripped and fell headlong, breaking his neck on the railings at the bottom of the stairs. Colin was rushed to the nearby Charing Cross Hospital; but he had died almost instantaneously.

'Oddly enough,' says Colin's close friend Edward 'Ted' Stead, sadly recalling a bizarre detail, 'the bottle of wine he was carrying was quite undamaged.'

Wilf Sharp, then the Head of English at Latymer Upper School, was informed of his colleague's fate the next morning on Sunday, 28 January. At first he couldn't quite believe it; he had only just received a letter from Colin the previous day.

The correspondence was about Colin's attendance at the funeral of their mutual friend, the painter Ruskin Spear, who had lived a few doors away from Colin in Hammersmith's British Grove.

There was to be a similar tragedy five years later on New Year's Eve, 1995, for a former Latymer Upper master who had lived in the same apartment block as Colin. Retired English teacher Jim McCabe died of a brain haemorrhage after falling and hitting his head on a stationary car in the car park. Alan Rickman attended his requiem mass at the end of January 1996 and later went back to the school to talk over old times.

When he had heard the news about Colin Turner's fatal accident, it was particularly devastating for Alan. Colin had been his mentor at Latymer Upper, joining the school at the same time as the then fatherless, 11-year-old Alan. Turner was 23. An English teacher at Latymer for the next 33 years, he would become Head of Middle School.

As a bachelor, Colin had treated his career as a vocation in the Mr Chips tradition. An Old Latymerian himself, he was a flamboyant and idiosyncratic actor and director in the school's Gild Drama Club. He had hoped to make a career in the professional theatre, but eventually trained as a teacher after National Service in the RAF and returned to his beloved Latymer.

'The school was staffed with frustrated actors,' remembers the writer, critic and broadcaster Robert Cushman, a pupil at the school in Alan's day.

'It was overwhelmingly non-fee-paying in my time,' adds Cushman, who left two years before Alan in 1962 but acted alongside him in Gild productions. 'The school was not class-ridden at all. It was a good time, the beginning of the 60s. It was almost like doing weekly rep, with a major show every term. The Gild met every week except in the summer exam term, and there was a great sense of comedy in the school. It was a fun place to be. A whole bunch of bachelor teachers bought us drinks when we were under age; in the Gild, we all felt like their equals.

'Colin Turner was a matinée-idol type, very good-looking with a light tenor voice. He was very tall – I remember him playing Sir Andrew Aguecheek in *Twelfth Night* when someone else dropped out.'

Opera fan Colin was just as likely to step into a skirt and send himself up as to play in straight drama. Among his most memorable roles at Latymer Upper were the sad schoolmaster and cuckold Crocker Harris in Rattigan's *The Browning Version*; the foul-mouthed fishwife Martha in Albee's *Who's Afraid Of Virginia Woolf?* and an outrageous succession of pantomine Dame parts, such as Sarah the Cook and Dame Trot.

A big and imposing man with an irrepressible sense of humour, he modelled his female roles on his favourite aunt, surrogate mother and holiday companion, Mrs Elsie Laws. Shades of *Travels With My Aunt*, indeed.

In *The Latymerian* magazine of Spring/Summer 1990, Ted Stead's tribute to Colin remembered '. . . the little touches which many people haven't time for . . . his gifts, a kind word, a joke, a glass of sherry, an arm round the shoulder, a present – often a flower, or even when needed, a sharp word of reality to cure self-pity and indulgence. There was always a welcome in his home and his hospitality through his parties brought together his wide circle of friends on *Twelfth Night* and on his birthday, when he sometimes ruefully counted the years but did not grow old.' Colin had the born schoolteacher's ability to seem as youthful in his enthusiasms as his pupils, hence his empathy with his boys.

It was Colin Turner who discovered the gawky young Alan Rickman, for whom he clearly felt a paternal concern. In later years he would also develop the talent of Melvyn 'Mel' Smith, Hugh Grant, Christopher Guard plus his brother Dominic and even a future Miss Moneypenny: actress Samantha Bond from Latymer's sister school Godolphin. Samantha's journalist brother Matthew, also one of his pupils, was later to write a tribute to Colin in *The Times Diary* on what would have been the occasion of his 60th birthday.

'There was a good creative buzz around the place, and Colin was at the centre of it. He was one of the great characters of the school. Colin was a great mentor to lots of people: he had a real eye for talent,' says *Mail On Sunday* film critic Matthew, an exact contemporary of Hugh Grant at Latymer Upper in the 70s. 'When you think of it, Colin had an amazing strike record for a drama teacher. It's sad that some of his former pupils only became great successes after his death; but Colin was interested in the progress of the journeymen actors as well.

'At 6 ft 6 in, it would have been difficult for him to be a professional actor. He was a very imposing pantomine dame; he took it very seriously and was good at it. He didn't mind being ridiculed in drag at the panto, but he had tremendous authority back in the classroom.

'I rather rebelled against acting because of my family,' explains Matthew, son of the actor Philip Bond. 'I did science A-Levels and Colin teased me about it. So I tended not to act much: I was the one who got away. It was the Arties versus the Hearties at Latymer, and I was somewhere in between.

'My career as a schoolboy actor reached its peak in *The Italian Straw Hat* when I played an elderly Italian gentleman; but I wore yellow dresses in the school Jantaculum with the best of them, Hugh Grant included.' The future pop star Sophie Ellis-Bextor and the actress Kate Beckinsale were among the Godolphin girls appearing in co-productions with Latymer. As Matthew recalls: 'They did allow girls in later to play female roles . . . but then they decided to ban the girls after some very unGarrick Club behaviour.' Despite that behavioural blip, girls have since been admitted to Latymer Upper's sixth form, with the eventual plan that the school will go fully co-educational.

From 1957–1964, when Alan attended the school, Colin inevitably became something of a father figure to him even with only twelve years' difference between them. Alan's bravura style and even the development of his unique voice can be attributed to him.

'It struck me that Colin's basic manner was not dissimilar to Alan's; both possessed this wonderful voice and presence. When you see Alan, there are echoes of Colin, because he is a mannered actor,' adds Matthew. 'But it might have worked both ways; it might have been Colin who adopted Alan's style, because he would have had great admiration for someone with such a natural actor's voice. The actor Simon Kunz has a great voice too, and he became another protégé of Colin's at Latymer; Colin must have thought that Simon would be another Alan Rickman.'

'Alan was very close to Colin, who really guided him,' remembers Ted Stead. 'Colin was one of my closest friends, and we were both invited to Alan's 21st birthday party as his friends. It's very unusual to invite your old teachers to your 21st, but he did.' Their former pupil even continued to act alongside Colin and Ted for several years after Alan had left Latymer Upper for Chelsea College of Art.

Alan and his new girlfriend Rima met up with Colin and Ted again in the Court Drama Group at a London County Council Evening Institute off the Euston Road, where Wilf Sharp and his wife Miriam ('Mim') were instructors in their spare time.

Wilf and Mim's daughter, Jane, played Juliet to Alan's Romeo in this amateur dramatics group, with Colin Turner as Mercutio and Mim directing. It was Latymer Revisited with females.

Alan himself recalls Latymer Upper in the 1960s as an exhilarating mini National Theatre, with teachers fighting pupils for the best roles. It was a glamorous sanctuary from the drab reality of poverty.

A former classmate of Alan's recalls that 80 per cent of the boys in Rickman's day were from a working-class background. 'They took the cream of the 11-plus from all over London. I came from a middle-class background, and I almost felt like the odd boy out. Most of the intake was from the C-D social groups: academically it was highly selective, but the social mix was like a comprehensive. It's a great pity that the direct-grant system has finished there.'

The school's motto is *Pavilatim Ergo Certe* (Slowly But Surely), which could sum up Rickman's slow-burn career. Founded in

1624 by the terms of lawyer Edward Latymer's will, it aimed to give a first-class education to able boys from all backgrounds.

Latymer worked in the livery courts. The income from the childless Latymer's rents in the hamlet of Hammersmith was bequeathed to the founding of a charity under which eight poor local boys were to be put 'to some petty school' to be taught English and 'some part of God's true religion' so that they could be kept 'from idle and vagrant courses'. The 1572 Vagabonds Act had deemed all unlicensed 'Common Players' to be 'rogues, vagabonds and sturdy beggars', no better than vagrants. One wonders just what the devout Latymer would have made of the famous thespians that emerged from his school.

Despite a certain working-class diffidence, Rickman's dramatic abilities were very obvious from the beginning. He was a regular performer in school plays as a member of the Gild Drama Club, held every Friday night.

The Gild was set up in the 1920s as a senior dramatic society, based upon the medieval trade guilds (spelt gilds). It was open to fifth and sixth-formers plus masters, with girls from Godolphin eventually playing female roles, though not in Alan's day.

The idea, very radical for its time, was to create 'Jantaculum' musical revues in which pupils and masters could compete as equals. Rickman's self-possession, interpreted by some as arrogance, stemmed from that terrific egalitarian start in life when boys were taught to take on the world. It almost goes without saying that, with that voice and that presence, he made an imposing prefect at the age of eighteen. Nearly four decades later, another Old Latymerian called John Byer, a teacher now for more than three decades, swears that the secret of Rickman's 'wonderful portrayal of the wicked Sheriff of Nottingham was the practice he had as my class prefect when I was in the fourth form!' As a poor boy from the wrong side of the tracks, Alan was self-conscious enough as a prefect to assume that aloofness conferred authority, as so many sixth-formers 'dressed in a little brief authority' tend to do. Tobacco helped the nerves, and Rickman puffed away at the ciggies as much as anyone. Byer recalls how 'Alan's fingers were nicotine-stained; smoking was de rigueur at Latymer then and it was allowed in the prefects' room. Although he treated me like dirt,' he adds good-humouredly, 'I think we were probably pretty awful – and it was what we expected!'

Latymer was a direct-grant school in 1957, with competitive entry by exam. 'You won a place here on merit,' says Nigel Orton, the school's former deputy head who went on to run the Old Latymerian Office that keeps in touch with former pupils. 'Most of the boys were on scholarship, because Latymer has always been renowned for taking boys from humble or lower middle-class backgrounds. The school is still selective, but the direct grant finished in 1976 and we became fee-paying – though the bursary scheme takes care of boys from poor backgrounds.

'When the Government started an assisted-places scheme in the early 80s, we bought into this in a big way. It's a totally academic, selective school.'

Alan made a memorably precocious Latymer acting début at the age of eleven as Volumnia, the overbearing and bellicose mamma of Shakespeare's *Coriolanus*. Later, he became a Gild committee-member, or Curianus, in the quaint Latymer parlance.

He was also Chamberlayne, the title given to the boy in charge of Wardrobe. The intricacies of costume design fascinated Rickman, whose talents as an artist were already obvious. The library still holds Curianus Rickman's own flamboyant signed cartoon of himself, heavily padded as Sir Epicure Mammon with a conical hat perched on his sharp Mod haircut for a production of Ben Jonson's *The Alchemist* in the spring of 1964, Alan's final year in the Sixth Form.

Not that Rickman was remotely the kind of teenaged weekend Mod who scootered down to the seaside for a ritual fight with greasy Rockers. The fastidious young scholarship boy was cosseted by academic privilege, and hated growing up on a rough-and-ready council estate. According to one friend, he still remains sensitive about the experience because acting is overwhelmingly a middle-class profession, even more so now that many drama grants from cash-strapped local authorities have dried up.

At Latymer, Alan could escape into a charmed life. Brian Worthington, a master from Dulwich College's English department, was a guest reviewer of *The Alchemist* for the school magazine, *The Latymerian*. He wrote: 'Sir Epicure Mammon's costume, though well designed, was made of a thin, meagre-looking material, quite wrong for the character. This grandiose and greedy sensualist should surely look as splendid as his verse sounds.

'Nevertheless Alan Rickman's performance compensated for this and his curious "mod" hairstyle. A lazy and smug drawl, affected movements and lucid, well-pointed verse-speaking succeeded well for this avaricious yet perversely sensitive booby. He knew how to throw away a line and deliver the famous speech – "I'll have all my beds blown up, not stuff'd, down is too hard" – without any indulgence in the voice, beautifully.'

The previous year, Alan played the female role of Grusha in Brecht's *The Caucasian Chalk Circle*, which was his first introduction to left-wing agit prop or agitational propaganda. 'He read with assurance, sympathy and complete absence of embarrassment,' noted Ted Stead, the director of the production, in *The Latymerian*.

Unfortunately, Alan fell ill and had to be replaced in the second half. He received his first dodgy notice when the late Leonard Sachs – who made his name as the deliriously alliterative Master of Ceremonies in the television variety series *The Good Old Days* and whose son, Robin, was a Latymer Upper pupil – seemed to find Alan just a little too precocious.

In a *Latymerian* review of a 1963 production of *The Knight Of The Burning Pestle*, Sachs had a somewhat equivocal response to Rickman's 'just too arch Humphrey'. Judging by the adjacent photograph, the foppish, confident-looking Rickman must have been hilarious.

'I used to bump into Alan on the Tube because we lived quite close to each other,' recalls Robert Cushman. 'Then I suddenly became aware of him as an actor in the Gild in 1962 when I played Sergeant Musgrave in a rehearsed reading of John Arden's *Serjeant Musgrave's Dance* and Alan played Annie the barmaid. He played her as a bedraggled slut, and there was amazing depth, tragedy and irony in his performance. I have this image of him cradling a dead body.

'He was a charismatic character at school: there was that voice and that authority. I don't know that I would necessarily have prophesied stardom for him. His individuality was always going to stand him in good stead, though.'

At the Speech and Musical Festival of 1964, Rickman was commended for having '. . . with studied nonchalance extracted every ounce of biting satire from Peacock's *Portrait of Scythrop*'. He's been studying nonchalance ever since. And as Grikos in *Cloud Over The Morning*, he won the award at Hammersmith Drama

Festival that same year for the best individual performance. The rap over the knuckles from Sachs had done him no harm.

'I first met Alan when I joined the school in 1962 and he was in the Lower Sixth,' says Stead, a Cambridge contemporary of David Frost, Corin Redgrave, Margaret Drabble and Derek Jacobi. Ted, who went on to teach at Gravesend Grammar School for Boys, gave Trevor Nunn his first acting job in Dylan Thomas's *Return Journey* when they were both up at Downing College.

Above all, Stead remembers Rickman's confidence, with an ability to camp things up as a schoolboy drag queen that nearly gave the Head of the time a fit of puritanical apoplexy.

'Alan was in the political panto *Ali Baba And The Seven Dwarfs.* He played the sixth wife of Ali Baba and one of his lines was censored by the headmaster, who was a northern Methodist and insisted it be cut from a family show.

'It was a line about Alan being the Saturday wife, since Ali Baba had one for every day of the week. Alan had to say "fat or thin, nearly bare, he doesn't care" of Ali Baba's taste in women. And he wore a diaphanous costume in a very flamboyant way, quite confidently.'

Robert Cushman reviewed that production for the spring issue of *The Latymerian* in 1963. 'Spy stories were very much in vogue then, and this was a riotously involved spy-spoof sketch. Alan infiltrated the sultan's harem as a spy, disguised as one of his wives,' he remembers.

A review in *The Latymerian* school magazine for Winter 1962 records that Alan took the role of 'a sultry spy from Roedean – a sort of do-it-yourself (Eartha) Kitt – played with a vocal edge that enabled him to bring the house down with a monosyllable.' That sounds like the Alan Rickman we all know.

'He was always laconic, wonderful at ensemble playing and tremendously popular with boys and staff. One could see he had tremendous talent,' adds Ted Stead.

'When he did *The Alchemist* in the Upper Sixth, it ran for over three hours. A schoolboy Alchemist is a recipe for disaster, but Alan had this panache in the role of Sir Epicure Mammon. He was very imposing indeed, but he didn't upset the ensemble. He was a very good verse-speaker even in 1964. Jonson is almost intractable, but he managed it.

'He always had a wonderful barbed wit, but it was never unkind. There was always a twinkle in his eyes; he never meant to hurt people. Really, he was a very reliable model pupil.

'Latymer was a very competitive school, and Alan wasn't a leader. He was just somebody who was popular, made people laugh. But he was university material, no question of it. In fact, Alan would have made a good teacher.

'But at that stage, art was his chosen career. He was so clear that he was going to Chelsea College of Art, so we didn't think of him in the theatre at that stage. The voice was there when I first met him: it made him unique.'

Chris Hammond, a chemistry teacher and the current Head of Middle School, came to Latymer Upper in 1966 two years after Alan had left with a mighty reputation. 'In Latymer terms, he was a household name because of his performances in the Jantaculum. He brought the house down; the audiences cried with laughter.

'The Gild doesn't really exist now in the old way. There are drama productions, but not with the staff and pupils acting together. There are no more Jantaculum cabarets: they called them light entertainments in those days. There's a new view that we ought to be doing proper drama. The great cabaret tradition is no longer there.

'When Alan came back to the school after Jim McCabe's requiem mass, he said that satire was very difficult these days. That's why the satire has gone from the Gild. Because it's all been done before, satire would border on the obscene these days. It has taken off in a strange direction.'

The school still displays a photograph of Rickman in a 1962 production, alongside examples of the early thespian endeavours of rugby captain Mel Smith and cricketer Hugh Grant, all looking absurdly plump-cheeked and misleadingly cherubic. For as Robert Cushman recalls, 'There was so much jealousy and competitiveness over theatre. I remember one contemporary, Michael Newby, who went on to York University. He was a marvellous natural actor, but he became very disillusioned.'

Newby figured in that *Ali Baba And The Seven Dwarfs* review from the Winter of 1962: 'This was a spy story, vaguely post-Fleming, and was handled with his customary skill and incisiveness by Michael Newby as a deadpan James Bond. His crisp timing did a great deal to hold the story together and he was given two excellent foils: John Ray, possibly the most original comic personality the Gild possesses, was marvellously funny in an all-too-brief appearance as a cringing British agent; Alan Rickman . . .' You know the rest.

Cushman, now based in Canada, has stayed friends with Rickman ever since their time at Latymer. 'My wife points out that Alan always helped with the washing-up . . . mind you, that was before he went to Hollywood,' he jokes.

Although Rickman still revisits Latymer Upper, he has a decidedly equivocal attitude towards the fee-paying school that gave poor scholarship boys like him a privileged upbringing.

His misgivings were to lead to an ideological falling-out with Latymer towards the end of 1995 when the school asked permission to use his photograph in a display advertisement placed in theatre programmes for three productions from October to December at the Lyric Hammersmith. 1995 was Latymer's centenary year, and the ads were specifically designed to recruit new pupils with an interest in drama. Hence the mug-shots of Latymer's most famous dramatic successes: Alan Rickman, Mel Smith and Hugh Grant.

The school wrote to ask Alan's permission to use his photo. 'We received a reply from his agent, one of those wonderful one-sentence letters that said Alan did not wish his photograph to be used in this way,' recalls Chris Hammond. 'Luckily we hadn't sent the display ads off to the printers, so we didn't have to reprint anything. We simply removed Alan's photograph.

'The strange thing was that Alan had already given permission for his picture to be used in a book about the history of the school, which was published in October 1995.'

Appearing in the school's history book was one thing; but joining in with its recruitment drive was a very different game of soldiers. Staunch Labour supporter Alan Rickman refused to cooperate with the ads because he didn't wish to be seen to be publicly endorsing a fee-paying school which no longer has the same quota of working-class scholarship boys that it did in his day. Paradoxically, that's because the Labour Party abolished the direct-grant system back in 1976 with the inevitable result that Latymer Upper took fewer poor pupils and became more élitist. The 300 assisted places that still existed in 1995 were abolished by Labour after it came back into power in 1997.

Ideally, of course, Labour would prefer private schools like Latymer not to exist at all. To add to the irony of Alan's dilemma, a member of his Labour councillor girlfriend's family was also educated at Latymer Upper. 'I think it was her brother or her cousin, I can't remember which,' says Chris Hammond.

In other words, though the system may not have pleased the purists, Latymer Upper proved to be the making of a lot of impoverished bright children . . . including Alan Rickman.

'Alan is a romantic,' says Chris Hammond, not unsympathetically. 'And every so often harsh political realities hit him, either through his partner or through logic. He has a romantic view of Latymer and of the Gild.

'He's ideologically in dispute with the concept of an independent-school education, the idea that money buys all. But after Jim McCabe's requiem mass in January, Alan came back to the school and stayed for three hours from which I deduce he's not personally in dispute with us. He didn't have to come back; nobody forced him.

'And when he was invited to the centenary service at St Paul's Cathedral in 1995, he sent his regrets that he couldn't come because of filming commitments.

'Harriet Harman's name came up when we were talking, and yes, you could certainly say that he wasn't exactly in favour of her decision to send her son to a selective school,' adds Chris of the educational own goal by a Shadow Cabinet Minister that split the Labour front benches for a while in February 1996.

'But I asked Alan how he would try to maintain Latymer in future if he were a school governor, and he reluctantly agreed that he would have done the same as us. He's ambivalent about it all, because he cares about Latymer.'

According to Chris Hammond, another issue that Rickman felt strongly about was the sacking of Jim McCabe in 1993; he thought Jim was poorly treated at the time.

'Jim was asked to leave,' admits Hammond. 'He was originally with us in the 60s, and he was fine then. Then he went off to teach at Crawley, Watford and eventually Singapore. He came back to Latymer for his final years. He was asked to jack it in at the end of one year; unfortunately he wasn't a good teacher any more. So he took early retirement; I would hope that Alan would see the necessity of that.' But Alan does like to play the white knight on occasion; it's a trait that does him no discredit.

Rickman was to demonstrate his commitment to Latymer still further by returning again in November 1999 for the gala opening of the school's new arts centre, including the 300-seater Latymer Theatre. With him were Rima and Mel Smith, with whom he has long been friendly. 'He wasn't remotely distant and aloof; it was a very warm occasion and he stayed for three hours afterwards,' says Orton. Far from being an élitist fixture for the use of the Latymerian boys and girls only, the theatre is used widely by local primary schoolchildren and drama students as a public resource open to all. Alan certainly approved of that; and one suspects that Edward Latymer himself might have done so, too. And Latymer Upper's new scholarship appeal fund, which Chris Hammond says has the 'keen' support of both Alan and Mel, is intended to replace the late-lamented assisted-places scheme to some extent.

Leaving Latymer for the outside world in 1964 was a great shock. Alan was later to recall the still, small voice that ignored his 'wild bruiser of a will' and told him he should take up art instead of doing a Drama or an English degree. In that, he was emulating his graphic designer brother, David. Family influences were strong: Alan was still living at home in Acton, much too poor to join in the emergent Swinging London scene of the King's Road in 1965.

Alan enrolled on a three-year art and design course at Chelsea College of Art, leaving in 1968, the year of Danny the Red and international student uprisings.

Alan was later to recall the wall-to-wall sit-ins, the fellow student who painted on an acid trip and the girl from the graphics department who cycled up and down the King's Road while dressed as a nun. He told GQ magazine in July 1992 how he 'wandered through those days wondering what on earth was going on . . . there was a bit of me that always wanted the painting teachers to come into the graphic design department and discover me as a great painter. But I could never get it together. I think there was a bit of me that was waiting to act.'

In truth, Rickman was a bit lost until he found his soulmate Rima. If Colin Turner gave him sophistication, she gave him self-belief.

'I always assumed that Rima and Alan emerged out of the diesel and smoke of west London, cosmically entwined,' says their playwright friend Stephen Davis, not entirely facetiously.

It was at Chelsea College of Art that Alan met a general labourer's daughter from Paddington, Rima Elizabeth Horton. She was small, dark, sweet-faced and snub-nosed, with a calm, self-possessed air that made her seem remarkably precocious. Alan was later to say, with a distaste for romantic gush that proved he was every inch his mother's son, 'It was not love at first sight; I'd hate for us to be presented as something extraordinary. We're just as messy and complex as any other couple, and we go through just as many changes. But I really respect her. Rima and I can sit in a room just reading, and not saying anything to each other for an hour, then she'll read something to me and we'll both start giggling.' In other words, they manage to be friends as well as lovers; the best, and the rarest, combination.

Like him, she was a clever, serious-minded working-class child who had suckled socialism at the breast. Alan and Rima instantly bonded like brother and sister; they thought alike and had the same dry sense of humour. They protected each other, and have done so ever since.

The relationship has been remarkably solid over more than three decades, outlasting many of their friends' marriages. Although Rima is a year younger than Alan, from the very beginning she always seemed the older of the two. Yet it's a relationship based on neck-strain, because he towers over her.

'When I first saw Alan with Rima, they didn't seem a very *coupled* couple. But I was wrong. I began to notice when I visited Alan in Stratford-upon-Avon that he seemed calmer when she was around. She centres him. She's very important to him,' says the playwright Dusty Hughes, who has known them both since 1981. 'She came up to do his garden at a cottage he rented in Stratford when he was with the RSC; she planted annuals everywhere.'

'Alan did a reading at our wedding in 1990,' says Dusty's ex-wife, Theresa Hickey. 'He read the Shakespeare sonnet, "Let me not to the marriage of true minds admit impediment" from the pulpit.

'He terrified everyone because he read it in a really sinister voice like Obadiah Slope's. I remember Rima had a bad cold, but she still came along to be with him. Alan is very much a one-woman man.'

Unfortunately, Teresa and Dusty's marriage lasted only three years; but Alan and Rima's informal arrangement is still going strong. 'Neither of them are slaves to convention,' says the actor and director Richard Wilson, explaining why they have never seen the need for a formal contract while friends' marriages crumble one by one. Another friend thinks that Alan would have married if he had wanted children. But in 1998, Rickman admitted in an interview with the journalist Susie Mackenzie that he would have loved a family himself; that fatherhood was not something he deliberately chose to avoid. Then, to protect Rima, he added hurriedly: ' You should remember I am not the only one involved; there is another person here. Sometimes I think that in an ideal world three children, aged twelve, ten and eight, would be dropped on us and we would be great parents for that family.' Mackenzie asked him bluntly whether he had ever been tempted to leave the 51-year old Rima for a 20-year old starlet. 'No,' came the very firm answer, clanging down like a portcullis on that particular conversational avenue.

Instead he set out to become the ideal uncle. In 2001, he told the movie magazine *Unreel* during a promotional interview for *Harry Potter and the Philosopher's Stone* that, far from being remote from children and children's interests as affluent Dinkies (Dual Income No Kids) so often are, he liked to spend time with his sister's young daughters Claire and Amy. Sheila had had the girls relatively late, and a middle-aged Alan found himself revelling in 'all those daft things – movies, McDonald's, Hamleys'. In a way, and with the distinct advantage of the wherewithal to pay for it this time, he was rediscovering his own face-pressed-against-the-glass childhood in the late 40s and early 50s when the magical Hamleys in Regent Street really did live up to its name as the greatest toyshop in the world.

When he took Claire and Amy there, however, he was in for a shock when they made a beeline for the kind of girlie toy that would give the gender politicians a fit of the vapours. Despite the fact that his sister didn't dress the girls 'in pink or bows', he recalled how Claire and Amy 'marched straight to the Barbie counter – I couldn't believe it – hideous little dolls with pointed breasts'. Yet even grungey old Alan was enough of an indulgent uncle – and a bloody-minded rebel – to declare, 'If I had children, I like to think I'd let them wear whatever they wanted. None of my friends would believe me, but I'd let them walk down the road in pink Lurex and gold plastic.' So much for his reputation for solemnity.

Rima was as passionate about theatre as Alan was, and they joined an amateur west London group called the Brook Green Players. She first appeared with him in a production of Emlyn Williams' *Night Must Fall* at the Methodist Hall in Askew Road, Shepherd's Bush.

He was the star as the psychopathic Danny, the seductive boy murderer who kept a head in a hat-box; Rima took the part of the maid whom Danny impregnates in Sean O'Casey's least favourite play. A cast photograph published on page three of the *West London Observer* on 1 April 1965 shows Rima wearing a huge floral pinny and standing demurely in the back row. The smallest member of the cast, she also looks the most assured.

That was deceptive, however, since she was never confident enough to take up acting full-time. The highly articulate Rima still finds political speech-making somewhat nerve-racking.

But acting was where Alan, of course, found himself in the ascendant. He is in the front row of the *Observer* picture, displaying that familiar sultry pout and looking ready to sulk the place down with the cross-looking face he so often presents to the world. His is easily the most dramatic presence in the line-up.

'What is one supposed to do when after watching a play, one finds oneself wanting to see more?' rhapsodised the gushing reviewer. 'For the registering of deep, heartfelt emotion . . . most of the burden fell to young Alan Rickman in the part of Danny, a rather mystifying young gentleman who is both the hero and the villain.

'He it is who is called upon at one stage to break down and cry. This Mr Rickman does so well that it's almost possible to see the tears in his eyes.

'It was Sir Laurence Olivier, I think,' hedges the reviewer, wallowing in the lachrymose theme, 'who once said this is the test of a real actor or actress. Of all the characters in this gripping drama, I think that Danny is the one upon whom most of the attention is focused.

'Of course, he is one of the central characters. So much so that the stage seems empty without him. Even when his part calls for no word or action, he dominates the stage.'

Nevertheless, Alan had persuaded himself that he ought to pursue an art career instead. In that, he was influenced by working-class caution: it seemed much easier to make a living from drawing than from the party-trick of performing. And if things didn't work out, he could always become a painter and decorator like his late father. However, Latymer had changed him utterly, much more than he knew.

In their spare time, Alan and Rima then joined Edward Stead and Colin Turner in the Court Drama Group at the Stanhope Adult Education Institute opposite Great Portland tube station. It was to become a little Latymer in exile for Alan.

Their seasons were amazingly eclectic. Edward remembers more of Rickman's camped-up shock tactics in the musical revue *The Borgia Orgy* at the Stanhope.

'There were some lines that went "Scoutmasters gay are we/ displaying a shapely knee/in our cute little shorts/we are known as good sports/from Queensgate to Battersea." Alan really threw himself into it,' he recalls.

'We acted together in Behan's *The Hostage*; and the Court did give Alan the part of Romeo, which he's never done professionally. Rima was Moth the page, Alan was Boyet and Colin was Don Armado in *Love's Labours Lost*; it was directed by Wilf Sharp, whose late wife Miriam requested in her will that Alan read from *The Importance Of Being Earnest* at her funeral.

'Alan was devastated by Colin's sudden death, no question of it,' says Ted, pointing out that Rickman read two speeches at a Service of Thanksgiving for the life of Colin Turner at St Michael and All Angels Church in Bedford Park on 23 February 1990.

'Alan came along and read the Queen Mab speech in honour of him, since Colin had played Mercutio in the Court's production of *Romeo And Juliet*. Alan even said, characteristically but wrongly, "Colin read it much better than me." It wasn't true but it was typical of his generosity. He also read "Our revels now are ended" from *The Tempest*.

'On *Desert Island Discs*, Hugh Grant mentioned the influence of Colin, though he didn't name him. Colin was immensely important for him, too. He's very different to Alan, though: Hugh is scatty and Alan is very in control.

'Alan can be vulnerable, but he's very strong and clear about what he wants to do. He has handled his career very well, he's avoided meretricious stuff. One could never say of him that he did it for the money.

'I lost touch for a couple of years when he finished at the Court, but then I heard he had got into RADA. We've kept up contact on and off since; he was there at the last anniversary of the Gild, there in person. Mel Smith sent a video.

'The voice was already there when I first met him. Initially it can sound affected, but it isn't. That's Alan. He's never patronising . . . even to the people from the Court Drama Group when they met him years later.

'A number of people say he seems aloof, which is absolutely wrong. When he was doing Achilles and Jaques at Stratford in the

1980s, I took along two boys who were mad about the theatre. Afterwards we had a bottle of wine in his dressing-room and he insisted on paying for a meal afterwards. He had a little cottage opposite the theatre and we had tea there. We also saw him in *Les Liaisons Dangereuses*; he couldn't have been nicer or more helpful.

'He made time to meet us, even though he had an hour's fencing every night before *Les Liaisons* to rehearse the final fight.

'I also took boys from my present school to see Alan's *Hamlet* in 1992 – even the Oxbridge candidates could do nothing but look at him and ask for his autograph. They wrote to him afterwards and he wrote back by return of post.

'People were kept out of the dressing-room so he could entertain boys from Gravesend Grammar whom he had never met. He had no reason to do it. He chided me and said, "You should have brought them all round" when I said, "Alan, there were 27 of them. I had to put names in a hat."

'He tried hard to defuse the feeling of him being the star when I took those boys backstage. There was no actory behaviour.'

After the three-year course at Chelsea, Alan studied graphic design for a year at the Royal College of Art to prepare himself for a career in art. Like so many others in 1968, he dreamed of changing the world with Letraset.

To this end, in 1969 he set up the *Notting Hill Herald* freesheet with a group of friends. The Editor was David Adams, the Features Editor Jeremy Gibson and Alan was the Art Editor, which meant he designed the whole thing.

It was surprisingly earnest stuff for those madcap times, with solemn think-pieces on the Kensington and Chelsea Arts Council and an undercover investigation by the *Herald*'s Managing Editor, Paul Horne, of the outrageous prices at Ronnie Scott's jazz club. There was also a leader-page article by the Sixth Baron Gifford, better known as Anthony Gifford QC, that called for the legalisation of cannabis. He has gone on to become one of the country's most prominent left-wing lawyers, setting up a radical set of barristers' chambers and running it as a co-operative that paid a flat-rate salary regardless of individual earnings. The experiment, unsurprisingly in the competitive world of the Bar, didn't last. But Tony did: since 1991, he has been dividing his work between Britain and ganja-friendly Jamaica, where he has a house.

The *Herald* had none of the subversive naughtiness that characterised, say, such radical magazines as *Oz*. Perhaps it longed to be taken seriously, like the alternative 'community' magazine I worked on in the 70s. Alan's design for the *Herald*'s front page looked like a Russian Constructionist nightmare, full of clashing capital letters of various sizes.

Published by the now-defunct West London Free Press, it grandly promised: 'Treat the *Herald* as an alternative to the other local papers . . . we exist to express all shades of opinion.' It purported to be non-politically aligned, but inevitably it became a forum for left-wing debate.

Its first issue carried advertisements about how to achieve sexual ecstasy and collect stamps, which certainly covered the waterfront in west London. Page two featured a holiday guide to Turkey and drugs, while the Liverpool poet, Brian Patten, provided a bit of local colour on page eight as a Notting Hillbilly.

The same group of friends also started a graphic design company called Graphiti. They hired a studio in Berwick Street, Soho, for £10 a week in an atmosphere where everyone smoked pot while working on such groovy design commissions as rock-album sleeves. 'We were successful workwise but absolute paupers because we foolishly went into it with no backing. Everyone paid us four months late,' Rickman ruefully told *The Stage and Television Today* in 1986.

Dave Granger, sales director of the present incarnation of Graphiti, remembers seeing Alan around while working in Berwick Street at the time. 'There were a hell of a lot of strange things going on at that time . . . a lot of drinking and drugs. But there were a lot of good creative people around. Rickman was a very clever cartoonist.'

'Our studio had white walls, sanded floors, trestle tables and no capital . . . and it was very heaven,' Alan somewhat self-consciously told the journalist Valerie Grove for a *Harpers & Queen* interview in April 1995.

As with so many of the rock stars whose portentous concept albums he helped to package, four years of art school had been Alan Rickman's university. Rickman's playwright friend Stephen Davis says rather wryly of his own more traditional days at Cambridge in the late 60s, 'British rock 'n' roll came out of art schools. I kept thinking, "If this place is so great, why isn't John Lennon here?" And Alan Rickman was probably the best undergraduate that university never had.'

To prove it, Davis later wrote the TV play *Busted* for Alan and another actor friend Michael Feast in which they portrayed old university mates from Soc Soc (the insufferably twee diminutive for every student Socialist Society) who had gone their separate ways after graduation.

But Rickman was restless in the middle of all the pot-parties: there was more to life than whimsical sleeve-notes, LSD lyrics and earnest debates on planning procedures in Notting Hill Gate. (The latter was to be Rima's speciality, lucky girl, when she later became a councillor.)

The acting instinct wouldn't go away, and Graphiti was not as lucrative as they'd all hoped. In the stoned atmosphere of the late 60s, it was difficult to make a tiny, under-capitalised cottage-industry work. They were small fry in a huge shark-pool where rock art was big business and the conglomerates were swallowing up the competition for the record companies' commissions.

One day Alan Rickman found himself posting a letter to RADA, asking for an audition. At nearly 26, he felt rather foolish about being a student again. Mothers, particularly working-class mothers, tend to ask exactly when you're going to get a proper job at that age. But it was now or never. 'I was getting older,' he later confessed to *GQ* magazine in 1992, 'and I thought, "If you really want to do this, you've got to get on with it." '

He had set in motion a chain of events that would change his life for ever, although it was to be a long slog. When he heard the news about his former star pupil, Colin Turner felt quietly triumphant. Alan was to phone 'home' regularly to Latymer Upper over the following eighteen years, letting Colin know everything about his progress from Leicester to Los Angeles.

3. 'HE'S VERY KEEP DEATH OFF THE ROADS'

He won a place at RADA by giving a speech from *Richard III*, a part that you could argue he has been playing on and off ever since. Certainly his cartoon Sheriff of Nottingham in *Robin Hood: Prince Of Thieves* was, in his own words, an amalgam of a crazy rock star and what the Irish call 'Dick The Turd'.

At 26, he was a mature student in comparison with nearly everyone else. By then, his art-school training had already used up his grant allocation from the local authority. So he lived at home, got by with the odd design commission and worked as a dresser to Sir Ralph Richardson and Nigel Hawthorne in the play *West Of Suez*, watching their work from the wings and spending more time at the ironing-board than John Osborne's Alison Porter. He not only fetched clean shirts for the men but also Jill Bennett's post-matinée fish and chips (no wonder John Osborne called the poor woman an overheated housemaid).

Sir Ralph, one of the true originals of the British theatre, was a big hero. 'He was fearless and honest and didn't tell any lies. And he was totally centred,' Alan told *GQ* magazine in July 1992.

It's only fair to point out that Nigel Hawthorne, later to act alongside Alan in the BBC's *Barchester Chronicles* plus a Peter Barnes play, told me that he couldn't recall his tall, lanky, morose-looking dresser. 'I do remember it being a particularly happy time, and that Ralph Richardson was always a source of great entertainment. I undertook the role of his secretary so I could be next to the great man and observe him at close quarters. It seems very much as though Alan Rickman was doing the same thing from the wings.'

The RADA acting course is renowed for its intensity, and Rickman admitted to *Drama Magazine*'s Barney Bardsley in 1984: 'You do get hauled over the emotional coals. But my body heaved a sigh of relief at being there. So much of your life is conducted from the neck up.' He loved the sheer physicality of the rigorous training, and he was old enough not to be overwhelmed. 'The stillness acclaimed in great actors in fact comes from a body so connected to mind and heart that in a way it vibrates. That's really centred acting. Look at Fred Astaire. You don't look at his feet or arms – you look here,' he said, pointing to a place between his ribs. He quoted the dancer Margaret Beals, who talked about 'catching the energy on its impulsive exits through the body'.

Alan won the Bancroft Gold medal (as did his friend Juliet Stevenson in later years) and the Forbes Robertson Prize. He also shared the Emile Littler award with Nicholas Woodeson at the end of his two-year course. 'There was always something special going on with him,' says actor Stephen Crossley, a RADA contemporary. 'I looked up to him as a brother, because my brother had been an artist at drama school. Alan was very mature as a student: he commanded a great deal of authority. Most people trust him: he inspires tremendous loyalty. He's the most complete man of the theatre I know. He's a tremendous listener, and he's still the steadiest person: that's what will make him a wonderful director.

'He won the Bancroft for generic performances: Pastor Manders in *Ghosts* and Angelo in *Measure For Measure*. Other people tried to imitate his style, but he's not easily imitated. He had a wonderful drawl at RADA – very laconic.

'I was Engstrand in *Ghosts* – the character has a club foot, and I had a very big, incredibly camp wooden boot. Alan said to me, "You'll get the reviews." There was a *Camden Journal* review and I was well mentioned or, rather, the boot was. He hasn't forgiven me for that,' cackles Stephen, not sounding too worried. He can bear testimony to Rickman's loyalty to old friends: twenty years later Stephen was cast in three roles for Alan's *Hamlet* tour in 1992.

Film producer Catherine Bailey – who profiled him on *The Late Show* in November 1994 and with whom Alan and theatre producer Thelma Holt drew up proposals for running Hammersmith's Riverside Studios in West London – was also at RADA at the same time.

'I was six years younger and I always wanted to go into stage management and production,' says Catherine, who looks rather like a younger version of Joan Littlewood (and said she had never been so insulted in her life when I mentioned this). 'But it was obvious that Alan was going to be a special actor; we've been friends ever since. People are fond of him: he's put a lot back into the business.'

And yet he struck some at RADA as rather grand. Deluded with grandeur or not, the 28-year-old Rickman started his career in the grind of weekly repertory theatre like every other aspiring actor. Very few people went straight from drama school to TV or film, as they do now, often to the detriment of their craft.

Patrick (Paddy) Wilson, now a theatre producer, was an acting ASM (Assistant Stage Manager) with Alan on their first job together at Manchester Library Theatre.

'He hasn't changed over the years,' says Paddy. 'There are no airs and graces about Alan. At Manchester, he played the Inquisitor in *St Joan* while I played an English soldier. As the Inquisitor, he acted everyone else off the stage. You got a sort of tingling at the back of the neck when he came on.' Indeed, the *Daily Telegraph* critic Charles Henn called him 'superbly chilling'.

'He was a very private guy: he was never one of the lads, going out to the boozer,' adds Paddy. 'He took things very seriously – acting was his life and he worked very hard at it. I played the butler in *There's A Girl In My Soup* and Alan played the Peter Sellers role. I knew I would miss a cue line to come on with a bag of bagels . . . and I was two or three scenes too early. Alan was so funny about it – Bernard Hill [Paddy was his producer for a revival of Arthur Miller's *A View From The Bridge*] would have chopped my head off.

'But Alan would discuss things if you've got a problem. He's never a frightening person.

'Alan was bloody hopeless as an ASM – wouldn't know one end of a broom from the other. But stage management was obviously not what he was destined for. Bernard Hill said to me "I'm going to be a fucking star" and he meant it. With Alan, when you have someone that talented, their career is marked out for them. The jobs come to them.'

Paddy and Alan claim to have really bonded when they played chickens together in the panto *Babes In The Wood*, although their shared socialism obviously helped.

'Alan is not a grand person; he's not on a star routine. There's no flashy motorcar. A lot of people change, but not him. He's just Alan Rickman. Bernard Hill has changed so much, and he was an acting ASM as well. When you first meet Alan, you think he's almost arrogant – there's an aloofness. He speaks very slowly: "Hiiiii . . . I'm Alan Rickman." I talk nineteen to the dozen, and it took me a while to get used to his way.

'You always feel there's something special about him. He had a fantastic presence on stage. I see him quite a bit still, and he's just the same. We think alike politically; I'm the only socialist theatre producer I know. Everyone else in the business wants to be a member of the Garrick Club.'

The theatre director, Clare Venables, was also an actor in the same company. 'I was St Joan to Alan's Inquisitor. We were never intimate friends, but he had a presence even then. Very calm, very much of a piece. He's changed remarkably little. I never got the feeling of him being grubby and stressed-out like most ASMs.

'Lock Up Your Daughters was a terrible production. I did the choreography. Alan played an old man behind a newspaper and sat on the side of the stage like a Muppet critic. He came out with acid comments about what was going on. I don't remember him ever doing the drama-queen stuff that most people do.

'There was something quite significant about him having had other irons in the fire, what with his background as an artist. He was someone who was looking rather quizzically at this profession that he'd entered.

'Controlled rage is quite a trick, and he had it. It was always pretty clear that he was a one-off – which is a sureish sign that there's real talent there. He has a very clear, self-contained way of speaking. That, and his stillness are two great qualities.'

Gwenda Hughes was also an ASM at Manchester at that time, along with the actress Belinda Lang (who is still a friend of Alan's and lived for years in the next street to his in Westbourne Grove). 'He was very clever – tall, brainy, talented and rather scary,' was Gwenda's impression of this aloof creature.

The tall, brainy and scary one moved on to two Leicester theatres, the Haymarket and the Phoenix, in 1975. There he made friends with a young actress called Nicolette (Niki) Marvin who is now a Hollywood producer. Both were late starters to acting, since Niki had trained as a dancer; and both became impatient with the empty-headed, unfocused time-wasters who didn't knuckle down to hard work. It was an obvious bond; and, if Rickman gets his heart's desire to direct a film in Hollywood, Niki Marvin will be his producer.

The two Leicester theatres were both run by Michael Bogdanov, later to be sued (unsuccessfully) for obscenity by 'clean-up' campaigner Mrs Mary Whitehouse as a result of putting bare-arsed buggery on the stage of the National Theatre, though she claimed a moral victory.

He cast Alan as Paris in a production of *Romeo And Juliet*, with the classically beautiful Jonathan Kent (who went on to run London's fashionable Almeida Theatre with Ian McDiarmid) as Romeo. Frankly, Alan just didn't *look* like one of life's Romeos, though facial hair was to improve him no end in later years.

'Alan wasn't actually very impressive as Paris,' admits Bogdanov. 'He was very rhetorical and not very good at fights. But there was a strength and stillness and controlled passion about him.

'We live in the same political ward. His lady and mine are very good friends. He's an absolutely natural person: there's no side to him. His own ego is not to the fore all the time; he has a sense of humour. The cult of "luvvyism" is vastly exaggerated; actors by and large are sober people.

'He was very striking-looking at Leicester, but I can't say that I thought he stood out fantastically, because I had a wonderful company of extroverts ... people like the director Jude Kelly and Victoria Wood's husband, Geoff Durham.

'But Alan was a wonderful company member, supportive of everything that happened. He mucked in with simple chores, a very prized quality that is quite often in short supply. He was very focused, intellectually very advanced, so he was able to get to the heart of a problem very quickly. He did street work with children, too.

'It was a very democratic company – even the cleaner had a casting vote for the programme. But after a while, I decided to abandon that because I thought being a dictator was good for the drama.'

A picture of Alan in a group shot for *Guys And Dolls*, directed by Robin Midgley and Robert Mandell, shows a Guy in long blond hair with designer stubble, flared trousers and plimsolls. Attitude is already his middle name. He's easily the most self-possessed of the bunch as he stares hard, almost challengingly, at the camera in a 'You lookin' at me?' kind of way. Another tough-guy role followed as Asher, one of Joseph's bad brothers in the Lloyd-Webber/Rice musical *Joseph and the Amazing Technicolor Dreamcoat*.

It was in 1976, when he joined the Sheffield Crucible, that Alan Rickman met an amusing mouth-almighty from Chicago called Ruby Wax. They shared a flat. He argued with her about the central-heating levels and all kinds of other domestic niggles; but she consistently made him laugh. She was not your average repertory company player; she didn't really seem to be a jobbing actress, because the personality was too big to play anyone but herself.

It was Rickman who persuaded her to start writing comedy. And thus was forged a lifelong friendship . . . most of Alan's friendships are lifelong. Ruby, forever playing the stage American, reckons that Rickman gave her a class that she might otherwise never have had (oh, come now). For his part, he admired her 'recklessness and daring'. In truth, she knocked a few of his corners off.

Alan needs funny friends to lift him out of the glooms; and the playwright Peter Barnes became another when Alan was cast in Peter's new version of Ben Jonson's *The Devil Is An Ass* for Birmingham Rep. Indeed, it's not too fanciful to see Peter, fifteen years his senior, as another surrogate father; he is certainly completely frank about Alan in the manner of a fond but plain-speaking parent.

'I have done eleven shows with him,' says Peter. 'We have been friends since 1976 and I've worked with him more than anyone else. 1976 was the first play, my adaptation of *The Devil Is An Ass*. He had a beautiful voice for the poetry and read it exquisitely. He told me, "I saw *The Ruling Class* on TV and it changed my life." So I said to Stuart Burge, the director of *The Devil Is An Ass*, "Well, we've got to have HIM."

'Alan has a humour of his own,' insists Barnes. 'He brings a great talent to comedy. The thing is that he's terribly, depressingly gloomy in rehearsal like other great actors of comedy – one thinks of Tony Hancock.

'Joy is not a word that springs to mind of him in the rehearsal room. He's a bit of a misery-guts. I want to enjoy art, want other people to enjoy it. I said to him, "You bring the rainclouds with you and it rains for the next four weeks." I have to be careful it doesn't spread; that's up to the director. But it springs from the best of motives: he's never satisfied and wants to get it right. Doesn't alter the fact that it's there. But Alan can laugh at himself,' adds Peter. 'When we were working together on the revue *The Devil Himself*, I said to him, "I hope we are going to have a lot of laughs, dancing and singing, with this one, but is that really you, Alan?" He burst out laughing at my image of him going around with a raincloud over his head; I remember it vividly.

'He's very "Keep Death Off The Roads". I find his gloom very funny – it's "Eeyoreish" and endearing. People feel affectionate towards his "Eeyoreish" personality, because they wonder what great tragedy lies behind it. He seems to have some private demons.

'One goes through various stages with friends, blowing hot and cold, but one of the reasons I like Alan is that he has a very good heart under that curmudgeonly exterior. When Stuart Burge, who was one of my favourite directors, died at the beginning of 2002, Alan phoned me up and said he would like to go to the funeral,' says Barnes, who wrote the 84-year-old Burge's obituary in the *Guardian*. 'It was very touching when Alan came, and it's one of the reasons I hope I will always be his friend. There are certain IOUs you pick up in your life and you should always honour them. Stuart was the one who really got Alan into London from the provinces with my version of *The Devil Is An Ass*, because it went to Edinburgh and then to the National; that was Alan's first exposure to the West End. I think it was very good of him to remember what Stuart had done for him; I think it shows a very strong loyalty which I place very high as a virtue. He has integrity. Some like to think they did it all on their own, but Alan doesn't make that mistake.

'Most actors have a feminine side. He manages to be feline without being camp, and does it very well. He designed the posters for my play *Antonio* in which he starred at the Nottingham Playhouse. I joked about the photograph of him as Antonio: "There you are, camping it up." But in fact he's not camp at all.'

It's rather difficult to credit that, what with Alan's eyes ringed in kohl, his hair bleached and permed and that pout in place. He looks like a decadent thirtysomething cherub suffering from orgy-fatigue.

'The vanity of an actor is endearing,' observes Peter. 'Alan doesn't really like being recognised, but he doesn't like not being recognised either. If they aren't recognised, they don't exist. It reminds me of a story about Al Pacino who took great pains not to be recognised – and then complained when he wasn't.'

It was in that hectic year of 1977 that Alan and Rima, still an item after twelve years, decided to move in together.

Although he was doing the dreary rounds of theatrical digs in the provinces, they wanted to show their commitment to each other. So they rented a small, first-floor flat in a three-storey white Victorian terrace on the edge of upmarket Holland Park. It was a quiet, private haven just minutes away from the gridlock of the Shepherd's Bush roundabout, a major west London intersection. Alan was to stay there for the next twelve years.

'With actors, you are buying their personality so you do want to know a bit about their private life. With a writer, it's usually only the writing that people are interested in. There were hundreds of girls waiting for Alan at the stage door when he was doing my version of the Japanese play *Tango At The End Of Winter* in the West End. One of the fans recognised me as the adapter one night and asked for my autograph – but only one,' says Peter with a mixture of regret and relief.

Another old friend from those days is the director, Adrian Noble, who first met Alan in 1976 when Alan and Ruby joined the Bristol Old Vic, where Adrian was an associate director. 'He was in almost the first play I ever directed, back in 1976: Brecht's *Man Is Man*. I stayed with him on a few occasions in an old town house that he shared with Ruby.

'Then he came to Birmingham and did *Ubu Rex*. He played the multi-murderess Ma Ubu, Mrs Ubu, alongside Harold Innocent. Alan was a hoot. There's a side to him that's a real grotesque, and it was first seen as Ma Ubu. I still have a photograph of Alan as Ma, sitting on the toilet and soliloquising with a wig on. Though he doesn't normally like wigs.'

In Bristol, Alan found himself playing next door to Thin Lizzy, and later confessed in a *Guardian* interview with Heather Lawton in 1986 to being 'knocked out by their high-octane excitement. I'm not trying to be a rock group, but there's got to be a version of that excitement – otherwise theatre is a waste of time.'

Rickman's association with Peter Barnes was auspicious from the start (*Tango At The End Of Winter* is, indeed, their only flop). Barnes' version of *The Devil Is An Ass* earned excellent reviews when it travelled to the Edinburgh Festival and the National Theatre.

Alan embarked on yet another drag role as Wittipol, the lovestruck gallant who disguises himself as a flirtatious Spanish noblewoman. The *Daily Telegraph* wrote from Edinburgh of the 'Superb effrontery by Alan Rickman', while Alan's Latymer Upper contemporary Robert Cushman's succinct *Observer* review said it all: 'Alan Rickman speaks breathtaking verse while in drag.' Well, he'd been to the right school for it.

In the *Glasgow Herald*, Christopher Small thought he looked like 'Lady Ottoline Morrell' – something of a mixed compliment, unless you're a tiresome Bloomsbury groupie.

'Alan Rickman is handsome, graceful and inventively funny as Wittipol and a couple of ladies!' noted another writer in the *Observer* of 8 May, while John Barber in the *Daily Telegraph* admired 'Mr Rickman's capital scene when, disguised as a Spanish lady, he imposes himself on society and reels off a wonderful recipe for painting the face.'

'Alan Rickman caresses Anna Calder-Marshall with the most honeyed, erotic words imaginable,' wrote the *Sunday Telegraph* in a ferment of lather. A photograph in the *Coventry Telegraph* proves that Alan looked more like Charley's Aunt than a Spanish lady, although the *Guardian* kindly compared him with Fenella Fielding.

The previous year, Alan had also played Sherlock Holmes for Birmingham Rep, still looking like an overpromoted schoolboy under the deerstalker. 'Although looking a little young for the part, he catches just the right combination of *fin de siècle* cynicism and scientific curiosity,' opined the *Birmingham Post*.

The *Sunday Mercury* was almost orgasmic over this new discovery: 'Holmes is played with superb coolness and languid authority by Alan Rickman in a performance which interweaves touches of melodrama with masterpieces of understatement in such an absorbing and funny fashion that it dazzles the audience. Others on stage therefore look grey and we have the odd phenomenon of a one-man show with a cast of more than 20.'

Castle Bromwich News also rhapsodised: 'The play is worth seeing for Alan Rickman's superb tongue-in-cheek portrayal.' But the *Express & Star* was vitriolic: 'Alan Rickman's Sherlock Holmes behaves like a supercilious prefect, whose deductions are one-upmanships more than shrewd observations. His most common expression is a smirk, which one longs for David Suchet's bald domed Moriarty to wipe off his face.' (Temper, temper!)

Yet *Redbrick*, the Birmingham University paper, knew a man who could wear a deerstalker when it saw one: 'Alan Rickman's brilliantly funny performance as Holmes . . . rightly dominates the stage and keeps the subtle humour flowing.'

All of which was most encouraging, so he took the logical next step up and auditioned for the Royal Shakespeare Company at a time when, as Adrian Noble recalls, '. . . it was an odd year, a fantastically competitive one'.

In 1978, Alan joined the RSC, and Ruby went too for a series of small roles that she was later to describe as 'chief wench'. It was a period in his life that was to prove disastrous for his development and very nearly led to him leaving the profession for good. Alan Rickman does not thrive on gladiatorial combat against other actors; an uncompetitive soul, he withdraws broodily into his shell instead. That passive aggression comes out when he retreats into his citadel as if he were playing life as a game of Chinese chess.

In 1994 he told his former Leicester colleague Jude Kelly at the West Yorkshire Playhouse in front of an audience of 750: 'I was miscast very quickly in national companies. I was unhappy very quickly and I ran very quickly! Within four years of leaving drama school, I ran away from the Royal Shakespeare Company and found the Bush Theatre and Richard Wilson, a wonderful theatre director who taught me stuff I needed to know.

'You go to places like Stratford and learn how to bark in front of 1,500 people. You're taught that talking to people on stage isn't very valuable and that what you should do is shout. I met Richard Wilson and he was my saviour.'

It was at the RSC that Alan first met Juliet Stevenson. She has since become such an inseparable friend and collaborator that the playwright Stephen Davis mischievously calls Rickman and Stevenson 'the Lunts of our day' after the rather grand Broadway actors Alfred Lunt and Lynn Fontanne, famously despised by anti-hero Holden Caulfield in The Catcher In The Rye.

'Alan was always rather intimidating,' Juliet told GQ magazine in 1992. 'We first met when Ruby and I were playing Shape One and Shape Two in The Tempest with plastic bags over our heads.

'I was quite frightened of him, but he was very kind and sort of picked me up in a non-sexual way. He had a talent for collecting people and encouraging them.'

He went there with what he called 'a burning idealism' and was inevitably disappointed. One RSC director told James Delingpole in the Daily Telegraph in 1991: 'When he first came to Stratford, it was terribly embarrassing. There was one season when he was so awful that we had a directors' meeting and we asked each other, "What are we going to do with him?" Then he just grew up and suddenly everyone wanted this wonderful new leading man.'

Clifford Williams, his director for a notoriously jinxed production of The Tempest in which Alan played the rather forgettable part of Miranda's suitor Ferdinand, remembers all the problems with a polite shudder.

The lasers broke down on the first night and Sheridan Fitzgerald, who played Miranda, cut her nose very badly on a piece of jutting scenery. The stage looked like an abattoir as a result.

'Alan was difficult in rehearsal; he even found difficulties in lifting logs,' admits Clifford. 'But there were problems with the production. We got on well, though.

'Mind you, I also thought I got on very well with Michael Hordern, who played Prospero. Then I went into Smiths to buy his autobiography and in it he had referred to me as "that boring man" – it was such a shock.

'I recall distinctly that Alan was very meticulous, anxious to rehearse everything inordinately. We ran out of time. I got rather impatient at the time, I must admit. He had terrific charisma, slouched about and had this deep slurred voice. He was always examining things. He questioned rather more than the part of Ferdinand warranted, frankly.

'This was the 1970s, yet he wasn't at all the hippie type. He was a contradiction in terms: extremely acute and questioning, and sometimes appeared almost antagonistic.

'But physically he was very relaxed, almost *louche*, slouching, with a slurred voice. He was an odd paradox. He struck me as a rather modern actor, by which I mean he questioned, he was his own man. He was not quite part of some RSC tradition.

'I think he was of the Jonathan Miller school: not keen on projecting. In the RSC's Royal Shakespeare Theatre at Stratford-upon-Avon, you have to push it out. It's not an intimate theatre. Eventually he was extremely good, though the production wasn't. I'm afraid it wasn't,' allows Clifford, 'the cat's whiskers. And Alan seemed to lack energy in rehearsal. But I couldn't be unaffectionate about him, though I certainly could about some other actors whom I won't mention.

'I think he was being deliberately laid-back: he wanted not to get too quickly involved in things, he was trying to pace himself. But you realised he was not relaxed at all. Yet he struck me as always totally sincere. I never felt he was playing tricks to conceal anything, as some do.

'He would make an extremely good Prospero now – he has the weight and the clarity,' adds Clifford.

'I remember him as always hitching up his jeans with his sweater hanging down over it, standing with hands on hips and looking out front and saying, "Weeeelll . . ." He was rather reserved. I have a feeling that he wished he wasn't there – he was not entirely happy. There was something in the environment of the RSC that didn't suit him. He was a bit in check, holding back. He certainly behaved in a professional way, but he was a bit stiff.

'He was uncertain, insecure. It's a *sine qua non* of their profession. Actors are dealing with their emotions, so perhaps they tend to get worked up more. They are cast on their physical appearance, no matter how one tries to avoid it. So they don't always get to play the parts they feel are within them. It's the Fat Hamlet syndrome.'

Peter Barnes offers another insight into that production: 'I remember him and David Suchet laying into the director of *The Tempest* in David's narrow-boat. Alan asked me for tips for stage business for Ferdinand, and I suggested picking up a really big log in the fuel-gathering scene. Clifford Williams cut it out. So I then suggested going to the other extreme to make a point and fastidiously picking up a tiny twig!

'Most theatre directors are arrogant and incompetent,' adds Peter, who has directed many of his plays himself. 'Over 50 per cent of the plays are directed by the actors. The arrogance and ignorance of directors is astonishing. Most of them come from the universities. Alan doesn't like directors either; he's diplomatic, but underneath he's as venomous as I am.'

Sheridan Fitzgerald left the acting profession to become a theatrical agent and has never regretted it. She traces her disenchantment to that season with Alan at the RSC and vividly remembers their unhappiness at playing such mismatched lovers.

'I didn't enjoy the role of Miranda, but I would never be a Juliet, either. That natural innocence is not me . . . I'm something of a practical beast. I went off to do a bit of TV afterwards, but I wanted to grow up. You have to remain a child for ever as an actor. It's a very victim position to be in. As an agent, I can grow old at my own pace.

'Acting is very vocational. I didn't have that vocation, and at first I wondered whether Alan did either. He was miscast the first time round at the RSC. I thought the place was like a boarding-school. I looked at him, and thought. "THAT'S my Ferdinand??!" He just wasn't a romantic young leading man.

'You can do Ferdinand if you come on looking like a dish. Alan, bless him, did not look like a dish.

'At first he looks quite evil' (and with Sheridan, this is meant as a compliment). 'So there he was, looking evil, and Miranda is supposed to be a complete innocent. Frankly I felt that his Ferdinand and my Miranda were heading for a shotgun wedding.

'It was a jinxed production: Clifford Williams had a motorbike accident shortly after we opened. And then an actress called Susannah Bishop tore an Achilles tendon, so Juliet Stevenson had to step in.

'A lot of egoes were crashing around in that production. Ian Charleson was sulking because he was trying to play the sprite Ariel as a political figure.

'Alan announced he didn't like playing young lovers. He tried to bring out the humour instead, and I developed my gallows-humour as a result,' says Sheridan with a wry laugh. 'I was never part of the wining, dining, clubbing set at the RSC that he seemed to be part of. He immediately took to Ruby Wax and Juliet Stevenson – I thought they could easily play brother and sister, or husband and wife. I was not part of Ruby's circle: they would punt down the river, do anything that was fun and vibrant.

'In fact, there was something slightly withdrawn about Alan. He was not part of the bridge-game clique. I had the impression that the girls were cheering him up and he was appreciating their qualities, especially Ruby. No one could see what she was doing at the RSC. So it was an almost charmed circle.

'Ian Charleson was another friend, they had the same political perspective,' adds Sheridan of the actor who went on to make his name in the Oscar-winning film *Chariots Of Fire* but later died, tragically young, of an AIDS-related illness. 'The common denominator with Ruby, Juliet, Alan, Ian and also Fiona Shaw is that they were all risk-takers. I remember when Juliet took over from Susannah at short notice. She was playing a part in the masque, and suddenly we realised she had something.

'That drawling university articulation in Alan's speech was not unfriendly, but I would never have guessed that he came from the working classes. I can't imagine him as a juvenile in rep. There was always a certain amount of maturity in him. I could never imagine him as a silly young man.

'He certainly had the capacity to be brilliant, but he was totally miscast as Ferdinand. He would have been a very funny Trinculo instead. Bless him, he tried. I think he knew he was miscast, but I think he felt he still had to try.

'And of course you have to learn to shout with the RSC. With Ciss Berry (Cicely Berry, the famous voice coach), you put five inches on your rib-cage.

'Alan's voice goes with his body-language – slow-moving. The arrogance that says, "I will not be hurried ..." There's an impression of arrogance. I found that arrogance quite threatening, but I remember his moments of gentleness too. His drawling voice and languid body seem contemptuous, but you eventually find that he isn't.

'It could have been a defence mechanism. Actors have to put on so many shells ... if they're allowed to keep their clothes on, that is. One of the first questions I ask new clients these days is, "Now how do you feel about nudity?"

'But Alan realised I was unhappy at the RSC, and we would go off together to try to make things work out. His whole voice changed then; he lost the actor's drawl and he became far more friendly.

'He had a lot of wit about him. He was into intelligent conversation, a wicked sense of fun. I came more and more to the idea of Alan really liking women: he likes their minds, and he had a big female coterie around him. He admires women's minds; so many men just want you for your body. He recognises talent; and he has a soft side. It's enormously flattering to Rima that he's interested in women's minds, because he's so witty and dry.

'It was mentioned that he had a steady girlfriend, but it was never overloaded into the conversation. It was just understood that he was spoken for. But none of the other men came into the Green Room or the dressing-room for long chats in the way that he would. There was this appeal about Alan. He would flirt, but in a non-threatening way. In an enormously flattering way. His moral code, his fidelity to Rima, is a grown-up side to him; so many actors remain children.

'He drew a very wide range of women around him – Carmen Du Sautoy, Jane Lapotaire, all very different. He brought a little bit of flamboyant gayness to the role of Boyet in Love's Labours Lost, but he was absolutely not gay himself.

'He's one of those very masculine men who never ever felt the need to prove his manliness and who is completely relaxed with women as a result. Some men feel like sex objects as well these days, and young actors are always mentioning their girlfriends to me just to make sure no one assumes they're gay.

'Alan doesn't flannel himself and flatter himself, even with all those female chests heaving out in his wake and all their grey cells fluttering out to meet his. I don't think I appreciated him enough at the time, and I don't think you can blame those who cast us. Both Alan and I were perfectionists; and we knew we were cheating at Ferdinand and Miranda.

'Had Alan been my first director, I might have been terrified of him because of the superficial first impression, especially if I had known of his hyper-intelligence. But he's a good 'un,' concludes Sheridan, 'despite the initial appearance.

'I did realise he was unhappy too, but he had the intelligence to get out of the RSC then. I was just so wrapped up in my own vulnerability. He's definitely a survivor. As an agent, I would have loved his initial attitude that an actor can and should be able to play anyone. We have something in common in that I used to try to make good boring girls interesting, while he has humanised villains.

'Michael Hordern was playing Prospero in our production of *The Tempest*, and even he was unhappy. He had difficulty in learning the lines. Everyone seemed to have their own ideas of how to play the role and no one would compromise. And the laser lighting went out of the window.

'On the first night, the blow from the scenery knocked me out . . . I came to as the lights went up. It was like Moby Dick . . . blood all over the place. The computer lighting broke down, so I lost my guiding light. And the dry-ice machines were slightly leaking. I stumbled off and Makeup gave me a false nose to cover the bleeding.

'Alan was great when I came back on stage like Cyrano de Bergerac. He would mutter through his teeth, "You are pumping blood again", and turn me round so the audience couldn't see.

'He was very good at thinking on his toes and being sympathetic; a crisis seemed to bring out the best in him.

'I really laughed at his card when he was leaving: it said "Alloa", because it was from Hawaii, and he wrote underneath, "Goodbye-ee". If I had been less vulnerable at the time, I think we would have become great friends.'

Needless to say, the critics had some fun with *The Tempest*'s opening-night problems, in some cases almost forgetting to review the play itself.

B. A. Young in the *Financial Times* was quite kind: 'Apart from an occasional habit of slurring two or three words together at the start of a speech, Alan Rickman is a personable, if not exactly magnetic Ferdinand ... Miranda is a brighter girl than we sometimes see, as Sheridan Fitzgerald plays her.' He even found Michael Hordern's 'down-to-earth' Prospero 'vivid and uncommon'.

But the *Daily Telegraph*'s John Barber found 'Alan Rickman's Ferdinand a gawky oddity', while Irving Wardle in *The Times* didn't mention him at all. 'Michael Hordern was able to leave a lasting impression, but little else did,' said the *Leicester Graphic*, which mustered a wonderfully unflattering cartoon of Rickman, Fitzgerald and Hordern trying to make themselves heard above the sound and fury of an out-of-control storm. Milton Shulman in the London *Evening Standard*, however, found Rickman and Fitzgerald 'suitably star-crossed as young lovers' ... perhaps he was impressed by Alan's tender ministrations in the First Aid department.

After a frustrating season of small roles, Rickman left the RSC in 1979 to strike out on his own. Away from the big companies, he hoped to rediscover his talent before it was too late.

He found it with the help of another late starter, the actor and director Richard Wilson, at a tiny experimental theatre over an unpretentious Irish pub in London's Shepherd's Bush. It was back to the future as he started all over again, earning a pittance at the age of 33.

4. 'THE WICKEDEST MAN IN BRITAIN'

'Alan is interesting because of the the very long wait he had for recognition,' says the playwright Stephen Poliakoff. 'Not until Obadiah Slope did he become known.'

Ah, yes: Obadiah Slope, the Victorian uber-creep whose devious, cringing sexuality made him a cross between Dickens' Uriah Heep and Mervyn Peake's Steerpike. One felt almost furtive about fancying such a snake-in-the-grass; but millions of female TV viewers most certainly did. And because there is always a connecting thread running through everything Rickman does, his characterisation of Slope was to lead on to one of his most famous roles in the film versions of J.K. Rowling's *Harry Potter* books.

'We all envied him that glorious part,' Nigel Hawthorne told me about Slope, 'but he was so absolutely right for it, and did it with such huge relish, that there was no doubt in anybody's mind that he was going to make a tremendous impact.

'This of course happened. And then it seemed peculiar, to me at any rate, who was enviously watching the acclamation given to Alan, that he turned down so many projects which were offered to him as not being the right step for him to take.

'It seemed to me almost as though he was squandering his opportunities by not taking them when they were presented ... and perhaps leaving things too late.'

Even as Rickman escaped from the RSC in 1979 to do the rounds of the rep theatre companies once again, he was on the brink of becoming a well-known face on British television.

His first foray into TV occurred in 1978 as Tybalt, Prince of Cats, in a television production of *Romeo And Juliet* that the BBC has long since wiped from the archives.

But his TV career really started in 1979 when he was specially written into a very erotic BBC serialisation of Émile Zola's *Thérèse Raquin*, starring Kate Nelligan and Brian Cox.

'In our production of *Thérèse Raquin*, we needed to give her lover, Laurent, a friend to talk to in his scenes away from her ... so Vidal had to be created,' says its producer Jonathan Powell, who went on to become Head of Drama at Carlton Television. 'The director Simon Langton cast Alan as Vidal. What struck us was that Alan brought a whole interior life to this made-up character. It was obvious you were in the presence of a major actor.'

'It was almost the first thing that Alan had done on TV,' says Simon Langton. 'My first impression of him was a laconic drawl, which is his trademark. At first I thought he was a little too contemporary for Vidal.

'But he had such a physical presence – a natural, unflustered approach. A man of the world. Plus he was humorous, which was very important.

'*Thérèse Raquin* is one of the first sexy novels ever written. It's very much the darker side of sex and illicit love, and we had to manifest that in every way. I don't like it on TV as a rule: you impose an anxiety on your audience,' says Simon, a veteran of *Upstairs Downstairs* and *The Duchess Of Duke Street* who went on to direct such acclaimed, award-winning series as *Smiley's People* and *Mother Love*.

In 1995, Simon had a huge popular hit with Andrew Davies' racy BBC1 adaptation of *Pride And Prejudice*. Although he thinks that now he probably couldn't get away with many of the sado-masochistic sex scenes in *Thérèse Raquin* in a politically correct climate that fights shy of sexual violence between men and women (although not, cynics would say, in a same-sex scenario), his dramatisation of Jane Austen's most popular novel famously plunged Colin Firth's Mr Darcy into a lake in order to cool his pent-up desires for Lizzie Bennet. You can always say it with symbolism.

'Since Vidal was an artist, we used a well-known artist's studio in Chelsea. We booked the girl who played the artist's model. She had to cross from one side of the room to the other and sit down as if about to pose. In the rushes, everyone was watching this naked girl: but the boom operator and the sound recordist were caught on frame, crouching in the corner. No one had noticed them at first because everyone was looking at the girl. It was quite funny.

'The shooting took two weeks. Alan's hair was cut in a fourteenth-century pageboy style. He wouldn't wear a wig. He had this marvellous, aquiline Roman nose and looked very haughty.

'He didn't have a scintilla of nerves with this naked model. Jonathan Powell said, "He's going places" and swore by him. And he did have a magnetism. He wasn't at all nervous, although it was only his second TV.

'It was all done in a rush, because we were behind schedule. We had to cut corners; but he was terribly unfazed by the pressure and sailed through it, whereas other people would get rattled. Most of it was done on tape: it was very fevered filming.

'Vidal's worldly-wise smile desperately worried Laurent, who had just killed Camille. You wondered just how much Vidal knew about his friend; there was always an enigmatic quality about him. Alan was very self-composed; you didn't have to guide him much. There was no agonising over motivation: he sees things quite clearly and directly. He doesn't go in for bullshit or any equivocation. He's no luvvie.'

The story of Thérèse is the story of a strong-willed, fiercely repressed, highly sexed woman who is stifled in a loveless marriage to Kenneth Cranham's pallid Camille, living with his elderly mother (played by the late, great Mona Washbourne). Kate Nelligan has a lethal inertia as Thérèse, just waiting to be awakened.

When she meets Brian Cox's moustachioed, ox-like Laurent, he becomes her lover behind the back of his best friend Camille. He's a rebel who appeals to her brooding nature; and his Bohemian friends, such as Vidal, have an earthy, worldly attitude towards women and sex.

Rickman's Vidal is a flamboyant fop who bluntly asks Laurent why he hasn't been to bed with Thérèse yet. In the fashion of the time, he has a luxuriant moustache and beard and wears a neckcloth. He has the worst haircut in living history: it looks as if he spent the night in curlers. He also wears an unfortunate fringe, which has the effect of making him look like Eric Idle from Monty Python. Somehow he carries it off.

Laurent eventually drags Thérèse down for burly sex on the carpet; it's all very animalistic and sexy and uninhibited for dear old 'Auntie Beeb'. They have sex games on the bed, when she prowls around on all fours in her frilly drawers and pretends to be a wild animal. These fleshly pursuits are brutally contrasted with the naked, decomposing corpses on the slabs at the morgue: on-lookers, including very young children, gaze morbidly at this almost pornographic display.

'She always comes early in case there's anything else I want,' says Rickman airily at Vidal's studio, gesturing at his naked model.

'Would you like her?' he asks Laurent. 'She won't cost much and she's as clean as a whistle.' Laurent is certainly attracted to her, but his yearning for Thérèse makes him turn down the offer.

Laurent and Thérèse conspire to drown Camille in a lake on a day's outing and manage to pass it off as an accident. His mother's circle of friends, never once suspecting foul play, eventually make a match between the widowed Thérèse and her late husband's best friend. But Camille's ghost comes between the lovers; and Thérèse is going mad with guilt.

Meanwhile Vidal has become rich and famous, with a fashionable salon. Laurent goes back to visit him, telling him he has set up in a studio to learn to paint like Vidal. He asks him for a second opinion. Rickman screws up his already hooded eyes and looks inscrutably at the daubs, still keeping us guessing about whether the ever-cool Vidal suspects the sweating Laurent of murder. Laurent is drawing tormented portraits of some skill and feeling, he says. But, remarks Vidal critically, he always uses the same model . . .

That is the last we see of Vidal, who has served his purpose. Cynic that he is, at least he was open about his desires. Thérèse, whom sex has imprisoned rather than liberated, has become a hard-faced, painted street tart. 'I'm as tired of life as you are,' she says to Laurent, offering to go to the police. The lovers, now bound together in hate, confront each other. They drink Prussic acid in a death pact as Camille's mother watches, paralysed, with the accusing eyes of her murdered son.

The role of Obadiah Slope in the BBC's *Barchester Chronicles* was still three years away. But the *Thérèse Raquin* team of Simon Langton and Jonathan Powell cast Rickman again in *Smiley's People*, the 1981 sequel to John Le Carré's *Tinker Tailor Soldier Spy*. If you blink, you'll miss his one appearance behind a desk. But even as a receptionist at London's Savoy Hotel in a scene with Alec Guinness as George Smiley, he still made an impact.

'The little parts always meant something in *Smiley's People*,' remembers Powell. 'The doormen etc. always had a personality. And of course people came along just to have a scene with Alec. Those who wouldn't normally do a part consisting of two lines did it in order to act with Alec. I had seen Alan as Trigorin in *The Seagull*, and remembered him from *Thérèse Raquin*. So all that decided it.'

Alan played Mr Brownlow, an upright young functionary with a luxuriant, almost military moustache. (I have a theory that he stowed it away in an envelope afterwards to recycle it for the part of Jamie in *Truly Madly Deeply*.) He joked with Smiley, a regular visitor whom he knew of old. Brownlow kept a shopping bag in the hotel safe for him, jesting that he hoped the carrier-bag wasn't ticking. Not exactly a part with a neon arrow over it, but another of those high-quality productions that Rickman prized above all else.

Which was why he dived back so quickly into theatre after leaving the RSC. Firstly, Nottingham Playhouse, then the Glasgow Citizens' Theatre and, afterwards, the Sheffield Crucible.

Peter James, now the head of the London drama school LAMDA, cast him when directing Stephen Poliakoff's *The Summer Party* at the Sheffield Crucible in 1980.

They had worked together before when James cast him as Jaques in *As You Like It* at Sheffield in 1977, with Ruby Wax in one of her many early 'wench' roles as Audrey. 'Jaques was absolutely where he lived,' says Peter. 'That quality of stillness that allowed him to be as aloof as you hope Jaques to be. He was brilliant, mature beyond his years.' He was 31 by then.

'You would listen to Alan for his opinion on design and a quasi-directorial feel for the overall, for what is going on.

'It's either a pain in the arse or a huge advantage. He was very sympathetic to the way things were being done, so he was a huge advantage. He was a marvellous company member, a terrific person to have in a group.

'In *The Summer Party*, Alan played a pop promoter called Nigel. It was well ahead of its time, a play about how top policemen were becoming media figures. Brian Cox played the lead and Dexter Fletcher was a pop star with Uri Geller properties. It was set in the backstage area, and showed how a pop star and a policeman turn out to be very similar.

'Hayley Mills and Alan were two city types who put on the concert. Hayley never got the chance to work in rep; she wasn't offered the roles. It's a shame.

'One felt Alan was going places because of the intellectual vigour he was bringing to the part. He expected very high standards of others, but that didn't manifest itself in impatience. There's a graciousness there; he would assume you were mortified if you missed your cue, so he wouldn't rub it in. There was no short-temperedness from him.'

'I don't remember having any audibility or clarity problems with Alan at all,' adds Pete. 'Sheffield and the Citz are smaller families than the RSC. They're not so competitive and probably more easily open to his influence. One can't imagine him pushing himself in any situation, but always having the same quiet modesty. The scenery in Glasgow was beginning to walk round the actors, he said; so he left.'

Alan had been cast in a total of seven roles in Giles Havergal's acclaimed Citz revival of the Bertolt Brecht play about the rise of Nazism, Fears And Miseries Of The Third Reich. Michael Coveney in the Financial Times noted how 'layers of authoritarian corruption are laid bare with merciless economy and real glee' by Rickman's performance as a judge wrestling with his professional conscience.

Prior to that, he had taken the role of Antonio in Peter Barnes' conflation of two plays by the Elizabethan dramatist John Marston: Antonio And Mellida and its sequel, Antonio's Revenge. That was the occasion when Alan designed the morbid poster of himself, half-naked in an almost crucified pose with a pronounced pout and an embarrassment of rich eye makeup. One of those collector's items that comes back to haunt you.

Marston wrote the two plays for a company of child-actors, Paul's Boys. There was indeed something of the precocious choirboy – as most of the young players had been – about Alan's melodramatic pose.

'Antonio is the Hamlet story done in a totally different way by John Marston,' explains Barnes. 'Alan came in, swinging on a rope: inevitably something went wrong and he was clinging to the scenery, suspended in the air. So years later, in Die Hard, he was the one that suggested swinging in on a rope. He never forgets anything.'

Rickman returned to work with Peter Barnes after The Summer Party at Sheffield, taking part in Peter's version of Frank Wedekind's The Devil Himself at the Lyric Studio in London's Hammersmith. Here, the Rickman singing voice was first heard by the public, wooing audiences with bawdy songs for a little-known but extraordinarily erotic interlude in his patchwork career.

Barnes recalls how another cast-member, Dilys Laye, 'saw Alan looking ashen-grey in the wings. He said, "God, this isn't easy, is it?"' But it was to prove the most extraordinary liberation for him. This uninhibited musical revue was a collection of songs and sketches on the theme of sex; Wedekind wrote a great deal of experimental cabaret material before embarking on his plays. Rickman played a punter at a brothel in several pieces, with his RADA contemporary Tina Marian as the young tart he visited. Charles Keating also appeared in what was to become Peter's very own repertory company for several of his radio plays.

In a sequence called 'The Sacrificial Lamb', Rickman asked for Tina's life story or 'confession'. Addressing her as 'My child', her john clearly got considerable kicks from posing as her priest. 'First I want you to uncover yourself completely, not only your clothes but your skin. Are you still in love with the man? The man you are going to tell me about?' he asked unctuously.

Then he launched into various ballads, sounding rather like a sonorous monk with a gloriously deep baritone that strays into the tenor range. This was Rickman letting his inhibitions down: one song carried a comic refrain about 'frayed trousers':

I slaughtered my aunt last week
but she was old and weak
The blood began to spout
as I shredded her like sauerkraut
I tried burning her
she wouldn't ignite

One song celebrated a boy/girl of indeterminate sex while Alan tap-danced around in the role of a happy drunk. In another liaison between Alan and Tina as a girl called Wanda, he breathed insinuatingly: 'I know your whole being . . . your way of loving . . .' He claimed to be able to tell what a woman is like from her walk, whether she's 'free or small-minded'. That languorous, highly suggestive voice was used to great effect on all these coded messages of love.

Above all, humour was paramount when he played a frustrated client with a bad case of ballsache: 'She almost kicked me out of bed . . . she won't strip! My flame is once again lit, but then she starts pulling back instead of pulling IT,' he added venomously.

A tape of the production records the rest of the cast corpsing at Alan's refrain, 'Oooh-ahh, the bugs are back again.' Nursing the mother of all hangovers, his voice slid over the notes of a Bessie

Smith melody in a wonderfully liquid way. 'I groan on my bed . . .
I feel dead . . . Oh, Christ, what a picture, I grit my teeth and reach
for Nietzsche,' warbled Rickman, archly adding a 'ha!' at the end
of the song.

There was always a sarcastic, slightly facetious tone to his
singing voice. Yet many of those flippant lyrics carried a deadly
serious sting: of Europe's war-mongering history, he declared: 'It's
a pleasure every year to rearrange Europe's frontier . . . politicians
believe that human beings grow like weeds.'

After that came the first of two formative stints at the tiny Bush
Theatre above an Irish pub in west London's scrubby Shepherd's
Bush, just down the road from where Alan and Rima had played
in an amateur production of Night Must Fall fifteen years previously
in 1965. The Bush must have felt like a homecoming. Its other
great advantage was Richard Wilson, later to achieve national fame
on British television as the comic grouch Victor Meldrew, among
its roster of directors.

'At that point my whole working life changed,' Alan was later to
declare of the move to the Bush for Dusty Hughes' play Commitments, the story of vicious in-fighting on the Left during the
ill-fated Edward Heath Government of the 1970s.

The Rickman/Wilson association proved a break-through partnership, though they did have one disaster together. 'Alan was my
assistant director on the Robert Holman play Other· Worlds at the
Royal Court. It had terrible reviews and emptied the theatre. Yet,
occasionally people say to me "What a great play that was" and I
say "Which night did you go?" ' says Wilson drily.

'When I first auditioned people for Commitments at the Bush,
Alan struck me as very centred and easy. If you take Alan, you take
his thoughts as well. He is never lost for a thought; he does speak
his mind. But I found him very easy to work with; we are on the
same wavelength.

'Both of us are into openness, a word we use a lot. It's working
from the inside, non-demonstrative acting. Minimalism, anti-
gestural. That's one of the problems with the RSC, one I'm not so
keen on. It's because of the problems of the large Stratford stage,
so I'm not surprised he had difficulties there. Alan is a minimalist,
so his style of acting works particularly well on film and TV.

'He's metamorphic in the subtextual sense. His thinking is so
accurate, his concentration is total. He concentrates on who he is.

He has a great physical sense of where to put himself. That comes back to his artist's eye.

'Unfortunately I lost him to the role when I did the TV version of *Commitments*; so I cast Kevin McNally instead. Alan had committed himself to *The Seagull* at the Royal Court Theatre. But he had become a member of the Board at the Bush by that stage.'

Indeed, it was at the Bush that Rickman became a script-reader or 'taster' alongside Simon Callow and first discovered the playwright Sharman Macdonald when she sent in the play *When I Was A Girl I Used To Scream And Shout* under the pseudonym of Pearl Stewart. The congenitally shy Sharman, who still speaks in a whisper, was very diffident about her writing abilities.

She renamed herself Pearl after a song by her heroine Janis Joplin, because the Bush's then Artistic Director, Jenny Topper, already knew Sharman as an actress. Alan suspected the old-fashioned name was bogus, given the new-fashioned, explicitly gynaecological material, but shoved the script at Jenny Topper, saying: 'I think you should read this. It has something.' It was his 'feminine' sensibilities again that had recognised the originality of this rites-of-passage play. The result transferred to the West End for a year-long hit run, won an *Evening Standard* Drama award and launched Sharman on a writing career. Years later, in 1995, Alan was to commission and direct another play by Sharman in the hope of beginning a new career for himself.

Dusty Hughes, former *Time Out* theatre critic turned director and writer, has been friends with Alan since that first meeting on *Commitments*. 'I ran the Bush; then I decided to do what I'd always wanted to do and write plays.

'The first play was fairly autobiographical. Alan came to the audition for the main part of Hugh in *Commitments*. He was far and away the best person we auditioned; no contest. We even saw Charlie Dance, who was unknown then. Alan's lightness of touch impressed me most, combined with a necessary weight – which is a very rare thing.

'I got the impression he had never done a huge naturalistic part in a modern play before. He got wonderful reviews and his career really took off. Hugh, the character he played, was me, really.

'Alan was studying all my mannerisms, pushing the floppy hair back the way I do. I didn't realise that he had been staring at me all through the run.

'Hugh is a happy-go-lucky liberal intellectual who becomes transformed as a fire-breathing Trotskyist. It was typical of Alan's sharpness that he spotted a weakness in the play, that we never actually got to see that transformation.

'He came on as himself: dry, droll and sardonic. I think he is a very strong personality and identity. A very likeable one. You wouldn't necessarily put money on either him or Richard Wilson being prominent one day. There's something archetypal about such actors: they are universal.

'It was a very quiet, ironic performance. He got on very well with Paola Dionisotti in *Commitments*; he's very much an actor's actor. He intensely dislikes actors who work on their own. He's a very hard taskmaster with actors who don't give you enough effort.

'There's a very clear seriousness about him; he's high-minded. But he's not remotely solemn. He's a wonderful gossip, with a droll sense of humour. There's a very funny, sly side to him.

'He's very unmaterialistic: he's a genuine heart-and-soul socialist. He loves nice food and wine like we all do, but doesn't make a big fuss of it. On a personal level, he's terribly sweet. I trust him completely. We are not terribly intimate, but we are fond of each other.

'There have been three phases to Alan. It took him a few years to come to terms with being a star; he's now as easy and relaxed as when I first knew him. In the first stage, he was terrifically exciting to work with; in the second stage, he was trying to come to terms with fame; and in the third stage, he was learning how to deal with a lot of pressure. He always has a ceiling-high pile of scripts: I don't know how you can possibly get through that lot.'

Dusty clearly feels protective about him, and suspects that Alan's socialism has put him beyond the pale in some showbusiness circles.

'He's not a member of the luvvie mafia; he and I don't belong to the set that they want to invite to the *Standard* Awards. Alan is not a member of that inner circle, so he will always be vulnerable. There are lovely people in that inner circle, don't get me wrong. But I think a lot of people have been sidelined. And being socialist or even mildly Labour is one of the reasons he's excluded.'

It is only fair to record that organisers of the London *Evening Standard* Drama Awards have reacted with incredulity – 'Absolutely not true,' snorts one of them derisively – to what seems like writer's paranoia. They point out that Alan is regularly on the guest list of the *Standard*'s annual awards. But he's away filming most of the time, hence the non-appearances. And six years after Dusty first made those remarks to me, Alan was a guest of honour at the *Standard* Drama Awards as one of the contenders for Best Actor for his performance in a sublime revival of *Private Lives*. So there was no dire conspiracy. Instead, because of a recurring stage fright that was to cast a shadow over his career in the late 90s after an unexpectedly disastrous production at the National, he had been a rare sighting on the London stage until that triumph with *Private Lives* broke the jinx and changed everything. And as for Alan's membership of the Labour Party, its leader Tony Blair attended one *Standard* Drama Awards ceremony before his landslide election victory in 1997 that felt rather like a Shadow Cabinet dinner and dance. Fired up on behalf of the arts, it was full of anti-Tory Government rhetoric. Alan's impresario friend, Thelma Holt, a lifelong banner-waving socialist, has a table every year at the event.

Alan was to be reunited with Dusty for the latter's university play *Bad Language* at Hampstead Theatre after stints at Oxford Playhouse and London's Royal Court in 1981, with his move to the latter proving crucial in getting Rickman spotted by the right people. Max Stafford-Clark directed him in Thomas Kilroy's Irish version of Chekhov's *The Seagull*, with Alan playing the Trigorin role under the new name of Aston. There he met another great friend, Harriet Walter, whose Nina became Lily in this transplantation to Galway.

The reviews, however, were very mixed. B. A. Young in the *Financial Times* opined: 'I couldn't understand how anyone could fall in love with Aston as Alan Rickman plays him. He is as passionless as a fish, even when he is making love.' The *Guardian*'s Michael Billington, on the other hand, thought that leading lady Anna Massey was 'superbly backed by Alan Rickman's Aston', and the *Listener*'s John Elsom wrote that 'Alan Rickman's Aston was a fine performance, clarifying Trigorin's fear of failure and his belief that the very nature of his art sucks life dry'.

Fellow Old Latymerian Robert Cushman in the *Observer* was of the opinion that 'Alan Rickman's Trigorin is . . . uncompromising . . . the analysis of his writer's disease is wonderfully lucid. Nina would have to be not only star-struck, but a bit deaf, to fall for him.'

Nevertheless, the playwright Christopher Hampton was to catch that performance and see in Rickman the dread seducer of innocent women for a daring stage adaptation of a notoriously corrupting French novel.

'Alan was enormously creative in *The Seagull*. As Aston, he had a self-loathing and obsession that was quite outstanding,' says Max Stafford-Clark. 'He has got a sexuality that is very particular. The role that created him was Valmont, a complete libertine, and Aston's cynicism played a part in that.

'You know where you are with Alan: if he's in a bad mood, you know he's in a bad mood. He used to be very candid about what he thought. The big companies do rather smother you, and he operates best outside big companies. In some senses he's a bit over-careful about his career. He should tour with my company Out Of Joint. I offered him Plume in *The Recruiting Officer*, but he said he didn't want to play any more parts with lace at the sleeves. It's the Valmont syndrome.

'The frustration of being an actor is that it's sometimes a passive life, hence his involvement with directing. The problem is that he's a brilliant actor, and everyone wants him to act. He's very special; and he's coped with power and comparative wealth with an elegance that eludes a lot of people.'

Having also caught his Aston/Trigorin at the trendy Court address, Jonathan Powell wanted to build on Rickman's impact in *Thérèse Raquin* and *Smiley's People*. The part that was to make Rickman famous on the small screen carried a sexual innuendo far beyond the original characterisation by Anthony Trollope. Obadiah Slope became a byword for beguiling sleaze, thanks to Rickman's insinuating performance.

Dusty remembers: 'Alan and I were having a drink at the bar in the Bush, while he was doing the Stephen Davis play *The Last Elephant*. Alan said to me, "I've just had the most extraordinary experience. An old man kept winking at me. I thought he was trying to get off with me. He came over and said he wanted to run this article on me as the wickedest man in Britain. I said no, thank you."

'Alan thought he was being kind to a tramp, that he was doing him a favour by speaking to him. It turned out to be a tabloid hack.'

Jonathan Powell admits that the casting of Alan as the slimy Obadiah Slope was a second choice, albeit an inspired one: 'Alan

Plater scripted *Barchester Chronicles* from the two Trollope novels, *The Warden* and *Barchester Towers*. We had cast all the major characters with some starry names: Donald Pleasence, Geraldine McEwan, Nigel Hawthorne, etc.

'I think we offered Slope to someone else who turned it down. We were up a gum tree. So I suggested this bloke . . . and the director, David Giles, said, "If you think he's good, cast him." I did think Alan would be brilliant. I also thought it would be nice, in this glittery cast, to have the interloper Slope played by someone who brought no baggage.

'In one article, Alan was quoted as saying "How boring to do a classic serial" – until he picked up the scripts. This was the star part. He was sensational: he had an ability to deliver comedy without upsetting the balance of the piece, to play the part full tilt without being overbearing.

'Of course he was virtually unknown to television audiences. He brought that repressed ambition to the role . . . but it was perfectly judged. It did reveal that he had the makings of a very great actor. It was very clever and perceptive of him to fear being typecast as a Uriah Heep thereafter.

'He's very parsimonious with what he will do, which is a pity for all of us. He says he won't do television now. He's a particularly special, very unique talent.'

Initially Nigel Hawthorne looked set to be the star of *The Barchester Chronicles* with the showy role of the harumphing, irascible Archdeacon Grantly, a part he played with a whirligig impatience. Everything changed, however, when Rickman made his entrance and caught the imagination.

'He has a lovely sardonic warm personality; ladies find him very sexy. He's a very straight guy, very unpretentious. I'm also a socialist, though I don't put myself on the line like he does,' Hawthorne told me.

'He's a dreadful giggler, which is a very endearing side to him. He's very warm, nice and enormously generous, a trait that's not always considered to be very common in theatrical circles. But theatre people are very supportive of one another. He's much more a theatre person than I am: you are constantly under scrutiny.

'He had an extraordinary presence as Slope. I didn't, however, agree with the way he said Slope's last line as if he were cursing like Malvolio: "May you both live for ever!" I always thought it would have been better if he had said it simply.

'Something like Slope sets up a situation you have wanted for a long time; and when it comes, it's not as easy as you think it is,' added Nigel, who found himself in the same position after becoming a great success on both sides of the Atlantic in the role of George III.

'You have to be very wary. You have suddenly been elevated into a commercial position. You have to ask yourself whether this is the right move. Alan wanted to stick out for better . . . he's got that integrity, a very sophisticated attitude that doesn't succumb to flattery. He's able to be aloof.

'But I couldn't believe at first that he would turn down so many roles some of us would give our eye-teeth for,' adds Nigel. 'I understand it now, though: you have to act with conviction.'

Our first glimpse of Slope is of the back of Alan's head: his greased-back hair, worn slightly longer over the collar than the allowable vanity of a bishop's chaplain strictly permits. When he treats us to a full-frontal of his face, Alan is frowning as usual.

Slope's first bid for power comes when he usurps the canon-in-residence's sermon in the cathedral by telling the bishop and his wife – Slope's patroness, Mrs Proudie – that the canon has been frivolously residing on the banks of Lake Como for the last twelve years instead of attending to his duties.

What gives Slope a unique advantage with the ladies is that he is the youngest man in the episcopal circle. His contempt for the bishop, Dr Proudie, is thinly veiled. A serpent in a provincial Eden, he hisses slightly during his maiden sermon at Barchester as he lifts his eyes up in false piety.

Alan's portrayal of Slope is infinitely smoother than Trollope's description, which is pretty damning. The original Slope's lank hair was 'of a dull pale reddish hue . . . formed into three straight lumpy masses . . . and cemented with much grease . . . his face . . . is not unlike beef . . . of a bad quality. His forehead . . . is unpleasantly shining. His mouth is large, though his lips are thin and bloodless . . . big, prominent, pale brown eyes . . . his nose . . . possess(es) a spongy, porous appearance . . . formed out of a red coloured cork. A cold clammy perspiration always exudes from him.'

That is the description of a Dickensian grotesque without any real appeal to women, for all his appalling pretensions. Alan's Slope is a consummate ladies' man, pursuing a protracted and very believable flirtation with Susan Hampshire's Signora Neroni. She, however, is sharp enough to see through him and plays an elaborate game with him as he 'slobbers' (in Trollope's words) over her hand. Alan even manages to make the kissing of her fingers an unusually bold and intimate gesture.

The audience is left to wonder about the exact nature of the intense relationship between Slope and the apparently invalid Signora. He bestows a lot of lingering looks upon her as she reclines on her couch, and she jousts with Mrs Proudie for his attention. He also infuriates the short-fused Archdeacon Grantly, who vows to his wife: 'I shall destroy him.'

'What were you doing with that painted Jezebel?' demands Geraldine McEwan's grande dame of a Mrs Proudie, all organ-stop eyes and shuddering consonants. For Slope has more effect on women than on men. That's his weakness, as Trollope points out: he should have cultivated the men for greater advancement. But he has a vanity, cleverly suggested by Alan's feline performance, that instinctively gravitates towards the distaff side.

He is, in fact, horribly attractive, with his boyish, sensual lips, almond-shaped eyes and sly, sideways glances. The bishop is weak and dithery, easily manipulated by the infernal alliance of his wife and Slope. Of course, Slope turns out to be a brandy snob – a sure sign of his great aspirations – when he declines an impoverished man's offer of some Marsala. Those piously downcast eyelids shoot up as if yanked by a hoist when told that the young widow he has been sniffing round is a woman of wealthy means. Slope slithers from one (im)moral position to another, forever changing his allegiance.

It is a delight to see how the fickle, flirtatious Slope has aroused even Mrs Proudie. 'Your behaviour with women . . .' she enunciates with awful majesty, almost unable to utter the unspeakable. 'At my party, your conduct with that Italian woman was inexcusable.'

In another telling piece of body language that Rickman has patented, Slope puts his face very close to other people's when he wishes to be intimidating. It's rather like one animal facing down another. He's a surprisingly physical performer, but elegantly controlled and tremendously instinctual.

In his serpentine way, Slope becomes the viper nestling at the bishop's bosom. He makes 'love' to Signora Neroni, declaring his passion. Slope bares his teeth amorously at her, another animalistic gesture, but he's a moral coward and she calls his bluff in a scene of unusual sexual intensity. Poor Slope looks vexed and pouts sulkily, with Rickman finding the vulnerabilities in even this slimy creature.

The ghastly man schemes to become the Dean of Barchester, but the bishop outmanoeuvres him. His only hope, thereafter, is the rich young widow, whom he treats with very unclerical passion. 'Beautiful woman, you cannot pretend to be ignorant that I adore you,' is his declaration. She slaps him hard for his presumption and he falls backwards upon the lawn with a look of such genuine surprise that, for a moment, one feels a pang of pity for Slope.

Not that Rickman sentimentalises him one jot; but, absorbed by his ambitions, he has no idea what other people really feel about him. For all his scheming, he's a hopeless innocent.

Signora Neroni, tiring of his machinations, finally humiliates Slope in public. 'I find your behaviour abominable!' he snaps and bangs the door behind him. 'Ambition is so tedious,' she says to her tittering friends by way of explanation.

Slope, now really nettled, is finally carpeted by the Proudies. The bishop makes it clear that he should seek some other preferment. There is an exchange of unseemly insults between Slope and Mrs Proudie; he has lost all caution and becomes a snarling animal. She suggests he become the curate at Puddingdale. 'PUDD-ingdale?' growls Slope, with Alan disdainfully emphasising the ludicrous sound of the first syllable. Obviously not an option for someone like him.

'May you both live for ever!' he snaps, after putting his shark-like face close to the bishop's in his usual intimidatory way. This is, in fact, the voice of the author's own ending, put into Slope's mouth instead by the adaptor Alan Plater.

It was a bravura performance of great subtlety and detail. And yet, as he defiantly told the London *Evening Standard* in 1983, Rickman crudely based the character on his favourite political hate-figures.

'You look in vain for any redeeming qualities in Slope,' said Rickman. 'Trollope himself grudgingly admits that the man has courage. And that's about it, really. He doesn't know fear at all.

'Although Trollope was ostensibly writing about the Church, I think he was actually talking about politicians. My performance as Slope was modelled on various members of the Government.

'If you just glanced at Norman Tebbit via Michael Heseltine and wiped a bit of Mrs Thatcher over the two of them, I think you might end up with something resembling Slope.'

This was the first political gauntlet that Rickman had thrown down; and there were to be more. Though he gives few interviews and guards the sanctity of his private life as if he were the custodian of the Crown Jewels, he does at least seize the opportunity to make his left-wing politics abundantly clear to the meanest intellect. But he's too imaginative a performer not to have revelled in the excesses of the character. Slope was a monster, and certainly a wicked Tory one, but he was scandalously enjoyable company. 'Playing Slope was like a wonderful holiday,' he admitted. 'It was such a rich character that you could just take a great big dive into it.

'I could see the potential danger that, after playing it, I'd never be offered any other sort of part . But in the end, it was too good to say no. There's one part which comes along and opens a door. Antony Sher was working brilliantly for years before he did *The History Man* – and zappo! It's the same with Bernard Hill playing Yosser Hughes in *Boys From The Blackstuff*.'

Slope opened not so much a door as a Pandora's Box. And thus began Alan Rickman's lifelong Faustian contract with the devil, playing the kind of deliciously evil character of whom he fundamentally disapproved. You could call it therapy, or just magnificently ironic fun. Maybe it's an exorcism. They're all raging sexpots into the bargain; he has never played, indeed, could never play, the kind of person who is dead from the neck down. He is a very physical being.

'I was rather surprised by the Obadiah Slope effect,' says RSC Artistic Director Adrian Noble, trying not to sound missish. 'I had an opening night in Tunbridge Wells that year for the opera *Don Giovanni*. Alan and Rima came down for it. There was a real frisson about him, especially among women of a certain age, and it was all because of Obadiah Slope.

'Rima was always fantastically philosophical about it; she found the female attention funny. I don't want to be sexist about it, but his Slope was fantastically charming and believable. There was a real sexual tension with Alan: he did keep you constantly wondering whether Slope does sleep with some of the women he flirts with, such as the Signora.

'As a result, it was the most extraordinary evening. All those Tunbridge Wells ladies definitely wanted to be misled by Alan Rickman.'

5. 'I WANT WOMEN'

In November 1983, Alan Rickman embarked upon his first nude scene with all the surface aplomb that one would have expected of him. He and Tracey Ullman were the leads in Snoo Wilson's marijuana play *The Grass Widow* in a Royal Court production by Max Stafford-Clark, a skilful director no more noticeably encumbered by inhibition than Snoo himself. All these years later, this dangerously funny play can now be seen as a precursor to *Sexy Beast*, the gangster film that begins with Ray Winstone lying in a heat haze next to a pool. Except that Winstone (the wuss) wore swimming trunks. Rickman opened the play by sunbathing in dark glasses and nothing else, delivering the first of many jolts to a startled audience. Later on in the same scene, his character Dennis clambered up on the roof of a house and perched there buck-naked except – as Snoo's stage directions helpfully pointed out – for his binoculars. Such completely matter-of-fact nudity, quite without the coyness that creates prurience, sent out a very efficient signal that anything was possible in a play which administered such early shocks.

'Alan was a perfect Dennis; he understood the humour,' recalls Snoo. 'And there's a quality of fastidiousness in Dennis's character which is very Alan. He did the nudity very well: there was no trouble at all, no stuff about wanting towels and so on. It makes a good stage picture to begin with nudity; people say if you are a leading actor you should be in full shot early on so that people can establish an idea of your character. So the character was completely starkers to begin with. And Alan was very much a pin-up anyway; there was already a bit of a buzz about him.'

Yet that cool which Snoo remembers was just a front: the only way Rickman could get through the nude scene was to pretend it wasn't happening to him. Years later, in *Antony and Cleopatra*, he was to envy Helen Mirren's ability to seem completely unaware of the audience – even when she went topless in the death scene.

'One casting director spent years arguing Alan's case, because a heterosexual director had said, "He's not sexy",' says the writer and director Stephen Poliakoff. 'Alan flowered when he got confident.'

Fellow playwright Stephen Davis has an interesting perspective on Rickman's fatal attractiveness for women.

'He is incredibly aware of his sexual charisma professionally. He has hordes of women writing to him, and there is evidence that it gets in the way. He wants to avoid being cast for it. He's not an exploitative person. In his private life, he's not in the remotest a sexual predator. He's incredibly vexed by this image.

'He has a matinée idol hold over the audience. But he has enormous self-control in his life – unnervingly so – and he's tried never to play a role where his sexual charisma is the ticket money.'

Somehow the roles of the Vicomte de Valmont, the Sheriff of Nottingham, Mesmer and Rasputin have slipped through the barbed-wire. Snoo Wilson is keen for Alan to play that uninhibited occultist Aleister Crowley, the self-styled Great Beast and 'the wickedest man alive', in a film Snoo says he has spent 'a lifetime' trying to get off the ground. Rickman has already agreed to lend his name to the project. Can we have Satanism without the sex? I think not. It would be such a waste.

Sylvia Plath caused a sensation with the posthumously-published poem 'Daddy' when she claimed that women craved the discipline of the fascist iron heel. The piece was a complex and belated response to the early death of her father, a German entomologist who had died when she was eight. With its incantatory rhythms, this was a dark and disturbing fantasy about the tyrannical power of a male parent with the prerogative of punishment. She breaks taboo after taboo, mocking the marriage vow as an incitement to violence and identifying herself with a Jew on the way to a Nazi death-camp. Despite its obvious ironies, the poem remains so controversial that I was refused permission by Plath's literary estate to quote from two stanzas.

This incestuous work was addressed to Hitler as a father figure. Plath was exorcising the fascist impulse, but the daring sentiments were still seen as an appalling lapse of taste and she would never have got away with voicing those uncomfortably sharp insights today. Even as they endorsed the attack on an aggressive male sex, feminists deplored the wallow in morbidity that accused the entire female sex of masochism.

Plath had caused an even bigger sensation when she killed herself by putting her head in the gas-oven. Her death was an accident, the last in several suicide-bids that were never intended to be successful. The man downstairs, who was due to knock on her door at a regular time, went to sleep because of the soporific effect of the escaping gas. And a returning home-help got caught in a traffic-jam. For all her rhetorics, Sylvia wasn't quite the masochist she made herself out to be. Her words, however, continued to resonate.

Certain roles do tap into disturbing undercurrents in the psychic electricity and turn some people on like a light-switch. There was to be nothing kinkier, or indeed funnier, on screen than Alan Rickman's black watered-silk costume as the Sheriff of Nottingham in the 1991 film *Robin Hood: Prince Of Thieves*. It was straight out of a domination-master's wardrobe at a suburban S & M party.

The tone was playful, not intended to be taken seriously, although Rickman was to throw himself with his customary gusto into the part. This became the performance that turned him into a worldwide sex-symbol.

A Peter Barnes TV play was to have an important influence in shaping the Sheriff, although Rickman was not among the cast. *A Hand Witch Of The Second Stage*, transmitted on BBC TV in 1989 as part of Barnes' *Spirit Of Man* trilogy on the pursuit of faith, God and the devil, set a medieval witch-trial in an underground torture-chamber. It was full of Peter's usual comic-grotesque conceits, with much savage humour. It was the black-clad torturer, who talked lasciviously about 'having my old master in the tight clamps', who was to prove an inspiration for the demented Sheriff, since Peter Barnes played a vital role behind the scenes of that film.

Alan Rickman's wonderfully suggestive drawl alone seems to wire some of his fans up to the National Grid.

'There are two piles of letters in his flat: one that he answers and one that he throws away,' says Rickman's old teacher, Ted Stead. 'Some letters are absolutely obscene: there's talk of him being in leathers, and so on.

'One woman was actually following him around. She sat in the front row of a play he was in and brought her son or nephew around to the stage door to ask for acting advice. He spent a few minutes with her and the boy, talking to them. He then got this abusive letter from her, saying he hadn't spent enough time with them. She sat down in the front row again for another performance of the same play, and he told me, "I don't know what to do." ' Although Peter Barnes has been badgered by the occasional over-zealous fan, he remains grateful for a writer's relative anonymity; as he points out, 'Actors get the worst of it because they get the very sick people.'

'His sexual charisma doesn't do anything for me,' quips Stephen Davis. 'I think he's rather embarrassed by all the letters. He has a very puritanical attitude towards the triviality of his profession. Look at how many people are destroyed by success; you'd think people would be more likely to be destroyed by failure. He doesn't like the notion of stardom, but he's fallen into it four-square because he has the gift of projecting his personality.'

Stephen Davis wrote his BBC play *Busted*, recorded in 1982 some months before *The Barchester Chronicles* and transmitted on 28 January 1983, for Alan and co-star Michael 'Mickey' Feast. It begins with a post-coital bedroom scene after Alan, playing a sulky-looking lawyer called Simon, has rung an old girlfriend up to suggest some lunch-time sex.

He's living with a manipulative child-woman called Roxy, well played by a fey Sara Sugarman, who never listens to a word he says. So Simon is really in need of a sympathetic ear rather than a touch of the other. 'I'm a bit fed-up,' he glooms to his old flame.

Rickman is still wearing his medieval pudding-basin haircut, which makes him look rather like an overgrown schooboy. As ever, he is sexy and intriguing despite himself.

Simon is a barrister, a Chancery law specialist in tax whose rebellious past comes back to haunt him. He receives a midnight call for help from a Dave Spart character: his old friend Macy has been busted. Simon and the scapegrace Macy were socialist activists together, Treasurer and Secretary of 'Soc Soc' at Oxford University. The police have found Macy's Derringer pistol on a spot street-search in a visit to an off-licence. 'You were always so bloody childish,' snaps Simon, exasperated by this unreconstructed rebel without a pause.

Simon leads a rather empty, unfulfilled life and envies Macy his primitive certainties. He discovers that Macy was planning to try to rob the off-licence, hence the gun. On a romantic, quixotic impulse that's very much at odds with his training, Simon does a Sydney Carton (after the example of Dickens' self-sacrificing anti-hero) and swaps clothes with Macy in his cell to enable his old brother-at-arms to escape. 'They will bust you right back to the ranks,' warns Macy. Yet there's still an element of risk-taking left in Simon, which is what gives the drama tension – and also release – at the end.

He settles back on the cell bunk to await discovery, a smile of relief on his face. He has thrown off his Establishment shackles and found freedom – of sorts.

Simon's air of self-containment suited Alan admirably, yet he also identified completely with that mad, quixotic urge.

'Alan is a bit of a gravitational force – the universe tends to shape itself round him,' says Stephen Davis. 'I thought that the activists, the student radical Trotskyite Left, were superficial and half-baked when I was at Cambridge University. I was a sceptical leftist in the middle with Jeremy Paxman on the right wing of the Left – if you see what I mean.

'I think that Simon would have been rescued by the Lord Chancellor in the end as a good man gone slightly bonkers. I was trying to write about that uncomfortable margin between ideologies and the various times of one's life, about characters whose sense of themselves is confused.

'There are nuances of distinction between Macy and Simon: Macy is a Manchester Grammar School type and Simon is Harrow. Essentially Simon is a Max Stafford-Clark type, very much in control.

'A certain element in Alan's success is genetic. If he didn't have that timbre of voice . . . Actors are dependent on what nature gave them, that's what they find out.'

Despite the bedroom scene with the old girlfriend (who was rather jeeringly known as Sociology Sara), Simon was hardly an overtly sexy character. He was one of those men that you would have to work hard to arouse, so overwhelming was his sense of ennui. On the other hand, women do respond to a challenge.

The seductive voice got the biggest reaction of all: it made him a radio star. Alan told Peter Barnes that he received more letters from teenaged girls for the role of a decadent Caesar on BBC Radio than for any other performance. Proof at last that the hypnotic drawl was working its caustic magic.

The work in question was Peter Barnes' free and witty adaptation of the Spanish playwright Lope De Vega's drama *Lo Fingido Verdadero*, translated as *Actors* – or *Playing For Real*. *Actors* was recorded in 1982 and transmitted on 3 April 1983. It began in the reign of the Roman Emperor Aurelius, the year AD 257. The cast was led by Denis Quilley, Timothy West, the late Harold Innocent, Alan's old RADA chum Tina Marian and Peter Woodthorpe.

Alan was cast as Aurelius's older son Carinus, a vigorous debaucher of senators' wives and vestal virgins (he particularly liked to defile property that was out of bounds). Lucky for him that lightning burns Aurelius to a crisp during a storm; he is found with his face blackened and his finger-ends still smoking.

So Carinus becomes the new Caesar, despite the fact that his life's work is 'Lust, sir, lust'. As he says disdainfully, 'Keep me from older women.' He goes only for the young ones in order to make absolutely sure he is soiling the goods.

'You begin to tire me,' he says to his mistress Rosada, sounding very jaded. Hubris looms, however. 'We are almost equal to the gods,' he says, using the royal 'we' as if suffering from delusions of Thatcher.

'I'm changeable as quicksilver. All Rome is open, waiting for my pleasure,' he adds in those languorous, caressing, insolent tones.

When an actor is ushered into his presence to perform in a play by Aristotle, Carinus shrieks: 'I've had enough of actors . . . I want women. Kill the husband and rape the wife.' Rickman throws himself like a mad abseiler into the role.

A cuckold whose wife was ravished by Carinus turns up to remonstrate with him, complaining: 'You told everyone, which was worse.'

Carinus is hardly about to deny it, and Rickman's voice shrieks with sarcasm. 'I did, I have SUCH a naughty wagging tongue. I grow bored. There is a suffocating stench of morality in the air.'

The cuckold, an outraged senator called Lelius, promptly adds to the stench by stabbing him in the guts. 'You have killed Caesar,' gasps Carinus.

'What a tragedy. I acted my role when Caesar, now I exit from the dirty theatre of the world. Take off the laurel crown of this actor king.' His mistress weeps over him, for no one else will.

'He's here for me now, fierce Death . . . what power can match yours? No one escapes you . . . not even kings,' he murmurs in a moment of sudden self-awareness that very nearly steals our sympathy. Others would have camped it up to the hilt – and the actor playing his servant Celio is pure Kenneth Williams – but not Rickman. He resists the temptation.

Radio was a great release, particularly for one who was so self-conscious about his looks. As his former co-star Sheridan Fitzgerald says: 'This is a lookist business.'

Rickman has subsequently recorded a total of eleven radio dramas, among them productions of *Blood Wedding* and *The Seagull* ... though you will listen out in vain for his voice-overs on lucrative TV commercials. He's too principled – and too recognisable.

The Obadiah Slope effect had given his confidence a huge boost, so much so that he had begun to gravitate towards directing. He had taken control of *Desperately Yours*, a one-woman show by his friend Ruby Wax, which played off-Broadway for a short season back in 1980. Although Wax didn't leave the RSC for another two years of playing wenches, the show was the beginning of Ruby's new career as a comedian with her own lines, rather than as an actress reciting someone else's. By 1985, Alan was making guest appearances in *Girls On Top*, the new ITV series that Ruby had co-written with fellow comedians Dawn French and the future *Absolutely Fabulous* writer Jennifer Saunders.

Having undertaken this new Svengali role, Alan felt he needed a crash-course in gurudom, which was how he became an assistant director to his friend Richard Wilson for a production of Robert Holman's play *Other Worlds* at London's Royal Court Theatre in May 1983. In the theatre, Richard is thought of more as a director than as an actor (the reverse is true, of course, for his TV and film). Yet all his expertise couldn't prevent *Other Worlds*, an ambitious epic set during the Napoleonic era, from being a flop.

'Alan was Richard's idea,' says Holman. 'Alan kept saying he wanted to direct, but then he didn't. But he was heavily involved in the casting: Juliet Stevenson, for example, was in it because Alan cast her.

'He wasn't a lackey; Alan will never be anyone's lackey. He took rehearsals on his own and Richard didn't mind, because Richard is the kind of person who is in full control of his ego.

'Fundamentally Alan doesn't tolerate fools. Some people do that with silence; he does it with contempt. You need ego to do that; I suspect he would show his contempt abundantly now.

'He's very rigorous on a script. On the script for *Other Worlds*, he crossed out the adverbs "happily" and "sadly" and said: "You can't put actors in strait-jackets". He's absolutely right: it's for actors to find the way to play it. He wasn't afraid to trample on my sensibilities if he thought his point was valid.

'I'm not good at changing stuff,' admits Robert. 'I play a waiting game. I wait for them to see my point of view. Alan always saw my point of view in the end. If he understands what you're saying, he's loyal to a fault.

'At the time, *Other Worlds* was the most expensive play the Court had ever done. It was a magnificent set built by the people who did *2001: A Space Odyssey*. Alan was very loyal and stuck with his own opinion. It had the worst attendance figures ever for the Court; and it was savaged by the critics. Then there was a rearguard action in the Press; it wasn't orchestrated, I had nothing to do with it. There were letters to the *Guardian* in defence of it.

'I had severed a tendon in my hand after cutting my finger; I came out of hospital, saw the first night and then went back in. At the time I was annoyed by the criticism; but I have no lasting grudge. It's the actors who have to do it night after night, and you have to support them. In the scheme of things, plays are not the be-all and end-all. They are not life and death. You take bad reviews with good reviews.

'But Alan is a perfectionist. He is driven because of that. I suspect he is as hard on himself as he is on everyone else,' observes Yorkshire-born Robert, mulling things over in his soft Alan Bennett voice.

'I always found him very interesting as an actor. I wrote a BBC film about the poet Edward Thomas for Alan . . . it was never made. We had various arguments about the director, then there was talk of Alan directing it. Had it gone ahead, Juliet Stevenson would have played the wife.

'Thomas was a loner who suffered from deep melancholy. His life was quite harsh. He married a younger woman, they had this spartan cottage in Hampshire near Bedales and grew their own veg. He would leave her with the children and have affairs, disappear without telling her.

'Alan would have been very good at that melancholia. People who think a lot, as Alan has, to a degree need their own space. I suspect Alan is quite spacious in that way.

'And I suspect that's why Alan has given directors a hard time. He was debating whether to become a director, what sort of work he was going to do as an actor and whether he wanted to be a star. All those things are slightly incompatible. As a star, you have control over what you do, but you're limited in what you do.

'Alan's performance is all behind the eyes, in a way. He can be his own rigorous person within the confines of a slightly daft movie like *Die Hard*.

'There's a degree of conceit in Alan, behind those eyes, and conceit is sexy. It's not arrogance, but it's a sort of rigorous conceit.

'His sense of humour is very droll. I think he's too spacious to be an actor; I can see why he's not completely satisfied with acting. Even with the directing, he would want more. He would be wanting to do everything, including the publicity.

'During *Other Worlds*, he said to me: "Your writing's on the line." In other words, there's no doubt in the actors' minds when they say something; they have already thought it. So you have to think hard between the lines, between the full stops. He was the first person ever to say that. The thoughts spring fully-formed; you can't be half-hearted.

'Theatre has an air of unreality; it's heightened reality. There's a suspension of disbelief. Theatre is about how you get people on stage and keep them there. And then the characters can't get off because of some emotional need. The trick is to keep them there, to sustain the scene. Why do those characters have to stay in that box? Alan understood that.

'It's a pity the Edward Thomas film never got made. It was written in 1987 and I was paid for it, but this was around the time when Alan was flirting with Hollywood and then agreed to do *Die Hard*.

'But I'm quite well balanced, I don't go in for troughs of anguish or highs. I suspect Alan would be very good if someone were throwing a wobbly. He is a political animal, and that grounds him.

'He would have been good at running Riverside Studios; he would have given the Board a run for its money. And I think he would be formidable if he went into politics. But I don't know if he would be diplomatic enough. He's undiplomatic about saying what he thinks. He's an actor, he shows off,' explains Robert. 'He wouldn't be a tough director like John Dexter was; he would care about the actors. Essentially, he's one of the good guys. He only plays bad guys because of his comic ability.'

Poor old *Other Worlds* did receive some good reviews, but most were along the lines of the *Daily Telegraph*'s withering intro: 'If you ever felt you didn't know enough about the rivalry of fishermen and farmers on the North Yorkshire coast in the late eighteenth century, go to the Royal Court Theatre immediately.'

The right-wing *Spectator* thought it 'a three-hour bore', while the left-wing *Tribune* considered it 'long, measured and thoughtful . . .

holds you till the last minute.' Charlie Spencer in the London *Evening Standard*, while deploring 'a perplexing and ultimately irritating enigma', conceded that 'there is a compassionate feeling for the strength as well as the weakness of human nature, of ordinary people's longing for other and better worlds.'

But there wasn't time to brood: another radio success came to Rickman's rescue. He had renewed his connection with Peter Barnes for the latter's adaptation of John Marston's play *The Dutch Courtesan*, transmitted by Radio 3 on 19 June 1983.

Once again Rickman was cast as a sexpot, his extraordinarily insinuating voice perfect for the role of the impudent chancer Cockledemoy. He robs Roy Kinnear as the inn-keeper Mulligrub for pure devilment, and lusts after every woman within reach. His lechery is presented as a comic counterpoint to the main story, wherein a seductive Dutch courtesan holds both the hero and his Puritanical best friend in thrall. As ever, Alan walks off with the show despite being part of the sub-plot.

Cockledemoy has a bawd, whom he bullies and calls 'My worshipful organ-bellows, my right precious pandaress, necessary damnation' (they really knew how to curse in those days).

Even Rickman's coughs are instantly recognisable and heavily pregnant with meaning, signalling the crafty approach of Cockledemoy. 'There's a smooth thigh, the nimble devil in her buttock,' he says of one 'punk' (tart), singing a carefree snatch of song in his smooth tenor.

Cockledemoy assumes a variety of disguises in order to outwit Master Mulligrub; and the range of accents here shows astonishing versatility from one who is so often thought of as a one-voice actor. He begins with a camp Scottish accent, straight out of Morningside, when he poses as a Scots barber called Andrew Shark.

Then he disguises himself as a French pedlar and languidly addresses Mulligrub as 'Merseeyur'. 'Turd on a tilestone!' is his muttered description of the unfortunate Mulligrub as he plans a raid upon his property. 'Conscience does not repine. I hold it as lawful as sheep-shearing; I must have the new goblet.'

Rickman then metamorphoses into a Mummerset peasant to annex the aforesaid goblet, gulling Mulligrub's wife. And he even gets to grope the Dutch courtesan: 'There's a plump-rumped wench! Kiss, fair whore, kiss. It's yours if you come to bed. Hump 'em, plump 'em, squat, I'm gone!'

There's more unbridled lechery when we hear Cockledemoy's haw-haw guffaw, as filthy as Leslie Phillips' snickers in *The Navy Lark*.

He sings a drunken song as he pretends to be a night-watchman. 'Maids on their backs dream of sweet smacks. I fiddle him till he farts,' he adds of Mulligrub. Cockledemoy reverts to the Mummerset accent, promising, 'I'll make him fart firecrackers before I have done with him. My knavery grows unequalled.'

Another disguise has Cockledemoy very plausibly impersonating an Irish sergeant at the foot of the gallows, picking the unfortunate victim's pocket. Eventually he reveals himself as a master of disguise, the Moriarty of Jacobean drama.

'All has been done for wit's sake. I bid myself welcome to your merry nuptials and most wanton jig-a-joggies,' he adds, inviting himself to a wedding. And Rickman speaks the epilogue too, saying that we may scorn such trivial wit . . . but cannot hope to better it. It's a virtuoso vocal performance. More than any other medium, radio freed Alan Rickman of all his uptight inhibitions as he allowed his instinctive sensuality free rein. No wonder Caesar had such an effect on those schoolgirls.

Sex was again the driving force when Alan returned to the theatre that August to play a bisexual Cambridge don in his old friend Dusty Hughes' play *Bad Language* at Hampstead Theatre.

Milton Shulman wrote in the London *Evening Standard*: 'Played by Alan Rickman as a world-weary ringmaster with a cageful of frisky animals, he keeps a wary eye on [the undergraduates] while carrying on literary feuds, furthering his own ambitions and having short-lived affairs with students of either sex.' In short, the kind of amoral seducer that Rickman was to make famous.

'Alan Rickman plays this lecherous rascal with chilling power and a shiversome disgust . . . in his snarling self-absorption,' wrote Eric Shorter in the *Daily Telegraph*, fascinated yet repelled. That mixed response would become a common reaction.

'Alan Rickman invests [Bob] with enough reptilian charm to explain his intellectual and sexual sway over his coterie of students,' was Rosalind Carne's verdict in the *Guardian*. Francis King in the *Sunday Telegraph* was snider: 'There is a tellingly acrid performance from Alan Rickman as the sort of arrogant, self-regarding don who has a mysterious attraction for his pupils of either sex.'

Radio had given him unparalleled opportunities, but he was still coming up against the prejudice of people who couldn't see his peculiar, offbeat allure.

Rickman's strong sense of style set the pace in *The Grass Widow*, which Alan began work on immediately after *Bad Language*. 'Alan was always the first choice for Dennis,' said Snoo Wilson. 'He has a genius for doing everything and yet nothing, which I'd seen him do in Dusty Hughes's *Commitments*. In *The Grass Widow*, his character Dennis is trying to hold things together: he's peaceful but that doesn't mean to say he's not opportunistic. There was a dreamy quality to the play which I think Alan got very well; this is a lazy man's fantasy of romance.' The first night was a famously jinxed one at the time, though it's fair to record that Snoo now can't recall it being more problematic than any other production. There was one cherishable moment, however, when Alan's co-star Tracey Ullman turned to the audience when the lights blew and said: 'At least there's something in this that'll make you laugh.'

Milton Shulman in the London *Evening Standard* found the characters '. . . as weird, disconnected and violent as a drug addict's dream'. But he was impressed by the way that 'Alan Rickman lolls with indolent ease among all these surrealist and scabrous images and chatter'.

But it was *The Lucky Chance* at the Royal Court in 1984, which reunited him with his actress friend Harriet Walter, that led directly to the role which changed the entire course of his career. Jules Wright launched her Women's Playhouse Trust (later known diplomatically as the WPT because of all the nuisance phone-calls from heavy breathers) with this rarely-produced play by the Restoration playwright, Aphra Behn.

Alan was cast as a lustful adventurer called Gayman, the kind of name that really doesn't travel well down the centuries. His rows with Jules over who was to run Riverside were still nine years away; her only battle here was over her unexpected choice of leading man.

'People said to me, "Why are you casting Alan Rickman as Gayman! He's so laid-back and contained." People have a strong perception of Alan as someone who sits back,' says Jules. 'But he has this tremendous range and he's not really been given that chance on stage. Alan is a really intelligent man, and so sensual. He's a complete maverick. People had stereotyped ideas about him, they didn't think that he could lead from the front and galvanise. But I knew absolutely that he could.

'I was 35 when I directed him in *The Lucky Chance*; I didn't then realise that he was nearly 40. In retrospect, that explains a lot. He even asked the stage manager Jane Salberg about me: "Do you think she knows what she's doing?" We had a couple of big rows, though he was very open. Mind you, Harriet Walter was also quite stubborn in rehearsal (Jules mimes stamping her foot and laughs). She was also incredibly bright, like him, and inevitably there were disagreements between them.

'We had a very short rehearsal period of four weeks. Alan said to me at the run-through, "There's a scene we haven't rehearsed." I said, "Who's in it?" And he said, "Just me." He laughed; so did I. It was about four lines – just him on stage. I suggested he pick up a candelabra and wend his way across the stage. He was impish, imaginative, he retained that playfulness and it was magical at every performance. He's a very game actor. His strength is that he still has incredible playfulness, fuelled by energy. He's quite an unEnglish actor, really. He would be just right for an Ingmar Bergman stage production – he fits into that. And a Woody Allen film. He's so funny and dry, yet that dryness is sometimes seen as throwing lines away.

'One row I had with him in *The Lucky Chance* was about him moving other actors around. Both Alan and I came to the theatre relatively late; I was 30 when I first started. We had had a hard week with two performances on Saturday; I was moving house on Sunday.

'I picked up the review in the *Observer* and I shouldn't have; I felt terribly upset. It said that it was not a feminist reading of the play, that it lacked political depth. I was inexperienced, even though I'd just had a huge success with *Masterpieces* that had transferred to the Court from the Royal Exchange. I was terribly hurt by the review. I think reviews are sometimes unnecessarily cruel, especially about actors.

'On Monday I had a big note-session with the actors in the stalls of the Court. Alan hit the roof and said, "Don't give me notes out of a Sunday review. We made this production together." We really bellowed at each other, and Harriet cried. He was right. Collectively we had made those decisions about the production, and he was very angry.

'I looked up to the Dress Circle and the entire staff of the building were peeping through the curtains . . . everyone enjoying the row. Especially Max Stafford-Clark,' says Jules of the then Artistic Director at the Court.

'But Alan you can take the mickey out of . . . With him, laughter is never far below the surface. He's very daunting; because he's a very bright man, directors feel threatened and don't take him on. If you don't take him on, he can be dour.

'Alan always works very hard, and a lot of actors don't. He comes with a very profound understanding of the material, and people probably find that difficult.

'He's a very generous person, and not just on stage. He's an actor who really makes a point of seeing other people's work. When someone has established himself in the way that he has, it really matters to other actors that he does this. They really want to know what he thinks of their work. The only other person I know who does that is Alan Bates. It's to do with being confident and uncompetitive. Not that Alan does it in a measured way; he's not a patronising person. He's very honest and disarming.

'He has a great sexuality and charisma on stage. Terribly sexy, to put it bluntly. I don't know whether he knows it. He's certainly always had a lot of women friends. In my experience, there are not many men who are not at some point patronising to women. Alan Rickman is never that.'

It seems an extraordinary paradox that, for someone so sexually constant in his private life, Rickman should be so successful at playing sexual predators. His narcissistic instincts revel in portraying manipulative show-offs; but his particular secret of flirting with danger is to give his vile seducers a superhuman self-control. He always knows how to leave an audience wanting more; it appeals to the dry wit and curious whimsicality of his nature.

Far from being just another boring old bed-hopper who enables us to read the washing instructions on his Y-fronts, Rickman's studied performances celebrate and prolong the noble art of foreplay. They hark back to an earlier age when sex on screen was implicit rather than explicit: cleverly, he appeals most of all to the imagination, refreshing our jaded modern senses. The lady-killing image he projects is in fact a fascinating throwback to the sneering Sir Jaspers of the barnstorming melodramas and Gothic novels, the so-called 'shilling shockers' whose influence lived on in the black-and-white films Alan saw as a boy.

'I've never heard on the grapevine that he's ever had an affair. I have always seen his relationship with Rima as incredibly solid.

They always seemed to me secure and close; it's a good relationship,' says Jules.

'And yet he was so brilliant and funny as this sexual predator Gayman. He was overcome by love and wanted to be smuggled into Harriet's bed; the audience were dying with laughter at that great lolling body. I really hoped he would win Best Actor for it, but he didn't.

'Yet I was really amazed by that outburst in Sloane Square, when he suddenly said to me at two in the morning after a meal, "Nothing's ever going to happen for me. No one will ever notice me. My career isn't going to go anywhere."

'He is shy, rather diffident. But he's a hard person to praise, because he gives the impression of being quite secure. His measured way of talking may seem pompous to some people. When on the few occasions that guard was let down, I felt startled by it.

'He genuinely didn't know how good he is. He doesn't look the vulnerable type, so people don't praise him directly. He waits for them to approach him . . . He's hard to pin down in terms of what he wants.

'What struck me was that his Gayman evolved into the Vicomte de Valmont in *Les Liaisons Dangereuses*. It was almost the same costume – the cut of the coat especially. Alan really can wear clothes and he's not fearful on stage. That rent-a-rake sexual being was there in Valmont.

'There's always something quintessentially him there in every performance – he always uses a bit of himself. Character actors do transform themselves. He doesn't. So he's not really a character actor.'

True, the *Observer*'s Michael Ratcliffe had a problem with the production and muttered about miscasting. 'Mr Rickman, whom none excels at portraying the horror of a man compelled to stagger from orgy to orgy without respite, plays Gayman, a one-woman man.'

But the *Financial Times*' Michael Coveney thought that 'He plays with a superb and saturnine grace . . . and force of personality. He still tends to swallow too many lines' – that muffled speech defect again – 'but it must be difficult to make all the material sing.'

The *Daily Telegraph*'s John Barber found 'That excellent actor Alan Rickman discovers a fine line in perfervid jealousy . . . and brings a splendid swagger to his character of a penniless but touchy and defiant adventurer.'

And even the *Sunday Telegraph*'s Francis King purred about 'the lank, sexually ravenous Gayman (a wonderfully sharp performance by Alan Rickman)'. The message about his maverick sexuality was finally getting through.

Laurie Stone informed the readers of the *New York Village Voice* about this wonderful new talent in London: 'Alan Rickman is an amazing discovery. His Gayman is an elegant comedian; he wears his thinness like a man too busy in bed to bother eating food.'

Ros Asquith in *City Limits* rhapsodised: 'Harriet Walter and Alan Rickman bring to their acid repartee the kind of bristling sexual equality that recalls great old partnerships like Bogart and Bacall.' The Bogie/Bacall connection was to be revisited much later by Rickman and Emma Thompson in the 1999 film noir *Judas Kiss*, when Alan joked that Emma was playing her part like Bogart while he was Bacall. But Michael Billington in the *Guardian* sensed a disturbing moodiness under the surface: 'Alan Rickman . . . lends the impoverished Gayman a dark, tortured, faintly misanthropic lust.'

Billington had sniffed the all-important whiff of danger in the performance that suggested even greater things around the corner. Despite all the witty fun and games and the coquettish ringlets added to his real hair, Rickman played Gayman like a man possessed. There was the ferocity, the unparalleled intensity of a manic depressive who is madly in love.

He had already made himself known to millions as the oleaginous Obadiah Slope, but it was a theatre role that immortalised Alan Rickman. The vicious Vicomte de Valmont beckoned.

6. VALMONT IN CURLERS

The unglamorous truth about *Les Liaisons Dangereuses* was that Alan Rickman took the role that made his name in the West End and on Broadway because he was facing unemployment at the time. With no other offers pending, he accepted the RSC's invitation to rejoin the company.

'He did have periods out of work in the early 80s,' remembers Richard Wilson. 'He said to me, "I don't know what to do: the RSC has asked me to go back, and there's this Christopher Hampton play." I think he went back because there was nothing else around.' This is not to say that Rickman, always a devotee of new writing and a very choosy picker of parts, failed to realise the potential of a part like Valmont. Although Obadiah Slope was not a charismatic character on the page, Rickman certainly made him so on screen in his peculiarly insinuating way. But Valmont was a vampire who fed on the emotions as well as the flesh. This dissolute aristocrat, who conducted his amorous intrigues in the spirit of the Marquis de Sade, captured the morbid imagination.

Les Liaisons Dangereuses, whose story takes the form of sly letters that positively invite you to read between the lines, was written by an obscure artillery officer with the cumbersome name of Pierre-Ambroise-François Choderlos de Laclos.

First published in Paris in 1782, the epistolary novel caused an immediate scandal; later, in 1824, a decree of the Cour Royale de Paris ordered this dangerous work to be destroyed. Its critics talked of 'the most odious immorality', 'a work of revolting immorality' and 'a book to be admired and execrated'. It leaves a taste of bitter ashes in the mouth, and also a feeling of tragedy that the two protagonists should allow themselves to become the engines of so much destruction. For there is no doubt that the Marquise de Merteuil and the Vicomte de Valmont are creatures of vitality and intelligence.

The poet Baudelaire was one of the few who spoke in its defence, but even he prudently judged it an evil book: 'If you could burn it, it would burn like ice burns'. Clive James quoted him on BBC TV's *Saturday Review* on 28 September 1985, just after the production had opened at the RSC's studio theatre The Other Place in Stratford-upon-Avon.

Laclos was a revolutionary Jacobin; and the French Revolution began seven years after the publication of this deeply subversive book about two cynics on a mission to corrupt.

Christopher Hampton says that he had first wanted to dramatise the book ten years previously in 1975. 'It's a play about institutionalised selfishness ... absolute indifference to needs, sufferings and emotional requirements of other people ... it's about ruthlessness.'

On the *Saturday Review* panel, Clive James rightly predicted: 'It's going to be an enormous world-wide hit.' That professional gainsayer A.N. Wilson was, as per usual, the only dissenting voice: 'Alan Rickman has not varied his acting technique one jot since Obadiah Slope.' But writer Paula Milne strongly disagreed: 'I can't see anyone else in the part.'

'He's very conscious of what critics say; I often tease him about it,' says Stephen Poliakoff. 'He was very upset by some review during his second RSC stint. It was just before *Les Liaisons*, when he was in *As You Like It*. I remember him saying to me that he read a review with his fingers spread across the page. Michael Ratcliffe in the *Observer* didn't like him.

'So his eventual success was sweet: it was almost a form of revenge for those of us who thought he deserved better. A revenge on circumstances, not on one person,' adds Poliakoff circumspectly.

'His Jaques was unfairly attacked by the critics; they didn't forgive him for that,' says Adrian Noble, his director for *As You Like It* in 1985 and *Mephisto* the following year.

'They attacked his voice; he was terribly upset by it. He is easily upset by bad reviews, although he won't admit it. They did the same with his *Hamlet* in 1992 – they objected to his voice.

'His Jaques was a deeply passionate character who lived on the fringes of society and was sought out by the great policy-makers and thinkers. That sums up Alan,' says Adrian with a giggle. 'He does court being a guru to a certain extent (is the Pope a Catholic?) It's a role that sits comfortably on him. He has always lived his career by his own lights, and it's difficult for theatre folk to do that. He's quite selective about things, mostly successfully.

'He can be railing against the world one minute and be at Neil Kinnock's supper-table the next. Well, most of us were,' admits

Adrian with another giggle. 'Alan does have a wonderful line in disdain. He doesn't corpse, but he's very funny. He retreats into his cave, as Jaques did, but he's sought after there. Young actors need people like that who say "You're going on the right path".'

Rickman's second attempt at that quixotic philosopher Jaques was unveiled on 23 April – the date generally assumed to be Shakespeare's birthday.

It was followed by that epic sulker Achilles in *Troilus And Cressida* on 25 June. *Les Liaisons* was the late summer 'sleeper', in Hollywood parlance, that finished the year's Stratford season with an opening night on 25 September.

In Howard Davies' production of *Troilus*, Alan was judged by some to have made Achilles even more of a heel than usual. He did not meet with Irving Wardle's approval in *The Times*: '. . . an unshaven Alan Rickman overplays the hysterical tantrums even for Achilles.' Similarly, Ros Asquith in the *Observer* wrote ambivalently of 'Alan Rickman's over-the-top but disarmingly rakish Achilles'. Significantly, Asquith had seen the sexual potential in Rickman's portrayal.

But the quills were sharpened for his Jaques in *As You Like It*: Michael Ratcliffe wrote in the *Observer* about how Rickman would 'talk through [his] teeth in a funny manner' and how he 'leaves the field of history standing for the outrageous contrivance of his Seven Ages of Man'.

Of course such a staunch socialist as Alan would always get upset about a bad notice in the *Observer*, though Michael Coveney in the *Financial Times* praised his 'languorous Jaques – now the sensational performance it threatened to become'.

Jack Tinker in the *Daily Mail* wrote of 'Alan Rickman's all-seeing, all-knowing, all-wearied Jaques'. Eric Shorter in the *Daily Telegraph* admired 'Alan Rickman's philosophical Jaques in a shabby dinner jacket who rules the entertainment with a refreshing relish'.

As if to confound the critics, Alan had set forth his views on playing Jaques in his only published work to date: one of a collection of essays by Shakespearean actors under the title of *Players Of Shakespeare*, published by the Cambridge University Press.

Jaques is all about attitude, which makes Rickman a natural for the role. He wrote of a Jaques 'who is perceptive but passionate, vulnerable but anarchic . . . He's very sure of himself and a bit of a mess.'

He admits in print that he made a meal of things in rehearsal: 'The other actors must have tired of wondering where I was going to enter from next, or if there would ever be a recognisable shape to the scene.' And there was an air of the dilettante about the character's self-conscious pose: 'Jaques seeks, frets, prods and interferes but he doesn't DO . . . he definitely needs the other lords to cook his food.'

Rickman saw him as an 'extremist . . . he might be in real danger of losing control. He's condemned to wander forever, endlessly trying to relocate some innocence, endlessly disappointed. Therein lie both his vulnerability and his arrogance . . . you are left with an image of complete aloneness . . .

'In some ways, it is a lonely part to play,' he concluded, recalling how he and Ruby Wax as Audrey had jazzed things up at Peter James' suggestion eight years previously at the Sheffield Crucible.

In a modern-dress production, they had sung 'Shake it up, Shakespeare baby' while eleven hundred people rocked with laughter. So much for the critics.

Light relief from Jaques' intensity came with another Peter Barnes radio play, an adaptation of Thomas Middleton's satire *A Trick To Catch The Old One*. Rickman played another shameless scamp, a Leicestershire gentleman called Theodorus Witgood who is constantly strapped for cash. Since his estate is under the control of his penny-pinching uncle Pecunius Lucre, he hatches a plot to gull him.

Rickman is a wonderfully Gothic combination of silken hypocrisy and pantomime villainy in the role. 'INN-keeperrr . . .! I have been searching town for you,' he utters shudderingly, fastidiously attacking each consonant as if spitting out cherry stones. Though the late Sid James need not stir uneasily in his grave at the thought of the competition, Rickman also unleashes one of his hearty and dirty belly-laughs again. So much for his laid-back image; once again, radio released him.

Alan has a working-class insecurity that has never left him, compounded by the usual doubts and fears that always assail the late starter. He's a great one for endless agonising in long, dark nights of the soul.

'In fact, he's a bit too concerned with what the world will perceive,' says Stephen Poliakoff. 'That's a drawback for actors even more than writers. He's very concerned with whether something is the right step.

'Nevertheless, *Les Liaisons* was pure luck for Alan,' he adds.

Poliakoff had lunched the year before with Daniel Massey, who told him that Christopher Hampton was dramatising the book for the RSC. Was Massey ever considered for the role? Howard Davies swears until his fax machine is puce in the face that Alan was his first and only choice; but it's tempting to speculate on Massey playing Valmont as a macaroni dandy in powder and high heels, in which case we would have lost one of the great sexual animals of theatrical history.

Christopher Hampton, however, insists: 'It was my idea to cast Alan. In fact, it was my wife's idea. She has a very good eye for casting. She had seen Alan in *Barchester Chronicles* and Snoo Wilson's play, then I saw him in *The Seagull* at the Royal Court. I suggested him to Howard Davies. The RSC was thinking of asking him to play Jaques anyway.

'It was a great boost to all our careers – Alan, Howard Davies and myself. All of us were at the same stage, same level and about the same age.'

The way Hampton tells it, *Les Liaisons* was the dark horse that crept up on the RSC and took it completely by surprise.

'Something remarkable was brewing. Howard and I felt like a subversive cell and the actors did, too. We were opening against Terry Hands' main-stage production of *Othello* with Ben Kingsley. The RSC thought of *Les Liaisons* as filling up its quota: it was the last play of the 1985 season in The Other Place. We were left on our own quite a lot.

'I can't tell you how dubious everyone was. Even Howard was dubious about directing it. It was a project we cooked up; I got him to commission me. The RSC had dramatised *Les Liaisons* in the 60s and called it *The Art Of Love*. It was a complete flop then. John Barton directed it, and Judi Dench and Alan Howard were the stars. It was a black polo-neck job, reading from the script.

'I suggested Juliet Stevenson as La Presidente de Tourvel for our version, and Howard suggested Lindsay Duncan as the Marquise de Merteuil.

'I first met Alan in rehearsals for *Les Liaisons*. I knew of him because we had various mutual friends, like Anna Massey. He comes from an unusual background, with very clear ideas and images – he's an artist like Tony Sher. Some actors are clothes-horses.

'Alan's voice suggests darkness; and it's expressive, not all on one note. There's a lot of variation. When he played the Trigorin role in *The Seagull*, it was the voice of a much older, more experienced man.'

Of Rickman's notoriously pernickety approach, Hampton admits: 'Alan was interventionist about costume. He was adamant that he wouldn't shave his beard, though an eighteenth-century aristocrat with a beard was of course unheard of. He wouldn't wear a wig either, so he had to sit in his curlers every night to get enough – what do hairdressers call it? – body in his hair.'

A backstage Valmont in curlers was quite a sacrifice to his dignity, yet Rickman's artistic instinct was impeccable. The result of all this carefully created 'naturalism' was a primitive, satyric, rough-trade Valmont, with the stubble and the long frock-coat of a (sexual) highwayman.

For all his elegance, there was something of the wolfish Captain Macheath from *The Beggar's Opera* about him. He even wore his boots on the bed in one scene as he discusses tactics with Merteuil. Rickman refused to play Valmont in the tights and high heels of the period, partly because he didn't want to make him a fop, and partly because Rickman has large, slightly bandy calves.

It was that sense of a werewolf in aristocrat's clothing that John Malkovich also picked up on for his performance as Valmont in Stephen Frears' film version of Hampton's play, although I also felt that Malkovich modelled himself on Mick Jagger . . . with a touch of the Japanese percussionist, Stomu Yamashta.

Alan later told Jane Edwardes from *Time Out* magazine: 'I always wanted the play to have the same effect as the book, and I knew I had to seduce 200 people in the audience as well as the women in the play. The quality of stillness and silence was a measure of how far we had succeeded.'

'There was an electric atmosphere at the first night at The Other Place,' remembers Hampton. 'The audience were on three sides: it was like being in the same room as the actors. The RSC have been touring it ever since. I said to them in 1995, please don't do it any more. Adrian Noble acknowledged that. It's been done all over the world. It's only last year that it's been released to the repertory theatres.

'Valmont's one moral act brings the whole house of cards tumbling down. He's in love with this Tourvel woman, the one decent instinct that destroys the whole business.

'I don't think you could play that part and be unaffected by it; but you never know with actors.

'Alan really conveyed Baudelaire's burning-ice description: he was very, very cold in the part, but also very disturbed. He was oiling that subterranean energy; it was palpable. I was tremendously impressed by the simmering violence.

'He was absolutely besieged by fan-letters. A typical letter would be from a grown woman, not a schoolgirl, and it would read: "I'm a feminist but I don't understand how you can have this effect on me."

'I'm not very good at answering those sorts of letter myself . . . though I didn't get nearly so many as he did,' adds Christopher modestly.

'Pressures had to be applied on the RSC, or it would have disappeared from the repertoire. You never saw Trevor Nunn or Terry Hands: they were so remote. It was just the pressures of running this huge company. They were certainly quite distant figures. At least we were left on our own and not interfered with, but I felt we were an unscheduled success and inconvenient for them. Most of my dealings were with Genista Mackintosh: I remember screaming at her, saying "You must do this or that".

'We were never really acknowledged by the RSC as a success,' Hampton feels. 'It was a terrific hit, yet to keep it alive in the repertoire, an inordinate amount of hustling went on. Alan was very active in all that, fiercely loyal.

'There were 23 performances in Stratford, 22 in London and then it was withdrawn from the repertoire. It was out of the repertory for three months, and there was a battle to get it on again. The RSC was opposed to a West End transfer, I believe. And I always felt they refused to approve the selling of the film rights. All we could think of was that there was this rage, because the RSC's *Camille* had been a flop. Frank Gero was finally allowed to do it in the West End. Alan was worried about the space in the West End and had a wheeze about the Almeida. He had a lot to do with the final choice of the Ambassadors.

'Then there were problems with the Broadway transfer. There was a lot of pressure from America to get an American company. Howard and I had a tremendous lot of argument about that. Jimmy Nederlander finally agreed to let the original RSC company go over. They were allowed 20 weeks by American Equity rules, and the play wasn't allowed to continue after that.

'Alan was very militant about that and attacked the Schubert Organisation's Gerald Schoenfeld about *Les Liaisons*' sell-out business. There was talk of Glenn Close taking over from Lindsay Duncan as the Marquise de Merteuil, but Gerry Schoenfeld uttered the immortal words: "Glenn Close means nothing on Broadway." This was just before *Fatal Attraction* was about to open . . .'

Glenn Close, of course, played Merteuil opposite John Malkovich's Valmont in the Hampton/Frears film version, *Dangerous Liaisons*. Close subsequently enjoyed great Broadway success as that other legendary vampire, Norma Desmond, in Andrew Lloyd Webber's *Sunset Boulevard*.

'I don't think anyone came close to Alan's performance as Valmont; and I don't think that Juliet Stevenson has ever given a better performance than she did as Tourvel, either,' says Hampton. 'Alan did it for six months in the West End and five months on Broadway. I think it was murderously difficult for him to adapt from the intimate Ambassadors to the Music Box on Broadway. I remember finding him in tears in his dressing-room from the enormous strain of the project in that big theatre. We only had three or four previews, but he was wonderful. Wretched Frank Rich of *The New York Times* insisted on going to an early preview. The night he came, Lindsay Duncan caught a panel in her dress on a nail and had to play a scene with her back to the wall. Howard insisted on turning off the air-conditioning because it was making a noise. So the audience was perspiring in the heat. When I saw a drip of perspiration on the tip of Jackie Kennedy's nose, I thought, "We've overdone it".

'But Alan really flowered in New York; and in this play, it's the man that does all the work. But although he and Lindsay were nominated, we got shut out of the Tonys – August Wilson's *Fences* won everything.'

Then came the greatest disappointment of Alan Rickman's career. Having made the role of Valmont his own, he was passed over for the film version. The story of how the screen role slipped through his fingers is yet another illustration of how timing means everything in this rackety business.

'We were able to use Glenn Close for the film version, and I slightly backed into casting John Malkovich,' says Hampton. 'The thing is that there was a tremendous battle over the film rights. I took a lower offer from the production company Lorimar in order to retain more control. I said we should rethink the whole thing and start again; and I said I thought we should have Alan Rickman. Lorimar said "Start again". Alan had made *Die Hard* by that stage, but it hadn't been released . . . and of course no one knew it would make such a huge difference to his career. And Lorimar wanted someone with a profile. The director Stephen Frears came on board at a late stage, and he was keen to do it with American actors.

'Another factor was the rival film *Valmont*, so we had to move with tremendous speed. I had seen Malkovich in the play *Burn This*. I know Alan was very, very upset over it,' admits Hampton, 'but it didn't affect our friendship. We were in New York one evening, on our way to the theatre. Alan had told me that people kept coming up to him in the street and saying, "It's terrible you didn't get to play Valmont on film, I don't know what to say to you." As we left the play, a woman came up to him and said "It's terrible you didn't get to play Valmont on film . . ." Alan just pointed at me and said "Ask him!" I think it was a very hurtful thing for Alan, but it's rare that a British actor could ever reprise a role in America; I think only Nigel Hawthorne has managed it with *The Madness of King George*. And I just didn't have the clout. But Alan's performance was unmatchable.'

Inevitably, playing an evil intriguer night after night had a terrible effect on Rickman's psyche. After a lifelong commitment to socialism, he belatedly joined the Labour Party in 1987 as if to distance himself from this degenerate aristocrat. Valmont was not a pantomine villain; that would have been easy to live with. It was his Byzantine intelligence, his insidious understanding of human nature and finally his moral despair that made the part so depressing for someone with such staunch principles. What made it even worse was that Rima had become a Labour councillor in 1986 for St Charles Ward in the Borough of Kensington and Chelsea. There's still a large element of puritanical working-class asceticism, the old Methodist hair-shirt tradition, in the Labour Party, as if you have to renounce all sins of the flesh – apart from eating mushy peas – in order to be taken seriously. With one or two exceptions – 'Gorgeous' George Galloway springs to mind – the Tories have always had the best sex scandals. As Rima embarked on a political career with a public profile for the first time in her work as an educationalist, her long-time boyfriend was seducing women on stage every night and finding himself buried under snowfalls of fan-mail. Of course, Rima appreciated the subtle joke and took it in her stride; but the contrast still made Alan uncomfortable. No wonder Valmont nearly gave him a breakdown. Those tears that Christopher Hampton saw had been just the beginning. 'It stopped being a play in a way, and became an event – especially on Broadway,' he told Sean French in *GQ* magazine in 1991.

'People came with such high expectations that a mountain had to be climbed every night. You are up there manipulating the audience in the way Valmont manipulates the characters. And when you're playing someone as self-destructive as that, night after night, it can't help but get to you to some extent. The body doesn't always know when it's lying. You know from the neck up, but you send the rest of you actually through it.'

The following year, he told the same magazine: 'You are really brushing evil with a part like that, you're looking into an abyss and finding very dark parts of yourself. Valmont is one of the most complicated and self-destructive human beings you would ever wish – or probably not wish – to play.

'Playing him for two and a half hours for two solid years eight times a week brings you very close to the edge. Never again. Never ever again. By the end of it, I needed a rest home or a change of career.'

He also told the *Guardian*: 'It's a part that ate you alive.' There's a story that he gave Howard Davies a hard time during rehearsals for *Les Liaisons*; but I'm inclined to think that it was more likely to have been the other way round. 'Howard is very cold and self-contained,' says Poliakoff.

Nevertheless, losing the film role to Malkovich was still an incredibly depressing experience for Alan. 'He became very withdrawn and broody, though he never said a word. You felt terribly sorry for him,' says a friend.

'It would be untrue to say he wasn't put out,' says Stephen Poliakoff judiciously. 'In 1989 I bumped into him on the street in Notting Hill; I had just seen *Die Hard*. He told me he had not gone to see *Dangerous Liaisons*; and out of solidarity, I hadn't either.' Stephen Davis goes further: 'He was terribly hurt.'

'I prefer Alan infinitely,' says loyal friend Theresa Hickey. 'Malkovich is this self-obsessed guy in Kung Fu slippers, whereas Alan is genuinely interested in people. He's very generous-spirited.

And he's so filmic: he would have made a wonderful Valmont on screen.'

For Alan, stage fright was the ever-present malignant monkey on his shoulder. In 1992, he told GQ that he had to 'struggle to find the character every time I walk on stage'. And the pressures of playing the vampiric Valmont, who must instantly dominate, only added to that.

Christopher Hampton's excitable view of how Les Liaisons Dangereuses had to fight for long-term survival against an intransigent, bureaucratic Royal Shakespeare Company makes a colourful story which is, of course, completely refuted by the RSC.

Adrian Noble, at that time associate RSC director, does admit that there was a problem with the transfer of Les Liaisons Dangereuses to the West End.

'The context of that year was that it was a truncated season. Trevor Nunn wanted to open Les Miserables and also Nicholas Nickleby in London in the Christmas of 1985, so all Stratford shows were cut short. The cast in a repertory system are cross-cast across different productions. The year we did Les Liaisons, Alan, Fiona Shaw and Juliet Stevenson were all in As You Like It as well. To free up all that cast – and Lindsay Duncan was also doing The Merry Wives Of Windsor – you have to wait for the shows to end in the repertoire, otherwise productions would be asset-stripped of their actors. Actors do prefer rep rather than doing the same thing eight times a week. So yes, there was a problem with the Les Liaisons transfer to the West End: endless problems with hoicking actors out of the rep. I don't know if Ben Kingsley, the star of Othello, was hacked off or not by all the attention Les Liaisons was getting. That's all speculation.

'As for the film rights, the RSC is always diligent about protecting the film rights of any production. We strike as good, and as hard, a bargain as we can.'

When I contacted the RSC's General Manager, David Brierley, he elaborated on that complicated transition to screen and the RSC's alleged delay. 'When we enter into a contract with a writer, part of the contract is to do with potential film rights.

'We negotiate a share of the sale of film rights that goes back to the original stage-producing company, which also gets consultation rights. Christopher's agent, the late Peggy Ramsay, was the best agent ever for ferociously protecting her authors. She did the deal and didn't consult the RSC. She was in a hurry because of the competing film *Valmont*, so it was a bit of a race to the tape. Plus Christopher's rights to be producer of the movie were also part of the deal.

'James Nederlander was by then the American producer of *Les Liaisons*. Peggy had cut us out – both the RSC and Nederlander. We asked her if she had the right deal, the best deal. We thought there wasn't necessarily a competitive approach here. At this point, Nederlander found a competitive offer. Christopher and Peggy were anxious not to accept this, because they had gone a long way down the road with Lorimar – who eventually produced Christopher's film version. But we said, "You can't just do the deal if there's a better offer. We can't approve of this deal until we have explored the competition as much as possible."

'So Lorimar upped their offer in cash by 50 per cent. Finally the deal was done with them, but the process had been slowed down. Chris had been willing to take a lower offer in order to have a position as a producer.

'The RSC and the Nederlander Organisation managed to up the ante in the end, but I think Christopher has never forgiven us,' says Brierley. 'It was a bit naughty of Peggy to go ahead without the RSC. Nine times out of ten, she would have done a good deal – but in this case, we helped secure a better one.

'James Nederlander is the commercial rival to the Schubert Organisation that owns the Music Box, the theatre where *Les Liaisons* played on Broadway. These are the two great theatre-owning organisations over there. Unusually this production brought the Schuberts and the Nederlanders together, so the RSC engineered a shotgun wedding. Normally they're like the Montagues and the Capulets. Nederlander thought the Music Box would be big enough. When we came to New York, our courage had grown and we wanted a bigger theatre – even though it only went on for 20 weeks.'

Trevor Nunn, then the RSC's Artistic Director, emphasises: 'Certainly no opposition to the work having an extended commercial life ever came from me. I saw Howard's production in both London and Stratford and thought it one of the best pieces of intimate theatre I had ever experienced. But I never had anything to do with the selling of the film rights, which I imagine had been retained by Christopher.'

'Everyone knew *Les Liaisons* would be a hit,' Adrian Noble insists. 'I don't remember Howard Davies being dubious; in fact, I can remember him fighting off the idea of anyone else directing it. I was pash [passionate] about Alan rejoining the RSC for *Les Liaisons* and I did have a say in that, although ultimately it was Trevor's decision. But it was because I've known Alan ever since he did *Man Is Man* for me at Bristol.'

With Valmont, as with Slope, Rickman had demonstrated the supreme art of showing the vulnerability in a multi-faceted villain. As Michael Billington wrote in his *Guardian* review of *Les Liaisons Dangereuses*: 'It is easy to say that Alan Rickman, with his air of voluptuous languor, is superbly cast as the Vicomte: what is really impressive is his ability to register minute gradations of feeling.

'He stiffens visibly as the Marquise de Merteuil denies him sex, literally shrugs an eyebrow at the news that people live on *56 livres* a year, allows his hand to hover over Cecile's body as if exploring a relief-map.

'But the keynote of Rickman's enthralling performance is growing self-disgust at his own destructiveness: he becomes a seductive Satan with a stirring conscience.

'Alan Rickman seems born to play the Vicomte. He endows him with a drawling, handsome languor and a genuine sense of spiritual shock at discovering he may be in thrall to love.'

Irving Wardle in *The Times* wrote: 'Alan Rickman, elegantly dishevelled and removing his mask of amorous melancholy to reveal a mirthlessly grinning voluptuary, carries the mask of death.' John Barber in the *Daily Telegraph* thought that 'languid, darkly handsome Alan Rickman makes a perfect Vicomte: plausible, cruel'.

Charles Spencer in the *Stage and Television Today* was ecstatic. 'Alan Rickman gives a performance of hypnotic brilliance as Le Vicomte. Fleshy and reptilian, languid yet prone to sudden bursts of feverish energy, he oozes charm and danger in equal proportions, an amoral predator who finally finds himself the prey of a stronger woman and the incomprehensible stirrings of his own soul.'

Only Barry Russell's review in *Drama* magazine's spring issue of 1986 dropped the classic clanger by questioning 'the casting of Alan Rickman as the scoundrel of the piece. He is too engaging an actor to play a "nasty" with much credibility'. (Oh yeah?)

In short, it was one of those reviews that you spend the rest of your life living down; though Russell at least noticed Rickman's 'endearingly unkempt quality, more fitted for Fielding's Tom Jones than for the aristocratic Vicomte de Valmont'. But surely that was the point: he was a wild animal in the boudoir . . .

Michael Coveney in the *Financial Times* gave 'thanks chiefly to Alan Rickman's predatory, dissolute Vicomte de Valmont, a languorous, squinting agent of destruction'. Sheridan Morley in *Punch* wrote of 'the silkily splendid' Rickman's 'elegant decay', although the late Kenneth Hurren was less convinced in the *Mail On Sunday*. 'Though Alan Rickman has been widely praised as the jaded vicomte, I feel he lacks something of a plausible seducer's practised charm,' he wrote.

Perhaps it was the glimpse of the conscience that Rickman's Valmont carried around with him which inspired so many women to write lovelorn letters to him. It's that potential for redemption and reformation which presents the ultimate challenge to female zeal.

Before Rickman's Valmont transferred to the West End and thereafter to Broadway, the RSC repertory system had given him the chance to play another Faustian character who had sold his soul to the devil. Rickman took the lead in Ariane Mnouchkine's didactic epic drama *Mephisto*, based on the Klaus Mann novel. As the actor Hendrik Hofgen, he found himself becoming the darling of the Nazi gods in pre-war Germany. The tale of how this former radical becomes Hitler's protégé is the story of an entire country's corruption.

Mark Lawson in *Time Out* considered that Rickman 'consolidates his status as a new RSC star', though some other reviewers expected a more grandstanding performance, finding him far too gloomy and depressive. Perhaps that old blood-sucker Valmont had sapped his energy; certainly it was crazy to play both in swift succession.

'Mr Rickman is merely bitchy when he ought to be demonic, pettish when he ought to blast everyone in sight or hearing with his rage,' wrote Francis King in the *Sunday Telegraph*. The *Daily Telegraph*'s Eric Shorter thought Alan had 'a compelling line in languid disdain and slimy hauteur', but others felt his heart didn't seem to be in this story of the Nazi rise to power and the equivocal attitude of the people.

Of course the voice, never to every drama critic's taste, came in for a hammering. Kenneth Hurren wrote in the *Mail On Sunday*: 'The chief focus is on a star actor and political renegade, played with enervating vocal monotony by Alan Rickman.'

As for Michael Ratcliffe in the *Observer*: well, he didn't like Alan's performance. Again. 'There are some attractive and truthful performances . . . all these sustain an evident humanity, but Mr Rickman chooses not to.

'Having frequently been accused in the past of camping it up, he has on this occasion put on sober attire and elected to camp it down, a dispiriting decision which leads to lugubriousness of voice and feature suggesting complete disillusion with past, present and future instead of a driving ambition to succeed at all costs. There isn't so much as a whiff of Mephistophelian sulphur all night.'

Barney Bardsley had written in *City Limits*, 'Mephisto is about the devil in us all.' But by this stage, the puritanical Alan was becoming revolted by the devil in Mr Rickman. Valmont was his darkest hour; his great film villains were tap-dancing scallywags by comparison. *Time Out*'s theatre editor Jane Edwardes pointed out in a 1986 interview for *Mephisto* that Rickman had become one of the hottest actors around by playing the coldest of bastards.

He took it all terribly seriously, as usual, and saw his character in *Mephisto* as a dire warning to those consumed by ambition. 'It's about how big a trough you can dig for yourself,' he told the *Guardian*.

Rickman had lost the battle to play Valmont on film and, in retrospect, it may have saved his sanity. Nevertheless, he was to win the Hollywood war in a strange and quite unexpected way, rediscovering his sense of humour in the process. His performance as Valmont on Broadway had brought him to the attention of a film producer who wanted a charismatic, intelligent, sophisticated baddie for his next action movie. Someone, in short, who would put up a truly satisfying fight, who would enter into mortal combat with a die-hard . . .

Despite having given us the definitive Valmont, Alan Rickman still felt as if he were a misfit outsider with a muffled voice in the snobbish caste system of the British theatre. It was to be in the more democratic medium of film, paradoxically enough, that he would be able to exploit his extravagantly theatrical roots. He had to go away in order to become truly honoured in his own country.

One is reminded of the famous brick dropped by John Gielgud when he talked about a very talented British stage actor called Claude Rains, who had been a West End star in the 20s. 'But he threw his career away,' said Gielgud plaintively, shaking his head sadly. 'He went off to Hollywood and completely disappeared. I wonder what happened to him?'

In Alan's case, he staged his 'disappearing' act in a sulphurous cloud of Mephistophelian smoke.

7. A DEAL WITH THE DEVIL

One sunny day towards the end of the twentieth century, Alan Rickman found himself being avidly stared at by a waitress while he and Peter Barnes were having lunch at a restaurant near their respective homes. They were sitting outside at a table on the pavement and the woman kept looking at Rickman, who maintained his customary Garboesque cool and pretended not to notice the kind of attention that had become an everyday occurrence in his life. Eventually, when Barnes went inside to pay the bill, the puzzled waitress said to Peter: 'I recognise your friend from somewhere, and I can't think where.' When Peter said, 'You might have seen him in *Die Hard* on TV recently,' she gave a tiny shriek of excitement and said, 'Of course, of course – it's Bruce Willis!'

'It's a great story about the fleeting nature of fame,' adds Peter. 'But Alan was just amused by it when I went back outside and told him; some people wouldn't be amused, of course.

'Actors don't like you saying this, but Alan's present fame is a matter of luck. There are crossroads in everyone's life,' points out Peter. 'If he hadn't had *Die Hard*, it might have taken him much longer.' Barnes has a particular fellow-feeling for Rickman because both had slogged away for years until one film completely transformed their fortunes. With Peter, it was his screenplay for *Enchanted April*. 'I had struggled for twenty years until *Enchanted April* opened the doors for me. It did huge business in America and was nominated for the Best Screenplay Oscar.' Later Peter finished a massive epic for Warners about the Medici ruler of Florence, Lorenzo the Magnificent; when he was asked his take on it in script conferences, he said, 'You should do it as *The Godfather* in tights.' He's learned the Hollywood pitch. These days he works like a demon, writing seven 'highly lucrative' American miniseries in just five years. Yet there's no danger of Peter living in an ivory tower: he impressed Alan by swapping his regular writing venue at the British Museum for the Leicester Square branch of McDonald's, much as the *Harry Potter* author J.K. Rowling first created her boy hero on scribbled notes in an Edinburgh coffee shop.

With Alan, it was the make-or-break movie *Die Hard* that changed his fortunes. It made his career – and it broke a cartilage in his knee after he performed eleven takes of a jump from a ledge on to uneven paving stones on his very first day on set. 'This torn cartilage is my souvenir of Hollywood,' he said afterwards, sounding like someone who didn't expect to be invited twice. For Rickman, always wary of getting carried away, had sternly told himself to regard the job as no more than a once-in-a-lifetime working holiday of the kind that never even happens for most British actors. He also took a Californian driving licence away with him as another souvenir after passing his test on his second attempt; he was failed on the first one for driving too cautiously through a green light. 'I think maybe that is a metaphor,' he told Karen Moline in *Elle* magazine, laughing at his own inhibitions.

'He's much loved by actors because he has a profound sense of irony,' says the RSC's Artistic Director, Adrian Noble. 'He can do trash and elevate it. Somehow he can keep above the shit. It's a deal with the devil. All actors have to do it. You have to do trash to survive, but he can send it up. Great Hollywood role models are so macho; but most people are not like that at all. Alan isn't macho at all.

'I was thrilled for him when it went so well in films. In many ways, he's an old-fashioned actor who can hand in a star performance – he has the intelligence and cut to create some of the great parts. He's very big, with a big voice.'

Die Hard producer, Joel Silver, preoccupied with casting his new movie, caught Alan's Valmont in *Les Liaisons Dangereuses* on Broadway. Rickman reeked of decadence, of course, and Silver professed himself duly asphyxiated. 'He was staggering. I was bowled over by the theatricality of how he played that role,' he told BBC2's *The Late Show* in November 1994. (Well, it was in a theatre.) 'For *Die Hard*, we were looking at conventional heavies . . . when we got Alan, it set the stage for a new evolution of the bad guy.'

In fact, it was all part of the long-established George Sanders and Basil Rathbone syndrome, in which suave British actors carved out a niche for themselves as the cads of Hollywood. (The fact that Sanders was half-Russian need not detain us.)

Claude Rains, of course, was clever enough to extend his range and make even the politically ambiguous police chief in *Casablanca* seem craftily sympathetic as he uttered the immortal 'Round up the usual suspects.' Even so, if you possess sharp features, narrow eyes and a drawling English accent, you are bound to be typecast thus.

Jeremy Irons won his Academy Award for the gallows humour of his performance as that suspected Bluebeard, Claus Von Bulow, a class act if ever there was one. Interestingly, Irons was later to play Rickman's vengeful brother in *Die Hard With A Vengance*.

American xenophobia has been blamed for the lazy habit of casting foreigners as the bad guys; but the preference for the theatrical disdain of those silky British scoundrels also betokens an inferiority complex on the part of a bedazzled Hollywood. It is as if they have to send out for their very best badduns, because they think they can't get them at home.

'When I was working in Hollywood, I got a call from someone saying he was a friend of Alan and that he had a script,' remembers the director Simon Langton, who had cast the then-unknown Rickman in *Thérèse Raquin* eight years previously.

'Alan, being a mate of this person, said he would meet me in a well-known bar in LA. It was an ultra-modern place, full of gleaming marble surfaces. He looked completely at home in the LA bar, but utterly English: rather *louche* and laid-back.

'We had a couple of beers and then he lounged back in his seat and said, "I have got this ridiculous Hollywood movie. It's called *Die Hard* and I play some crazy East European fanatic. It's non-stop explosions – the actors won't get a look-in. And I'm appearing with Bruce Willis! I play the lead baddie . . ."

'He was very self-deprecating and very friendly; almost too laid-back. I'm sure he doesn't suffer fools, though. He hadn't changed a great deal, he was physically leaner. That haughty-looking exterior had become even haughtier: hooded eyes, aquiline nose. I don't think he quite understood what was going to happen. He was quite unfazed by the enormity of it all, and yet this was his first-ever picture. Normally, you disappear in a cloud of burst fumes and flames when the film bombs, but this one didn't . . .'

After playing Valmont solidly for two years, your man was just about ready for the funny farm. *Die Hard* was, he confessed to *GQ* magazine in 1992, 'a great big present, with eight lines to learn every two days and a lot of Los Angeles sunshine. It was like being offered a glass of ice-cold water when you have been in the desert.

'I had never been in a movie before,' he told Catherine O'Brien in the *Daily Mirror* in 1992. 'Suddenly I found myself on a set in the middle of Los Angeles, surrounded by hundreds of people at 10 o'clock at night.

'It dawns on you that millions of dollars are at stake and everyone is watching and waiting to see if you balls it up.'

It was certainly a wonderful consolation prize for not winning a Broadway Tony for Valmont and for losing the film role to his imitator, John Malkovich. Die Hard was a huge success whose fortunes at the box office surprised everyone. It propelled the former television actor Bruce Willis into the supernova league and pushed the unknown Rickman to the very forefront of inventive screen villainy.

Alan always behaves exactly the same, regardless of his surroundings. If he's annoyed about something he's asked to do, he'll say so. He saw no reason not to have his usual frank and free exchange of views with the director on this, as on any other production. This movie beginner nearly stopped the filming one day when he refused point-blank to throw heroine Bonnie Bedelia to the floor, telling director John McTiernan that the violence was both offensive and inappropriate. Rickman combined male feminism with an instinctive gallantry towards women that was to make him an ideal Jane Austen hero eight years later.

'A big victory was won on that film set in terms of not conforming to the stereotype on the page,' he told GQ magazine. 'My character was very civilised in a strange sort of way and just wouldn't have behaved like that.

'Nor would Bonnie's character – a self-possessed career woman – have allowed him to. It was a stereotype – the woman as eternal victim – that they hadn't even thought about. Basically, they wanted a reason for her shirt to burst open. We talked our way round it – her shirt still burst open, but at least she stayed upright.'

Which was more than another unfortunate female in the cast did. Hurled across a desk by one of the other terrorists, her strapless party frock fell down and she ended up topless. But at least Alan Rickman's dabs weren't on her.

Nevertheless, Die Hard is still a simple-minded, xenophobic, Neanderthal film, which carries the subliminal message that workaholic feminists – i.e. career women – rot the social fabric of America. Until a cowboy comes to the rescue.

Rickman was there to add the gloss of class. 'All sorts of people asked me why I wanted to be in a film like Die Hard,' Alan told the Guardian in 1989, revealing a lot about the high-minded circles he moves in. 'I thought it could turn out to be a fabulous film, something like the best ride at the fun-fair. That's why.' He is certainly a thrills addict who loves the most death-defying fairground rides (as his *Mesmer* co-star Simon McBurney was later to testify).

For all his lordly insouciance in this alien culture, gloomy old Rickman was still convinced he was going to be sacked the first week.

'The first shot I did, and this is significant, was one where I had to produce an American accent. If I hadn't produced an acceptable accent, I'm sure I would have been got rid of. I mean, when a film's costing $30 million, no one's got time to waste.

'On the other hand, once they've decided you're all right, they'll make sure they've got it all in the can before they do the shot where they might kill you. The very last shot I did in the film was one where I was dropped from 40 feet.

'I'd certainly never picked up a machine-gun or even a hand-gun before. And we lost a lot of takes because I had a habit of flinching as they went off.' In fact you can catch him flinching in one split-second of fear as he fired a shot; and neither was his elusive American-German accent all that hot. They must have decided they just liked his voice anyway. But the tongue-in-cheek humour of the film was right up Rickman's boulevard; he and Willis got together with various scriptwriters to add jokes and ideas as the production got underway.

'When I met Willis, my immediate comment was that they're such cartoon-like characters that it would be much more interesting if they could make each other laugh. There was no emotional development to chart with my character, so it needed something extra. That came as the script was rewritten. In fact the script was rewritten so much that I could hardly say we filmed the script I agreed to do.'

The result of making it, he says, 'was endlessly surprising and endlessly enjoyable'. His name is the second to be credited, followed by Alexander Godunov and then Bonnie Bedelia. Very much a boys' picture.

We first see Rickman's character Hans Gruber emerging from a group of terrorists who seem to have fallen off the back of a lorry. They walk mob-handed out of the truck. Suddenly, this crowd parts like the Red Sea and he emerges from its centre. This is a cinematographer's cliché, but Rickman carries it off well, conveying just enough nerves under the professional cool to suggest a human time-bomb who might explode prematurely.

(Gruber was an inspired choice. There is a rumour that Hitler's family name was Schicklgruber, since his grandfather Johann Georg Hiedler married a peasant girl from Lower Austria whose name was Maria Anna Schicklgruber. Five years before, she had given birth to an illegitimate child.

According to the accepted tradition, the father of the baby was in fact Hiedler himself. But he never bothered to legitimise the boy, who continued to be known by his mother's maiden name of Schicklgruber until he was nearly 40 and who was brought up by his father's brother. The latter later took steps to legitimise him and asked the parish priest to cross out the word 'illegitimate' in the register, putting Hiedler's name down as the father.

Yet twelve years before Hitler was born, his father had started calling himself Hitler. Little Adolf was never known by any other name until political opponents discovered the old scandal and jeeringly labelled him Schicklgruber.)

The epitome of a designer terrorist, Rickman has his hands buried deep in the pockets of a long cashmere overcoat as he emerges from the mob. Gruber wears a Mephistophelean goatee beard and moustache. In fact he is Valmont revisited, with the same facial hair. The sideburns and beard form one long seamless stripe of fur round the chops of this sexy weasel.

After gatecrashing a Christmas party given by Bedelia's Japanese-owned firm on the 30th floor of a skyscraper, the neo-Nazi admires a scale model of a business project in Indonesia. 'I read an article in Forbes magazine,' he name-drops suavely. 'I could talk about industrialisation and men's fashions all day, but I'm afraid work must intrude.' A lovely camp flourish. Gruber is after 640 million dollars of negotiable bonds locked in the company vault. 'Who said we were terrorists?' he asks rhetorically, as if playing an elaborate game. He turns his head in slow-motion to glower at his henchman Godunov when the latter says 'It's not over yet' to Bedelia's captive Japanese boss. Rickman then shoots the latter in the head. 'See if you can dispose of that,' he orders, switching from the conversational to the callous in the abrupt way that is supposed to be the hallmark of the psychopath.

His suit reveals Rickman's surprisingly narrow shoulders. He's big-boned but his lean body has absolutely no pecs appeal, although Alan does work out at the gym – reluctantly, according to him. Though he believes fundamentally that the best career advice to a budding actor is to stay fit and healthy, to look after 'the instrument' of your body, he finds the grind of gym a tedious business. In a 1995 *Premiere* interview, he told Duncan Fallowell that he goes to his health club 'in secret – and I dutifully bore myself rigid on the machines'. Rickman's Gruber travels light, with high cheekbones and a hawkish nose to confer authority. Willis looks like Popeye in comparison, though the sweaty vest (which surely should have won Best Supporting Performance) stands up quite well.

Gruber has a rather contorted, very Germanic insult ready for Willis' character John McClane: 'Another orphan of a bankrupt culture who thinks he's John Wayne,' he sneers. On the contrary, McClane calls himself Roy Rogers, a Hollywood in-joke that's just a little too smug. But then that's Bruce Willis for you, revelling in the cat-and-mouse game McClane plays with Gruber.

Hans is pragmatic and not uncivilised, however, just as Rickman insisted: when he takes the staff hostage, he graciously allows a sofa to be brought in for a pregnant woman at Bonnie's request. Rickman's feral face is well used here. A TV picture reveals Gruber to be a former member of an extremist German underground movement until his expulsion, too radical even for the radicals. It shows him with hair combed unflatteringly over his forehead, looking very drab and downbeat ... this is Alan Rickman in real life as a superannuated student revolutionary, sloping down to buy his veggies at the Portobello Road market in Notting Hill Gate. With such a style makeover since his early days, clearly Hans is more in love with capitalism than he lets on.

A welcome touch of satire has a crass Gareth Cheeseman type, of the kind created by the comedian Steve Coogan, emerging from the hostage group. He boasts to Hans that he can broker a deal by giving him McClane, 'the guy on the roof' who is the one man that can stop the terrorists. Gruber shoots the fool when he realises that he doesn't know where the detonators are.

They risk more subversive humour when Gruber barks at the police and the FBI that he wants 'colleagues' round the world released – in Northern Ireland, Canada and even Sri Lanka, conjuring up such groups as 'Asian Dawn'. ('I read about them in *Time* magazine,' he stage-whispers with perfect comic timing to

Godunov, who has mouthed the name in facetious surprise.) It really must be like this with some terrorists, making the revolution up as they go along.

Gruber shows his mettle by posing as one of the hostages when McClane, toting his machine-gun, turns up to ask 'How ya doin'?' in that homespun, all-American way.

This little detail is ridiculous: Gruber has altered his accent slightly, but surely McClane would recognise that rich drawl anywhere? He's heard it enough times. And how about the lethal-looking teeth, revealed in a wolfish smile? McClane hands him a gun, whereupon Gruber ominously grounds out McClane's cigarette with his shoe (another cliché) and speaks in German (always a bit of a giveaway) on his mobile.

'Put down the gun and giff me my detonators,' he demands. It would be laughable in the mouth of anyone else but a deadly serious Rickman, who has both the intensity and the integrity to make you believe in his villains.

Alan uses a machine-gun to shoot the glass out of a window in a movie with more than its fair share of defenestration. Again you're suddenly very aware of Hans' jangling nerves under that studied cool: he's the student revolutionary who has hit the big time.

The FBI men are the usual unbearable egomaniacs and McClane is no less smug in his rivalry with them, so much so that you almost feel perverse enough to want Hans to win – especially if he could wipe out some of Bruce Willis's smirks. The villain is supposed to smirk, not the hero; Alan keeps his dignity by contrast. His best line comes when he realises Bedelia is McClane's wife and makes her hostage-of-the-week with a gun to her head. 'You are nothing but a common thief!' she accuses him. 'I am an exceptional thief, Mrs McClane,' he hisses, putting his face close to hers like a furious lover. 'Since I'm moving up to kidnapping, you should be more polite.' But dear old Brute Willis keeps coming back for more punishment, covered in blood like Banquo's ghost. McClane makes all the terrorists laugh, distracting them with a bit of male bonding for one vital moment. As a result, it's all over. Gruber finds himself travelling backwards through yet another window. His head swivels slightly as if he were an angry snarling animal, and then he goes into freefall, imitating the rapid descent of that malignant comic cat Lucifer in Disney's Cinderella.

He vanishes like a magician into the ether, dropping 40 feet. All this and Rickman's own stunts, too, as a first-time action man. The RADA fencing lessons had paid off; perhaps they put the vest on the wrong guy.

'I got *Die Hard* because I came cheap,' admitted Alan to *GQ* magazine. 'They were paying Willis $7 million, so they had to find people they could pay nothing.' However, it planted Rickman's flag on the international map with a scene-stealing performance that began his new Hollywood career in grand larceny. 'I wasn't prepared for the reaction,' he told Sean French in the same magazine the year before. 'I flew to New York for a preview, and the audience just stood up and cheered and threw things at the screen. I walked into that cinema and I could have just been someone with a ticket, but when I walked out I couldn't get to the car.

'My girlfriend and I went to Anguilla at Christmas and you're on this little West Indian island and everyone knows who you are. You're not Alan, you're the guy in *Die Hard*.' He was still bemused when he told *The Times* magazine of 12 March 1994: 'Black New Yorkers loved Hans Gruber. They come up to me and say: "Yo! My main man!" I don't know what it is. They want him to get away with it, I suppose.'

Yet he went from there straight back to BBC television and the intellectual comfort of a Michael Frayn play, *Benefactors*, which was transmitted on 28 May 1989. It reunited him with Harriet Walter, a member of the Rickman 'harem' whose inimitably dry little-girl voice was perfect for her role here. *Benefactors* was a miniature state-of-the-nation play – or perhaps just a state-of-South-London play – about the collapse of idealism. It told the story of how a tower-block architect – played by Michael Kitchen, with Barbara Flynn as his pragmatic wife – fell to earth. Rickman's character was an ex-senior classics master at Eton, now the bad-tempered editor of a woman's magazine. Harriet was his girlfriend, the archetypal dippy hippie-chick with a wonderfully vacuous and dithery manner and a maddeningly enigmatic air. They both sponge off Kitchen and Flynn, almost living round at their place. Harriet eats her hair and watches *Z-Cars* while the other couple, furious at her constant presence, argue about just whose friend she is. Kitchen and Flynn are capable, confident; the other two are incredibly disorganised, with smelly children we never see. With her long bell sleeves and curtains of hair, Harriet looks like the moping lady of Shalott. She whimpers a lot and tells herself she has held Alan back in his career.

Of course she begins a relationship with Kitchen, and Alan gets his first chance – but by no means his last – to play a cuckold. He's bitter and defensive, baggy-eyed and haggard.

'Life goes round like a wheel: what we have done once, we do again,' he says doomily.

Kitchen's anti-social skyscraping plans are leaked to the papers by Alan via Harriet. Alan goes to live in a derelict house in the middle of the redevelopment area, squatting there.

'Welcome to the war,' he snarls at the visiting Flynn and fires off an angry monologue to camera. 'I see in you a little of the bleakness I have in me,' he says provocatively to her. 'That's why you don't like me.'

He's menacing, shaggy, sexual, insinuating: a natural subversive and tinpot urban guerrilla. It is to Frayn's credit that he is not so obvious as to allow Alan and Barbara's characters to end up in bed together, but it's a natural conclusion to draw.

'Don't scrape the sky, just sweep the streets – a whole philosophy of government in eight words,' Alan says, using his headline-writing skills. But, by the end, this vulnerable malcontent is drily reflecting: 'We had all kinds of supporters by this time – but not all of them had heads.'

Nevertheless, he becomes famous as a spokesman for the campaign and attacks 'North London cultural imperialism'. He even survives two attacks by boiling brown stew from the hysterical Harriet, which would have scalded anyone with a thinner skin. Eventually Flynn fixes him up with a new job, while Kitchen's practice withers in this nicely cynical but over-long piece.

So much for the revolution, indefinitely postponed. It was in 1989 that Alan Rickman became a member of the property-owning classes. He was 43. After half a lifetime in the theatre, it was the first time that he had been able to afford a property. He and Rima had shared the rent on her Holland Park flat since 1977, but *Die Hard* had made a significant difference at last to his finances. Rima stayed put because she was required to either live or work in the borough of Kensington and Chelsea in order to remain a councillor.

Though he was worried about how Rima would feel if he moved out, Alan bought a maisonette near a garden square just over a mile away from Rima. They lead such different lifestyles that it's hardly surprising they find it difficult to share; but it was his burgeoning film career that made the real difference.

Once you start playing the Hollywood game, you have to make yourself available to work around the world at very short notice. The restless Rickman is forever on the move, while Rima is permanently home-based by virtue of sitting on no less than ten council committees, not to mention her governorship of Barlby Primary School and her involvement with a canalside project and a community centre. Her speciality is education, despite, or because of, not having had any children of her own.

'We were all very worried about them at first when Alan set up on his own, but it seems to have worked out,' says the close friend.

Indeed, there is a longevity to all his loyalties. Alan said no to several overnight movie offers on the back of *Die Hard* and returned to Britain and his old mentor Peter Barnes for three remarkable BBC projects: two period television dramas and a disturbing radio play, *Billy And Me*. He believes in causes, and he certainly found one in *The Preacher*.

The latter was the third of four Barnes monologues under the series title of *Revolutionary Witness*, based on eyewitness accounts of ordinary men and women caught up in the French Revolution.

Alan played Jacques Roux, a radical priest who officiated at the execution of Louis XVI and organised food riots in 1793. This was – and still is – the most passionate performance he has ever given, laying his emotions bare in a wonderful fusion of head and heart.

Roux is standing in a pulpit in an apparently deserted church, with his dog Georges at the foot of the pulpit as his only audience, apart from us. He is a true terrorist from history; this is the real thing, as opposed to Hans Gruber's entertaining ersatz version.

'God created rich people first and then showed them the world they would own,' he says through clenched teeth. He has wild hair and looks incredibly unkempt, the epitome of the turbulent priest. 'Your slavery is their liberty,' he adds in a spell-binding incitement to righteous violence, based upon Roux's own writings. 'The church offers fear and punishment for ever and ever. Religion is a liar and a cheat. Mad Jacques, Red Roux, sower of sedition, subverter of all law.'

His first sermon in a new parish is being preached in this ruined church. He goes before the tribunal tomorrow, charged with revolutionary excess. 'It seems I'm too revolutionary for the revolution,' he says with a bitter smile. 'Do not forgive me, Father, for I have not sinned.'

His own father had twelve children; Jacques was the cleverest. He was a priest at the age of fifteen years and became a professor of philosophy. Eventually he was arrested, he tells us, for a crime he didn't commit. 'This is how fires are kindled,' he warns menacingly. For he was not given a trial.

'Revolutions must be violent . . . the only way to end the greater violence,' he says, banging his fist on the pulpit. As the title of one South African film put it, *Death Is Part Of The Process*.

He lives, he tells us, with a good woman and is now a pamphleteer; she sells them. They adopted a son, Emile. The close-ups reveal Rickman's sensual, well-defined lips, the upper one slightly lifted in that characteristically animalistic way. 'Don't be fooled by those who set themselves above you. Look at the bill they present you with. It's not my purpose to be popular. I am here to sting.' As Rickman himself is; he's not a beige personality.

'To stop me stinging, the Assembly hired me to write the report of the King's execution . . . the rich we will gobble up, tra-la-la,' he sings. He tells us how ordinary people die in the mud and calls King Louis a toe-rag.

'We must appropriate the land and money from the rich, who have it in excess. We have to push the revolution as far as it will go and then further . . . and that's never enough for me.'

He tells us he wrote a pamphlet condemning the revolutionaries for banning women from power; so he's a male feminist as well as a socialist. 'I shun fame . . . it costs too much,' says this passionate, ruined romantic in his last confessional. Not Alan Rickman's own words, but certainly his sentiments. 'Making love or making revolution . . . but with a revolution, you have to be right.'

He waves a sword in the pulpit and says he will strike himself down if he's condemned by the tribunal. 'Living well is so much harder than dying well,' he says of the friends that he expects to 'move on' when he is dead. 'I have tried to create a people who are sceptical, rational, critical.

'We are of the generation that so transformed the world that it can never be the same. One last word . . . the revolution is not complete. Don't sit back. Act. For God is an active power. We do his work in fighting.' Roux committed suicide in 1794. You could almost fall in love with such a man, as conveyed by the Rickman brand of full-blooded romanticism that finally gives the lie to the image of this actor as the archetypal cold fish. Roux knows he's condemned, but he has no self-pity. His friends will move on because they have the difficult task: to live. It's a barricade-storming performance that sets out to change lives, just as he swears his was changed by Peter's play *The Ruling Class*. 'Alan's Roux was Lenin and Danton rolled into one. He was too left-wing for Robespierre, who had to get rid of him,' says Peter Barnes.

The radio monologue *Billy And Me* was the familiar story of a ventriloquist who is taken over by his dummy, yet Rickman played it very effectively on a rising note of hysteria.

'Yes, of course it's my wife ... would I have a maid so ugly?' went his patter, very much in the spirit of Archie Rice in John Osborne's *The Entertainer*. He proved an unexpected virtuoso at the music-hall innuendo; as with all great actors, Rickman has a strong vulgar streak of the grotesque in him. 'I'm depressed. I feel so dull, I can't even entertain doubt,' he moaned; Alan's natural lugubri-ousness is well employed here. Master Billy Benton is the creepy schoolboy dummy who exercises a sinister control over him. The 'vent' has had a nervous breakdown and becomes a schizophrenic as a result. He starts having visions and gabbles wildly about a row of dummies all singing Handel's *Messiah*, as camply funny as it's frightening.

However, it was the third Peter Barnes project, the TV drama *From Sleep & Shadow* in a Screenplay trilogy entitled *The Spirit Of Man*, that was to provide a fascinating foretaste of his performance in *Robin Hood: Prince Of Thieves*. Rickman often cannibalises himself: here, in this playful madman, is the genesis of his barn-storming Sheriff of Nottingham.

'Peter Barnes is our most Gothic of writers,' as Rickman's co-star Nigel Hawthorne pointed out to me. '*From Sleep & Shadow* was a very complex religious thing, but we had a great deal of fun doing it and laughed immoderately throughout – which I don't suppose was totally proper or totally what was expected of us, but it was certainly very good fun.'

Alan was cast as a seventeenth-century Ranter, one of those travelling demagogues who sprang up in vast numbers during the apocalyptic New Age turmoil of what the Marxist historian Christopher Hill termed the English Revolution. The Ranters were a primitive branch of ultra-zealous Methodists who split from the prim ranks of the Wesleyans; most of them were barking mad, and there were many great pretenders among the sane ones.

Rickman made his flamboyant entrance in twentieth-century sunglasses; it still amuses Peter Barnes that no one has ever spotted this camply anachronistic detail. 'For the Ranter, the costume was made up from bits of different countries. I believe historical accuracy is not as important as dramatic accuracy, though some of the dialogue was from the pamphlets of the time.'

Hawthorne played the right-hand man of the regicide Oliver Cromwell. He is mourning the sudden death of his beautiful young wife Abegail, played by Eleanor David. Now a pastor, he questions his faith. 'This is God's revenge for some unknown sin.'

Upon which cue, Rickman bursts in like Monty Python's Spanish Inquisition. 'You sent for me and I am here . . .' he says excitedly. 'I'm naked before women . . . proclaiming the word of God.'

Whereupon this extraordinary figure has a seizure, spluttering that Hawthorne had him whipped out of Southwark for enjoying bawdy mixed dancing and wearing shaggy hair and a hat during prayers. Hawthorne upbraids this lunatic upstart. 'I'll still rant with the best of them,' shouts Alan, leaping around the room as if the bugs are biting his bum.

He is Israel Yates, a tatterdemalion mountebank with a witty and paradoxical turn of mind. He mesmerises Hawthorne with his mad staring eyes, urging him to believe in faith-healing and telling him that Abegail is in a cataleptic coma. With his jigs and capers, it's a preposterous but beguiling performance of enormous charm.

'Curing carbuncles and haemorrhoids, capering up and down in the gutters of the world,' is how he describes his vocation. He produces a quartz stone on a chain and waves it above her, a gesture that is very Mesmer. He sweats, and that quiescent hazel snake-eye suddenly becomes bright and human. Unfortunately, he's brought the wrong woman back to life – Abegail is possessed by the spirit of Hawthorne's first wife Sarah.

Rickman is a cunning charlatan with a touch of genius, not quite in touch with his gift. Again, very Mesmer. He shouts in Abegail's ear, playing the voice of God, and then kisses her violently on the mouth. She faints. Then she comes back to life, restored by the sheer randiness of this apparent exorcism. Brother Israel-of-the-ten-tribes-Yates then boasts: 'We Ranters who cling to the bright lights of liberty and love.' He exits, but then suddenly bursts in again with a thought for the day. 'There can be no happy glad-man compared to a madman.' He sings and dances on the table. 'I'm shaking off melancholy soul-dust, sister.' And the three of them form an all-singing, all-dancing, table-top chorus line.

After this strange BBC interlude, Alan went straight back to Hollywood, but his inexperience made a bad mistake in choosing *The January Man* as his second foray. This lethargic and whimsical thriller about a serial killer might have worked if Rickman himself had been the murderer. Instead, he was the artist friend of Kevin Kline's ex-detective-turned-fireman, who is reinstated by his police commissioner brother, Harvey Keitel, in order to find the murderer.

Rickman was attracted by the cast – Susan Sarandon played Keitel's wife, on the rebound from Kline – and the prospect of portraying an artist once more was such an easy gig that he nearly did it in his sleep. Perhaps he followed Sarandon's advice rather too literally, for he later recalled, in a *Los Angeles Daily News* interview, how she had advised him not to think about it too much after seeing him agonise and pace back and forth before doing a scene. As he rationalised it, 'You have to let the animal part of an actor have its head.' Eventually Rickman was to patent a peculiar animal magnetism of his own, but in *The January Man* he was more of a good-humoured sloth than a prowling panther.

The first scene recalled Vidal in *Thérèse Raquin* ten years previously. Rickman is an eccentric bearded painter with a dilettante air whose studio has a lush nude model installed on a sofa. 'Just languish there, darling, don't molest anything,' he instructs her. Kline offers him a job. 'I resent the fact I need money,' Alan sniffs, and spends most of the movie squinting at a computer: '. . . trying to get the hang of this'.

He is supposed to be Kline's assistant, offering mumbled insights here and there. To add to the insult, he's dressed like a kooky clown – baggy check trousers, violently clashing neckerchief. He looks like a German artist with his spikily-cut, shaggy hair, beard and moustache. But he makes much of raising a lone eyebrow and producing goodies from a hamper with a sardonic flourish – Alan always manages to manifest signs of humour somewhere.

'I'm an artist, I watch the women,' he jokes heavily when he declines to enter the murder apartment. As if to mean business, he's now clad in a leather jacket that makes him look like an East German dissident with the faintest echoes of Hans Gruber. Essentially, he was paid to hang around as a spare part that became an embarrassment to him, judging by Alan's inert performance. The film was a box-office disaster.

It seemed that his Hollywood career was over before it had really begun until the Australian Western *Quigley Down Under*, released in 1990, rescued Rickman's fortunes.

'On *Quigley Down Under*, I hear he was so hysterical and anarchic that they loved him and he took over the film as a result,' says theatre director Jules Wright.

He had recovered his energy and intensity for another great scene-stealing performance in a movie that he took only, so he disingenuously maintains, to 'visit the Outback'. Later he would talk about the 'pull' of the Australian desert landscape, the so-called red centre whose mysterious vastness would attract anyone raised in Acton. Movies are often chosen by actors for their location alone, but in this case Rickman chose the right vehicle. Its politically correct perspective was an obvious attraction for him; but he couldn't resist the subversive urge to jazz it up.

Quigley Down Under has to be the slowest Western since *Dances With Wolves*, which was made the same year. Rickman gives it a giant jolt of electricity as the guy in the black hat, the psychopathic land baron Elliott Marston. He has shaved off the beard but kept the Valmont moustache and tuft under the bottom lip, which makes him look rather like Eli Wallach at his most weaselly.

His artistic eye insisted on changes immediately. 'When I arrived in Australia, they had me dressed in a purple jacket and white trousers as this indolent ne'er-do-well who sat around drinking glasses of wine,' he told the *Guardian* in July 1991.

'I didn't see Marston like that. He lived in squalor. He might drink wine, but from a dirty glass. My idea was to have him dressed all in black, which turned out to be a good choice but a hot one!' The result was a rather sexy character straight out of a maverick spaghetti Western.

Elliott has hired Tom Selleck as the finest long-distance marksman in the world. He wants him to wipe out all the local aborigines, for whom Marston has conceived a pathological hatred after the massacre of his parents. His mother, he reveals on a note of rising hysteria, was even butchered while holding her sewing.

English hunting-parties did in fact conduct a campaign of genocide against the aborigines of nineteenth-century Tasmania; it remains an appalling blot on Australia's human-rights record.

Quigs, a fine, upstanding Wyoming cowboy of no little sensitivity and nobility, is so furious at this churlish commission that he hurls Elliott out of the nearest window. That's another fine defenestration Alan's agent got him into . . . And this after Elliott has even tried to make friends by offering Quigley 'mint jelly on your lamb – it's my own creation' over a chummy meal. Every reasonable person would agree that Elliott has no choice thereafter but to leave Quigs plus leading lady Laura San Giacomo stranded in the broiling heat of the Outback desert as punishment, and none too soon so far as she is concerned. As the childish heroine Cora, Ms San Giacomo is seriously embarrassing . . . as well as being half Tom Selleck's size. Only his gentlemanly upbringing makes him put up with this prattling circus midget when most of us would have dumped her in the Outback ahead of schedule; it makes one speculate wistfully about the rather more hilarious sparring partnership that the irascible Elliott would have had with the brat.

When Quigs and Cora escape, Elliott's men make the mistake of breaking the news to him while he's being shaved at the barbers. Hence another entertaining outburst of peevishness from Rickman, who – be he never so villainous – makes a point of observing the proprieties. 'Don't bother to knock, will you? Oh SHUT up,' he snaps.

'He's going to spring something on us during the night – all right, nobody sleeps,' he snarls.

Quigs, however, is captured and dragged back to base on the end of a rope pulled by a horse. 'Good of you to drop in again,' is another example of Rickman's exquisite sarcasm. But Elliott is such a shameless showman that he insists on organising a duel with two Colt guns, which he mistakenly assumes Quigs has never used before.

The excitement of the occasion makes Elliott wax philosophical, another endearing trait in Rickman's laterally-thinking villains.

'Some men are born in the wrong century. I think I was born on the wrong continent. Oh, by the way, you're fired,' he barks with superb delayed timing.

That's his last word on the subject – or any subject. He is dispatched with indecent haste, and the film ends with a scene that pays self-conscious homage to *Zulu*. An endless line of aborigines, armed only with Stone Age spears, appears on the horizon. This magic circle surrounds the hostile British soldiery and provides Quigley with a safe passage.

'No animals were killed or injured during the making of this film,' say the credits at the end of the most right-on B-movie ever made (if you count *Dances With Wolves* as an A-movie).

The life goes out of it when Elliott finally catches that bullet, but Alan Rickman had now established himself on the movie map as the definitive die hard. Twice.

8. HOW THEY SHOT THE SHERIFF

Behind the scenes, Alan Rickman takes pains to behave like a real-life Robin Hood. He quietly gives away proceeds from his rich films to poor theatre projects, an orphanage in Romania and other pet causes such as Glenys Kinnock's One World Action campaign against poverty and Children On The Edge. When he secretly agreed in 2001 to voice the Genie of the Lamp in Philip Hedley's production of *Aladdin* at the Theatre Royal Stratford East on a strictly-no-publicity basis, Alan recorded it at RADA where he has long been quietly involved with fund-raising for his old theatrical alma mater. Yet his sharp looks made him a natural Sheriff of Nottingham.

Everyone in the business has fallen for the rumour that Ruby Wax rewrote Alan's dialogue for the Sheriff in the Kevin Costner movie *Robin Hood: Prince Of Thieves*. Nearly every person I interviewed for this book muttered conspiratorially, 'Did you know that Ruby . . .?', so it's travelled a long way. It's a great story, save for one thing: it's not true. To be fair to Ruby, she herself has never claimed the credit; instead it was claimed on her behalf by friends and/or admirers who made the logical deduction: 'The dialogue is funny, Ruby is Alan's friend, Ruby is funny, so . . .'

The real truth behind the Gothic humour of such bravura lines as 'Cancel the kitchen scraps for lepers and orphans. No more merciful beheadings – and call off Christmas' is that Alan's old friend, Peter Barnes, was the author.

Alan called him in to help as a script-doctor. A downmarket Greasy Spoon caff in London's Bloomsbury was the improbable operating theatre as Alan spread pages of the script over the table and Peter rolled up his sleeves (very characteristic of Peter, this) and set to work.

'I wrote the dialogue for the Sheriff,' Peter confirms. 'Alan and I have been friends for twenty years. I used to work a lot in the Reading Room of the British Museum. There's a working-men's café nearby and we went through the script together, because Alan said it needed some work on it.

'So there we were: I said, "Look at us, we've ordered egg and chips and we're working on the dialogue of a $40 million movie!" Alan, slightly misunderstanding me, said "Don't worry – I'll pay for the egg and chips." And he did.

'I made it more speakable. Kevin Costner was clonking around because his dialogue was a bit heavy-going. It doesn't trip easily off the tongue. Alan is a mixture of Claude Rains and Basil Rathbone in the role. There was something about a teaspoon in the middle of one speech – cutting a heart out with a teaspoon. It was a bit oddly positioned, so I made it work. In an action movie, everybody kicks in with the dialogue. The poor old writers are very much relegated.'

The results of that barnstorming session in a Greasy Spoon were such choice witticisms as 'I had a very sad childhood, I never knew my parents, it's amazing I'm sane', 'You – my room at 10.30 tonight. You – 10.45. And bring a friend' and 'Now sew – and keep the stitches small' to a physician.

The year 1991 was Alan's *annus mirabilis*. Four Rickman films were released, and only one of them – the little-known *Closetland* – was a flop. *Truly Madly Deeply*; *Close My Eyes*; and *Robin Hood: Prince Of Thieves* all enhanced his reputation to an extraordinary degree, so much so that influential film critic Barry Norman named him British Actor Of The Year. All three films were in the Hollywood Top Ten.

It was *Robin Hood* most of all that caught the imagination, though to my mind Rickman has never bettered his performance in Stephen Poliakoff's *Close My Eyes*. Therein he gave a cuckold – that traditional figure of fun – an unprecedented dignity and complexity. *Truly Madly Deeply* completed the Top Ten triumvirate, remarkable for its raw emotional intensity. Few people know that it is also the story of Alan: the man you see on screen is his real self (save for the fact that he's not a ghost and he hasn't had an affair with Juliet Stevenson).

Of course his mad, ranting, glam-rock Sheriff of Nottingham was a huge popular hit, and so completely upstaged Kevin Costner that there are stories circulating to this day about how Costner removed Rickman's best scenes from the final cut in the editing room. What's left is so wonderful anyway that one hardly needs to bitch about the missing bits.

Kevin Costner didn't really know who Alan was – the name meant nothing to him. But when filming started, Costner realised what a formidable actor Alan was. Costner has a reputation in Hollywood for being incredibly physically well-endowed. That's why he didn't wear the traditional tights in the role of Robin of Locksley; they made him a pair of breeches instead. However, Alan Rickman still upstaged him with his wonderful roguish quality and powerful presence.

Rickman's single-minded intensity responded to the need for speed in filming the £25 million project. 'The film lacked enough time. We were filming at the time of the year in England when you only have light until 3.30 p.m., so it was very difficult to get everything done,' he admitted to Jeff Powell in the *Daily Mail* in 1991.

Yet his Sheriff almost never happened. 'He turns a lot of things down, fussing a lot,' says the playwright Stephen Poliakoff.

'He tends to be a bit of a pessimist; he has mellowed a lot in the last year or so. He's very honest; he sees the pitfalls perhaps a bit too much. He doesn't bullshit and he's very self-critical. And he said to me gloomily that he was about to ruin his career by signing to play the Sheriff of Nottingham in a new film about Robin Hood. I said to him, "Is Prince John in it? No? Do it!" '

So he did, persuaded only by an offer of some control over his lines with help from Peter Barnes. And the preview audiences at early screenings cheered for Rickman, not Costner, hence the notorious cuts in the editing suite.

'At first I thought "Robin Hood – again?" I just turned it down flat. Then I started to hear of some of the names involved and I could see the way forward for having fun,' Alan told *People* magazine in 1991.

And have fun he most emphatically did. 'I tried to make him certifiable and funny – a cross between Richard III and a rock star,' he explained to the *Daily Mail*. It was that Thin Lizzy Crotch-Rock memory again . . .

Director Kevin Reynolds, who had manifold problems in getting Robin Hood to the screen and lost the friendship of his old chum Costner in the process, wisely gave Rickman his head.

Closetland, *Truly Madly Deeply* and *Close My Eyes* were in the can by then. 'So it felt okay to go back into the primary colours and just stride about in two dimensions for a while and have fun,' Rickman told the *Sunday Express* in 1991.

For someone who is popularly supposed to be politically correct, Rickman has a lot of subversive humour. He's one of the few actors who could turn the Sheriff's attempted rape of Maid Marian into an absolute hoot without making it tasteless. 'It has to be treated with humour,' explained Alan. 'You give it a particular tone, so that it's one of the more fun scenes. The only difficulty, to be honest, was getting out of the costume.'

Dressed in black, with sprouting ebony wig, beard and moustache, his Sheriff looked like the proverbial Bluebeard. 'I thought about Richard III and a rock guitarist and I said, "Let's make [his costume] raven so you know who's coming,"' he told Ann McFerran in an *Entertainment Weekly* interview. 'It was a cartoon . . . I didn't want the film to disappear into all that historical business.' Once again, as with Elliott Marston in *Quigley Down Under*, Alan instinctively understood that the Man in Black always won the style wars when it came to imposing your presence on screen. Would you ever catch Cruella De Vil in verdigris or Darth Vader in violet? I rest my case.

But Rickman's Sheriff made his first entrance as a wolf in sheep's clothing, as it were, by posing as a masked, white-cowled monk on a horse, confronting Brian Blessed's Locksley Senior with the snarl 'Join us or die' and a quick flash of his shark-like sneer.

The monks close in on Blessed with a pincer movement, their costumes and burning tapers deliberately evoking the Ku Klux Klan for the benefit of Middle America. Poor old Costner wears a duvet (known as a pelerine cloak in medieval times) and bird's-nest hair. Needless to say, he doesn't stand a chance in comparison with Rickman's lacquered glamour. Nottingham Castle is depicted as Dracula's lair; the horizon is studded with shrieking bats. Rickman is discovered nuzzling a girl's body as if chewing ruminatively on a chicken-leg. His head is cocked bird-like on one side at an interruption, a typical pose for him. His chest is bare but casually framed with black fabric: the effect is very kinky and straight out of a bondage shop. 'I trust Locksley has visited his manor and found the home fires still burning,' he says suavely.

His entourage consists of Geraldine McEwan in a white wig as the wizened old witch Mortiana; they make a wonderful pantomime double-act. The terribly po-faced Robin, by contrast, carries a blind retainer around with him: the self-conscious effect is that of King Lear, lumbered for life with Gloucester.

The Sheriff was raised by the witch, and scenes that ended up on the cutting-room floor disclose that she was in fact his mother.

'Zounds,' he exclaims in horror at the moment of death, 'who was DAD?'

Rickman's old school master Ted Stead says: 'You cannot get out of him what happened in the editing of *Robin Hood*, because he's very professional. But he did say, "You should have seen the eyework that Geraldine and I had." '

The Sheriff casts coquettish sidelong glances at Maid Marian in the cathedral; very reminiscent of Richard III and Lady Anne. 'You shine like the sun, my lady,' he snarls over Mary Elizabeth Mastrantonio's hand. The smile is like a rictus grimace, eyes suddenly flashing as if a snake had awakened with a start. He also has the beaky look of a bird of prey, his head so often cocked on one side that one begins to wonder if he's slightly deaf in one ear. 'Locksley, I'm going to cut your heart out with a spoon,' he promises. He slides on the floor in his haste, swats at people in his rage and frustration and repeatedly bashes the guard who let Robin through the gate. As the luckless flunkey falls, his feet catch the end of the Sheriff's cloak and there's a hideous rending sound . . . this is a Sheriff who's almost endearingly accident-prone.

'Now sew – and keep the stitches small,' is this piece of vanity's instruction to a doctor about to patch up his face. A fury of nervous energy, he flagellates himself with rage and stabs at some meat on a plate as if trying to skewer an enemy. 'Something vexes thee?' enquires McEwan's hag demurely.

He even glowers threateningly at his own statue, trying to wipe off its scar. 'You – my room at 10.30 tonight. You – 10.45. And bring a friend,' he tells two wenches.

The Sheriff skewers his useless whingeing cousin with a Spanish blade – 'at least I didn't use a spoon,' he hisses. Even Costner's bare bum can't compete; both he and it are far too stolid. For, in truth, Robin's ponderous tale is in dire need of Rickman's diabolical inventiveness to jazz it up.

'Tell me, Mortiana, am I thwarted?' the Sheriff asks McEwan rhetorically, with a smile like a saw-toothed portcullis as he realises he can hire Celtic thugs to fulfil a prophecy and marry Marian by kidnapping her. So a mercenary band of cider-heads makes an appearance, brandishing bloodaxes on the edge of the forest. One is again reminded of *Zulu* and the shot of the assegai-carriers wrapped around the horizon as far as the eye can see. 'Get me prisoners,' grates Rickman.

As his men send flaming arrows into Robin's Iron Age village, Rickman is caught gnawing his nail obsessively and fastidiously – as in real life. (One suspects the Sheriff was probably a late bed-wetter, too.)

For there is constant human detail in Rickman's villainy. Howard Davies, director of *Les Liaisons Dangereuses*, says that Alan once rang him up in a fury to disagree after Davies had told a magazine that actors needed to find a trait they could love in a character. 'On the contrary,' admitted Davies to Allison Pearson in the *Independent on Sunday* magazine in 1992, 'Alan sets out by exploring the pathology of a character. He cuts them open and looks for what makes them weak or bad or violent.' Indeed, there is a crazy, deluded gleam in the Sheriff's eye, almost as if he really does half-imagine that Marian has fallen in love with him. Rickman's Sheriff has been frivolously compared to Basil Rathbone's Guy of Gisborne in the Errol Flynn version of *Robin Hood*, but Rathbone was incredibly stolid by comparison.

'I had a very sad childhood, I never knew my parents, it's amazing I'm sane,' Rickman glibly tells a child whose life he's threatening in front of Marian ... such an obvious bid for our sympathy vote that it's breathtakingly funny. There's a hint of cynical contempt for such fashionable psychological sob-stories, too.

'If you fail, I will personally remove your lying tongue,' he tells the spy Will Scarlett, who is now suspended by his ankles in the torture chamber. Rickman turns his own head upside-down to talk to him. At one point Rickman goes cross-eyed with exasperation (don't we all). 'Shut up, you twit!' he shrieks. And when Mortiana slaps Marian's face, he rasps proprietorially, 'That's my wife, crone!'

'For once in my life, I will have something pure . . . will you stop interfering!' he tells Mortiana, insisting that he won't ravish Marian until they are married in the eyes of God.

His biggest weakness is revealed at the marriage ceremony: the Sheriff of Nottingham's Christian name is George, which explains a lot. He desperately tries to unstrap his sword in order to subject Marian to marital rape as soon as they've exchanged their vows. 'I can't do this with all that racket,' he says fretfully, trying to penetrate his bride while a battering ram bashes down the door in hilariously symbolic counterpoint. Geraldine helpfully puts a cushion under Marian's head – better for conception, perhaps? Whatever, it's another wonderfully funny detail.

'Dew yew mind, Locksley? We have just been married,' he sneers with a look of ineffable exasperation as Robin crashes through the stained-glass window of the tower to make a widow of Marian. Some of Rickman's flamboyant curls are sliced up by Costner's sword, but he hasn't given up the glamour role yet. He kisses Marian violently in front of Robin and pulls the fatal dagger out of his own chest . . . quite heroic, really.

He goes fleetingly cross-eyed again and finally swoons with pain, lying like a broken-winged crow on the floor and looking oddly pathetic. Rickman's full-blooded performance and quirky insights have made the Sheriff strangely lovable: you just know he was bullied at school and passed over for promotion. Yet the performance is never sentimental.

Neither was he to succumb to sentimentality in a film that would make a stone statue weep without recourse to any religious miracle. 'The Sheriff of Nottingham is a troublemaker with a murderous streak, all right – but goodness, this is a costume melodrama, not Shakespeare. I believe this particular villain needs to be a little laughable, lest we mislead the audience into taking things too seriously,' said Alan in an interview with the *Fort Worth Star-Telegraph* in 1991, adding plaintively that he wished more people knew about his performance in another movie called *Truly Madly Deeply*. 'I'm looking to defy as many expectations as I can, in case the people who liked my turn in *Die Hard* should take that character as the only thing I'm capable of doing. That's what I'm doing so much of the broad comedy-villainy for in *Robin Hood* . . . Kevin Reynolds and I worked out where I could get away with mugging the camera and sticking my nose into the audience.'

It was the modestly budgeted *Truly Madly Deeply*, which made £20 million from its cinema release, that established Juliet Stevenson as an international name; unlike Alan, however, she has not yet followed up that initial impact on the international stage. Anthony Minghella directed and also wrote the screenplay for the BBC-funded film, which is the most personal, autobiographical work of Alan's career.

'We used our own relationship in the film,' Juliet admitted to *GQ* magazine in July 1992. 'I really am the Nina character, juggling a hundred balls in the air at the same time and driving Alan potty with my scatterbrained way of doing things. He is much more selective and sure in his tastes, which can be equally infuriating. But he's a great anchor in my life.'

The enigmatic Juliet, whose forthright independence had long made her an idol of the Sapphic community, now has a little daughter by her husband, American anthropologist, Hugh Brody. Director Jonathan Miller nicknamed Stevenson, Harriet Walter and Fiona Shaw 'the nuns' while they were at the RSC; and all three are great friends of Rickman. Such good friends, in fact, that he felt relaxed enough to remark years later, 'Actually, I've kissed some of the greatest actresses around – Fiona Shaw, Harriet Walter, Juliet Stevenson', without making it sound like a vulgar boast. And he was to claim that he and Stevenson had – with the aid of the famous BBC radio sound effect department, of course – performed 'the first oral sex scene on radio in an Anthony Minghella play, *A Little Like Drowning*'. With bonding like that, no wonder Alan and Juliet went on to make *Truly Madly Deeply* with Minghella. The actor and director Philip Franks is another Stevenson buddy, and even he felt the need to explain himself thus: 'I'm not gay . . . but I have a number of strong friendships with a number of women.' Alan is just the same: a man who attracts all kinds of women, straight or gay. They are easy in his company because they enjoy being treated like equals.

Socialism is another common denominator for Rickman and Stevenson, a brigadier's daughter who went to Fergie's old school, Hurst Lodge, and has been trying to live it down ever since.

Both Juliet and Alan took part in the Labour Party TV broadcast for the General Election in April 1992, and she joins him on crusades: they hosted a party at the Red Fort Indian restaurant in London's Soho to help black South African children. They are embarrassed by what they see as the trivia of showbusiness, and they're forever trying to prove that they are serious people. Inevitable, then, that they would make a film together . . .

It's true that Juliet, with her fierce, offbeat beauty, is what the French shrewdly call a *jolie-laide* (in its literal translation, pretty-ugly) . . . very much like Alan himself. And there are other similarities.

Truly Madly Deeply was filmed in Bristol and in Juliet Stevenson's Highgate flat in North London. Minghella encouraged the actors to

Humble beginnings. Alan Rickman's school nativity play, West Acton, 1951

Alan Rickman (*far left*), a poised presence in *Guys and Dolls*, Leicester, 1975

Left: Alan on tour with the rep at the Crucible, Sheffield, in Ibsen's *When We Dead Awaken*, 1976

Below: First stint at the RSC in *Antony and Cleopatra*, with Glenda Jackson and a girlish Juliet Stevenson, 197?

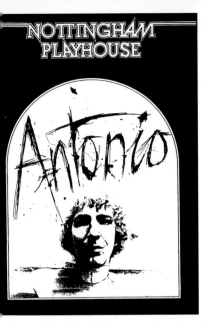

Above left: Alan Rickman, who also designed the poster, as Antonio in 1979
Above right: Looking decidedly menacing as Achilles in *Troilus and Cressida*, 1985

Left: The cast of *Lucky Chance*, with Alan Rickman as the quaintly named Gayman, starring with long-time friend Harriet Walter, 1984

Right: Gayman evolves into the dissolute aristocrat Vicomte de Valmont in *Les Liaisons Dangereuses*, 1985

Below: The screen villain: Alan Rickman's first cinematic role sees him cast as Hans Gruber in *Die Hard*, 1988

1991 was Alan's *annus mirabilis* with three successful film releases:

Left: Truly Madly Deeply with Juliet Stevenson

Below: Close My Eyes, as the cuckolded husband of Saskia Reeves with Clive Owen

Overleaf : Robin Hood: Prince of Thieves, as the psychotic Sheriff of Nottingham

Above right: "I'm too old but what the hell." The ultimate challenge: as Hamlet a[t] the Nottingham Playhouse, 1992

Below: Alan Rickman's first cinematic lead role in Dennis Potter's *Mesmer,* 199[2]

Above: Alan Rickman, as Colonel Brandon, finally awakens the love of Marianne (Kate Winslet) in *Sense and Sensibility*, 1995

Left: With Rima Horton his partner

Alan Rickman continues to make his name in Hollywood: in *Galaxy Quest* (1999) and the hugely successful *Harry Potter and the Philosopher's Stone* (2001) ...

... but he doesn't forget where came from. Alan Rickman and Mel Smith at the opening of the new Arts Centre at their old school on 19 November 1999

draw on their own experiences, introducing their own quirks into the film. Thus Juliet is a scatty, highly strung woman; and Rickman is the calm, slightly caustic control-freak in her life.

This scaled-down British version of *Ghost* tells the story of how Juliet's character Nina learns to come to terms with the sudden death of her lover Jamie, played by Rickman. What makes it particularly difficult is that he returns to her several times in the guise of a ghost, accompanied by his friends from limboland.

The movie begins at Highgate Tube station and the long climb up the stairs from the underground tunnels into the wooded, slightly spooky exit. Nina is talking to herself: 'If I'm frightened, then he'll turn up,' she reassures herself. 'He always was forthright. I would have been feeling low and hopeless . . . and he's there, his presence, and he's fine. And he tells me he loves me . . . and then he's not there any more. I feel looked after, watched over.'

This almost makes him sound like a Christ figure, except that the film has far too much humour for that. In fact, it exactly replicates Alan's central role for his mates. 'He's an important figure in the lives of all his friends,' says the playwright Stephen Davis. We realise that Nina is in fact talking about Jamie in this intense way to her psychiatrist. Then the camera cuts to Alan, feigning playing the cello (the sounds are not his). He frowns in concentration, his hair long, bleached fair and floppy and his moustache dark. The contrast suits him. The mourning Nina is surrounded by solicitous men who are desperately concerned about her: her language-laboratory boss Bill Paterson; a lovestruck, slightly mad and totally unsuitable Pole called Titus; Michael Maloney as the psychologist she meets in a café; and even the elderly oddjob man who has come to sort out the rats in her flat.

Indeed, Jamie is the only one who is never sentimental about her; and this is very much a Rickman characteristic.

'He's into the Tough Love Department,' says Davis, who plays lead guitar in his own rock band and tells the story of how Alan told him to pull himself together during a panic attack for one gig. 'I played live to an audience at London's Pizza On The Park for three nights, and it was the most nerve-racking thing ever. I said to him, "This is killing me, I'm so nervous." He looked at me and said, "No one's making you do it." We share each other's troubles a lot. He says, "Don't be negative". But he is, too . . . and I listen to him. It's a one-way street.'

Nina finds herself crying without warning, and they are real, uglifying tears that make her nose drip and her face flush red. This is very Juliet Stevenson. 'I miss him, I miss him, I miss him, I miss him . . .' Her pain is so raw that it hurts to watch. She's angry with him for leaving her, a typical reaction of the bereaved. 'I can't forgive him for not being here.'

But this mood is counterbalanced by tantalising moments of fleeting happiness, such as when she is with her beloved young nephew. 'You aren't getting posh? Say bum and Trotsky twice a day,' she teases him, joking but deadly serious at the same time.

Juliet is so committed that she was reported to have left the Labour Party in 1995 because she felt its modernist stance was compromising its politics. Alan, so far, stays firm.

Nina won't give her nephew Jamie's cello, however. It's all she has of her dead lover . . . and she won't let go. As she plays the piano, Jamie materialises behind her, playing his cello. He stands motionless as she cries, her face scarlet with grief. Then he hugs her as she weeps piteously. 'I kept thinking,' he says drily, 'just my luck . . . dying of a sore throat. Maybe I didn't die properly, maybe that's why I can come back. Didn't hurt.' She gingerly feels him to see if he's real.

'Are you staying?' she asks meekly. 'I think so.' 'Can I kiss you? Your lips are cold.' 'This is a terrible flat,' he grumbles. 'And you've got RED bills. And you never lock the back door . . . driving me crazy.'

This is pure Alan, who keeps his flat in Westbourne Grove incredibly tidy and would lecture Ruby Wax about monitoring the central heating when they shared a flat together. 'Thank you for missing me,' Jamie says morosely, but not without lugubrious humour.

'Your pain . . . I couldn't bear that. The capacity to love that people have . . . what happened to it? I blame the Government. I hate the bastards,' he ends with a growl.

'You died and you're still into party politics?' she says, amazed. 'I still attend meetings,' says Jamie defensively.

He makes himself scarce as Titus arrives at the door and invites her to Paris for sex. 'Now I'm depressed. I book tickets. Man with big emotion, big heart. I love you,' says this ghastly character, a sexual harasser by any other name whom well-bred women are too polite to rebuff. When she comes back after tactfully getting rid of him, Jamie has apparently gone. 'Who was that?' he asks, emerging from underneath the bedspread and laughing almost evilly as she screams with fright. He warms his lips for her by breathing on his hand and then touching his mouth. They kiss.

They sing at each other, rather raggedly in that cracked, ironic way of close friends, droning their way through a Sixties/Seventies medley: The Walker Brothers' 'The Sun Ain't Gonna Shine Anymore', Buddy Holly's 'Raining In My Heart', Joni Mitchell's 'A Case Of You' and Bob Dylan's 'Tangled Up In Blue'.

They play the childish games of lovers as they vie with each other to declare their passion: 'I really-truly-madly-deeply love you.' He pushes her away playfully then pulls her back imperiously into his arms.

Rickman plucks a guitar and sings again with that strangely musical cawing-crow voice of his, slightly reminiscent of the late Jeremy Brett, the definitive incarnation of Sherlock Holmes. Stevenson dances wildly. The rats have gone, perhaps terrified of his ghost – or their singing. Later he drips a glass of water on her face to wake her up and pushes her out of bed in his benignly bossy way. This is the essence of Juliet and Alan's relationship; indeed, his relationship with everybody. He has tidied up and lit the fire for her. Jamie comes and goes with no warning. Nina's handyman friend George, played by David Ryall, confides that he still talks to his wife who died in 1978. 'And death shall have no dominion,' he quotes sombrely.

Jamie next pops up in the most surreal way when Nina is in the bath with a face pack on; he appears over the edge of the bath. He pokes a plastic toy animal in her face, and it whirs as it sticks its tongue out at her. 'Oh come on, don't be coy . . . I know you shave your legs,' he says, asking casually whether he can bring some guys back to watch videos. Bizarrely enough, the spirits turn out to be huge film buffs who wrap themselves up in duvets and watch *Brief Encounter* intently before taking a vote over whether to see *Five Easy Pieces* or *Fitzcarraldo*. Jamie huddles up in bed next to her: 'You smell so nice.' He even brings a string ensemble back to play a Bach suite. She fetches him a hot-water bottle because he feels permanently cold, the only sign of his otherness.

These quirky interludes are beautifully handled, though the contrasting 'real life' episodes with Michael Maloney have a slightly embarrassing whimsicality as he tries to jolly her along and bring her back into the land of the living. Rickman seems more real than any other man.

Nina briefly glimpses Jamie again, but it's just another cellist on the South Bank next to the National Film Theatre. Her dead love is then discovered sitting by the fire at her flat again. Nina is driven to distraction by his disorganised friends, who are playing chess and generally causing mayhem. Alan is even taking up the carpet to expose slightly mildewed floorboards, just as he did in their relationship. 'Could everybody just go?' she finally says. They all waddle out like offended penguins in the John Smith beer commercial on TV.

She asks Jamie to remember their first meeting, and there's a real intensity between them. 'I want a life,' she says; it is her bid for independence and freedom from his memory.

Suddenly you notice that Rickman is grey at the temples. 'Do you want me to go?' Jamie asks softly. 'No, never, never, never,' says Nina fervently, thinking she means it. But the fraternity of ghosts does go; and she is finally over him as she rushes off to Maloney's class to meet him.

The rat is back; a pet one called Squeak, supplied by a company called Janimals. It's a sign that the ghosts have truly gone. They come back briefly, with Rickman at their centre, to stare out of the window at the sight of Juliet kissing her new man in the garden.

Rickman has never looked more romantic than here, like some sulky Russian dissident artist, but he made the part an anti-romantic one. The tug of nostalgia is very powerful, but his astringent personality gives the ghost of Jamie solidity. By contrast, though Maloney's character lives in the real world – and you can't get much more real than someone who works with Downs' Syndrome adults – he has a gentleness about him that offers Nina an enticing escapism. As ever, Rickman's instinct is to play against the character he is given, to introduce surprise and tension.

By contrast, his next project was a big mistake. The low-budget Hollywood film *Closetland* was written and directed by a woman, Radha Bharadwaj; and, as with Kathryn Bigelow's ultra-violent *Strange Days*, perhaps only a woman could have got away with it.

Rickman plays a Fascist interrogator trying to break the will of Madeleine Stowe, the nearest he has got so far to the kind of Torquemada figure that some fans crave. All the action takes place in one room, a gleaming, high-tech affair that bears no resemblance to the moth-eaten Gothic dungeons favoured by the Sheriff of

Nottingham. The victim is blindfolded, so that Rickman's voice, slipping into different parts, confuses her. His character, according to the *Variety* review of 11 March 1991, is no brute, however, but 'a complex, highly civilised man who displays a range of emotions and talents'.

Stowe plays a children's author whose work stands accused of feeding subversive ideas to infants in the guise of innocent stories. Rickman is an agent of the oppressive government. It becomes a contest of wills, with Stowe determined to awaken his conscience and Rickman trying to break down her resolve. *Variety* made the point that it is an essentially theatrical piece, difficult to sell to cinema audiences and perhaps better suited to TV. Amnesty International was the consultant and participated in the film's marketing campaign, so it's easy to see why Alan became involved.

Rickman was praised for his multi-faceted performance; but he was very unhappy with the end result. 'He said it was awful after it was edited, and he told me not to look at it,' says his old Latymer Upper English teacher Edward Stead. 'He hoped it would never open in England.'

It had been a gruelling year. On the back of that disaster, he made Stephen Poliakoff's incest drama *Close My Eyes*, taking the part of the betrayed husband that Poliakoff created specially for him.

Poliakoff had first come across him in 1976 when Alan played one of two middle-class drug addicts in Stephen's play *The Carnation Gang*. 'I then ran into him at the RSC during his second time with them in the mid-eighties. I did a starry workshop with Alan, Tilda Swinton and Juliet Stevenson. I was interested in doing a play about dreams, so we did a workshop. He and Juliet were very compelling as a weird, dark couple: brother and sister. She was druggy, he was dragging her down into a dark spiral. Essentially it was a portrait of the 70s and the 80s.

'I gave Alan quite a lot of space when I was directing him for *Close My Eyes*,' adds Poliakoff. 'I made him feel secure; and I got the impression that not a lot of people had done that. Actors are always being judged on their physical qualities, so they're very vulnerable.

'Alan has big vulnerabilities. He worries that people are doing the work intelligently, and he and Juliet are big smellers of bullshit. It was the combination of *Close My Eyes*, *Robin Hood* and *Truly*

Madly Deeply that finally made him known to the man in the street. With success, he expanded enormously in terms of his confidence. For an intelligent man, it's difficult to sell yourself. Improvisations for directors are very tough for someone who's intelligent. At least a writer doesn't have to sell himself physically to a complete idiot.

'Alan didn't make any suggestion for the dialogue in *Close My Eyes*, but he did suggest wearing a baseball cap in the garden-party scene. And some of his sister's children played the kids running around. I offered him the role of the husband Sinclair before I cast the brother and sister, and he's renowned for being one of the longest drawn-out yes-noers in the business. He came in halfway through the shooting, and Clive Owen was slightly terrified of him. Sinclair has an opinion on everything; that's slightly true of Alan, too.'

Close My Eyes is a (very effectively) overheated tale of incest between a brother and sister, separated when young and only meeting later when both are grown up. Their grabby intensity could be taken as a metaphor for the Yuppie 80s, particularly as parts of the film were shot in the fashionable surroundings of Docklands London. Clive Owen plays the brother and Saskia Reeves the sister, married to Rickman's watchful but enigmatic Sinclair.

He's supposed to be a high-powered City solicitor, though Alan was careful not to include any detailed clues to the character.

Alan used his own artistic background to collaborate closely with the costume and production designer so that Sinclair could not be put into any rigid social pigeonhole, according to an interview with Sean French in *GQ* magazine. 'I didn't want people to learn anything about him through where he lived or who his friends were.' In other words, he is creating an archetype in this morality tale for our times.

In his own quiet way, Sinclair is having the big adult breakdown while Owen and Reeves indulge in the screaming, shouting, childish melodramatics. He finds their relationship intense, but at first he doesn't suspect . . . or doesn't want to. At one point, we see him pushing a cart round the supermarket and questioning certain details that don't quite make sense. Then he sits abruptly on the floor of the shop as the truth registers. It could almost be a scene from a Woody Allen film. There is another scene on a riverbank in which Rickman's long look at Owen says everything he dare not quite admit to himself. It's a devastating combination of suppressed rage and vulnerability.

As Sinclair's suspicions fester behind that outwardly calm facade, the tension becomes palpable . . . as James Delingpole pointed out in the *Daily Telegraph*, 'You suspect that at any moment he might be about to commit some monstrous act of violence.' This is a one-dimensional reading of the performance, however. It is Sinclair's tremendous restraint that impresses: you know he knows, but he's holding back all the time and trying to be civilised, not just for the sake of his dignity but because he feels like a clumsy, helpless outsider between the siblings. He is powerless to intervene . . . in a kinky Greek tragedy. Anyway, who wants to admit that you've been cuckolded by your brother-in-law? Particularly if you're as rich – and as suavely attractive – as Rickman's well-heeled character. Indeed, the only surprise is that Reeves finds Owen more attractive.

On the BBC's Gloria Hunniford show in 1991, Rickman said the film showed 'how uncertain our lives are. It's a story about Britain in the 90s, and my character is an arch-Yuppie.' All the torrid sex is reserved for Reeves and Owen; Rickman admits to Gloria that he kept his knickers on and Saskia her nightie during a bed-scene. 'I remember us all giggling a bit at that point,' says Poliakoff. 'I've done a lot of hopping in and out of bed naked, but this was my first actual sex scene,' recalled Alan. 'Saskia whispered to me, "Did I have any knickers on?" I did. I mean, God forbid there should be any real contact.'

The female screams and whistles from the studio audience when he made his entrance on Hunniford's show suggested that perhaps the wrong guy got his kit off (not that anyone in full possession of their faculties would kick Clive Owen out of bed). Rickman took the homage with gallantry and humour; despite the explicit letters, he tries to be polite to his fans and always signs autographs at the stage door.

'We hadn't even had a conversation; we had only just met again; and suddenly Alan was in bed and we had to begin that scene. It often happens like that if you go into Makeup and then straight on to the set. So I said, "Sorry, I'll keep my underwear on," ' remembers Saskia Reeves, who first encountered him at a play-reading at the Royal Court Theatre back in 1988. So Alan decided to preserve a bit of decorum too.

'I like being around him because he's such an extraordinary individual. He's calm and extraordinarily eccentric – so different to anyone else I know,' she says. 'He makes me feel very relaxed. He always brings out a cheeky side in me: I tease him to make him laugh. He was very sturdy and confident and helpful on *Close My Eyes*. He's a great socialiser. I invited the cast over to my flat and we sat up till all hours. I was quite surprised: he stayed the distance for lunch the next day and left in the evening.

'It's nice to find a kindred spirit. He's a latter-day philanthropist, he brings people together. He's not a parent figure, he's my playmate. I tease him. I think he's great.

'In many ways, I sometimes wonder if there's a hidden agenda with Alan. He can be quite removed: he's like a character in a Pinter play, where the strongest person is the one who says least. I do that childish thing of teasing and tickling him. I teased and tickled my granny's dog and eventually it bit me on the chin. But Alan has never bitten me yet . . . I try to make him laugh. I try to give him what I see him giving to others. He has this huge support-network whereby he supports and looks out for other people.

'Sinclair in the film was a calm, solid, eccentric, tender man, rather like Alan. I'm not shy of him. I have never found him intimidating; that's Alan. He and Rima came to see me in Stephen Poliakoff's play *Sweet Panic* at Hampstead Theatre in 1996, and he's the kind of person who always knows nice places to eat. That sort of thing fascinates me about him, though I couldn't begin to say what he's about. I always feel very positive about him; I never feel intimidated by him.

'Sometimes I feel as if he's playing a game of being aloof on purpose, but it's just the way he is. Sometimes he takes his time before he's worked out what's going on.'

After wall-to-wall filming, Rickman was ready to head back to theatre with the Japanese play *Tango At The End Of Winter*, the story of an actor in crisis. His old friend Peter Barnes adapted it for the Edinburgh Festival and the West End stage, with the legendary director Yukio Ninagawa directing it.

Rickman played Sei in the Kunio Shimuzu play about a famous matinée idol whose wife urges him to go back to the stage in order to stay sane. 'He has the usual actor's madness,' Rickman told Jessica Berens in the September 1991 issue of *Tatler*. 'You know, the voices inside the head. The usual . . . this is terrible, why on earth are you doing this?' What a prophetic question; and very appropriate in these circumstances.

His hooded eyes already looked the part; he was perfect for an Asiatic role. Unfortunately, even Peter Barnes' adaptation couldn't save this ponderous theatrical metaphor for life. Why did Alan do it? Because it was produced by his old friend Thelma Holt, who has been called 'the last true impresario' of the British stage. Like Alan, she's a dedicated internationalist. But ultimately the name of Ninagawa, the Japanese Peter Brook, sold the project to Alan. There is a mystique about Ninagawa, as with Dennis Potter, whose own flawed script for *Mesmer* would later involve Alan in a major law-suit and creative stalemate for the first time in his career.

Amid much publicity about rehearsals stopping for Japanese tea ceremonies, one sensed a case of the Emperor's New Clothes.

Rickman had seen Ninagawa's *Medea* and thought: 'This is what the word "unforgettable" means.' Not everyone agreed: I remember a fellow critic muttering 'This is the campest thing since *Sunset Boulevard*' as he and I fled to file copy at the end of the show as though our trousers were on fire.

But Rickman rationalised it to himself in an interview with Peter Lewis in *The Sunday Times* in 1991: 'If you have such an experience watching someone's work and are then asked to work with him, you are not being true to yourself unless you do,' he said. Usually he's too analytical and too aware of his working-class roots to gush, but this appealed to his quixotic side.

'It wasn't an easy decision. But there's a voice somewhere inside that eventually packs the suitcase. It said, "If you are any good in films, it's only because of what you do in the theatre." Hence the sideways move in what many have seen as a quirky career. But as Albert Finney once pointed out, actors don't ascend a great golden staircase to the heavens – it doesn't work like that.

Rather more prosaically, Ninagawa had chosen Rickman for the lead after seeing him in *Die Hard* – wherein he shot a Japanese tycoon in the head. He had also caught a preview of *Truly Madly Deeply*.

Ninagawa is clearly not cocooned from reality, even if he does issue such statements as: 'The playwright is the mother, the actors are the father, and between them they bear the child called Theatre. As director, I am only the midwife.'

And the critics played King Herod. I reviewed the première at Edinburgh for the *Daily Express*: 'Only the legendary status of Yukio Ninagawa can have persuaded Hollywood's favourite British villain Alan Rickman to star in this empty domestic epic about a Japanese actor's mid-life crisis. Yet even he flounders in a cliché-ridden play laden with pretentious symbolism.'

Yet Ninagawa had directed, in Japanese, an unforgettable world-class production of *Macbeth*, with the fall of the cherry blossom symbolising the death of the tyrant and a Samurai parallel with medieval Scotland's war-like hordes.

Tango At The End Of Winter was Ninagawa's first production with a British cast of actors. He didn't speak English, so they communicated via an interpreter. Ninagawa did his own casting by making people talk about themselves at their auditions while he watched their facial expressions.

Tango was a popular hit in Japan in 1988, but the predominantly female audiences there worship actors. A play on such a subject was bound to succeed, whereas in the West we see it more as a self-referential indulgence. The action was set in the shabby auditorium of a defunct cinema, with tattered curtains fluttering at the entrance to symbolise the transience of life. Figures from the actor's past appeared and reappeared as if in a dream, summoned by memory, as he struggled with his madness. Acting styles varied wildly, given the language barrier between director and cast. Sylvia Syms' talented daughter, Beatie Edney, played Rickman's mistress, having appeared alongside Alan on Broadway in *Les Liaisons Dangereuses*. Friends believe that Beatie had a big crush on Rickman; an impression strengthened by the fact that later she dated his lookalike, a morose young actor called Ronan Vibert who is frivolously known as 'Moanin' Ronan'. He has never quite forgiven the London *Evening Standard* for calling him the poor man's Alan Rickman in the BBC bodice-ripper *The Buccaneers*. Ronan certainly has a piratical smile but not, as yet, Alan Rickman's gracefulness and subtlety.

The elliptical *Tango* was not popular with either reviewers or public at the Piccadilly Theatre, at the time a somewhat jinxed venue that had had more than its fair share of flops (it has since recovered its fortunes with a string of hits).

David Nathan in the *Jewish Chronicle* wrote: 'Sei's plight is not gripping, especially as conveyed by Alan Rickman, who . . .

declines from his usual melancholic lassitude into terminal leth-argy.'

Benedict Nightingale in *The Times* thought it lacked coherence as Rickman reeled about, 'filling the stage with his sardonic self-absorption', in the role of the actor who goes mad because he fears he has lost his talent. Could this be a dry-run for *Hamlet*?

' "This is embarrassing," announces Alan Rickman halfway through, and the guy ain't joking,' wrote Lyn Gardner in *City Limits*. Jack Tinker in the *Daily Mail* found Rickman 'languid to the point of torpor'.

Yet Michael Billington in the *Guardian* felt that 'the play is a dense tissue of allusions to *Hamlet*, *Six Characters In Search Of An Author*, *Casablanca*, *Limelight* and an old Ronald Colman movie . . . Rickman exactly captures the Hamlet-like melancholy, the doomed romanticism, the exquisite narcissism of this falling star. It . . . makes me hope someone will cast Rickman as Shakespeare's gloomy Dane forthwith.' Someone did: Thelma Holt a year later.

Although the finale featured a beautiful transformation-scene, most critics, nevertheless, felt the journey there wasn't worth the effort.

The lack of narrative drive made it a difficult vehicle for the West End, which at least demands a good story from its artier endeavours. So the production was a commercial failure, despite a strictly limited season that turned out to be something of a loss-cutting exercise. Alan's old English teacher Ted Stead feels strongly about it to this day. 'Alan was very disappointed with the reaction to *Tango At The End Of Winter*,' says Stead, who took a party of schoolboys to see Alan's performance. 'Alan found eight performances a week very trying and demanding, and the recep-tion was lukewarm. He was going to do *Peer Gynt* with the same director, but that never materialised.

'I'm convinced it flopped because Alan wasn't allowed to have star billing in the West End; it was the director who got the billing,' argues Ted, who believes that the crowds would have come if Alan's name had been prominently displayed. Certainly, Peter Barnes testifies to the enthusiasm of the Rickman fans that did make it to the stage door. But Thelma Holt explains: 'Alan specifically didn't want star billing. It was an ensemble company, therefore the billing was alphabetical.' And Alan himself had gamely told the *Sunday Times*' Peter Lewis on 4 August 1991: 'I'm trying to make myself like an empty vessel, a piece of equipment labelled actor.' This was test-tube theatre.

In Japan, Ninagawa is a god whose word is not questioned. For once, Alan didn't argue; and he was also obliged to submit to the strict regime of the Taiwanese director Ang Lee on the film *Sense And Sensibility* five years later. All very noble in the cause of good global relations, but such self-effacing modesty just didn't make commercial sense in the West End where Alan Rickman would have brought the faithful flocking to theatre's equivalent of Eric Cantona, had the billing deified the right guy. Alan's fans had to search for his name near the end of the list underneath the banner headline 'The Ninagawa Company'. In retrospect, it was pointlessly purist of him. His talent and personality elevate him.

In a curious twist ten years later, the Texas frontwoman Sharleen Spiteri was to recruit him as her dancing partner in the video for 'In Demand' and thus enhance his street-cred even more. As she explained, 'I thought it had to be someone who would rip your coat off and pull you into the tango, so I thought of Alan Rickman.' Well, quite. Who wouldn't? He does rather throw himself into these things, as Emma Thompson found out when he whirled her round the room at a *Sense And Sensibility* location party.

But the bold experiment in international theatre was not to be the last for Alan and Thelma. They had taken the hint about *Hamlet*.

9. IMMORTAL LONGINGS

The foyer of the Royal Court Theatre in London's Sloane Square is well accustomed to the odd loud-mouthed wino who comes in from the cold steps outside. No problem. Even after it reopened in February 2000 with an urban-chic redesign which included a front-of-house revamp that left the box-office looking more like the *maitre d*'s desk at a fashionable restaurant, the home of the theatrical angry brigade can still cope with noise pollution on any scale. If the evening – either on or off the stage – has been completely devoid of what Dr Feelgood used to call firkin this and firkin that, I never feel I've had my money's worth from the Court. The old 70s chocolate-and-orange decor of the main house used to scream at you, of course; and if you're a sensitive vegetarian, the gorgeous new leather seats now scream at you instead. And even after its refit, the late-Victorian building that first introduced George Bernard Shaw's loquacious jaw-jaw to British audiences still regularly rattles to the sound of the tube trains entering and leaving the underground station next door. It's not a place to go for a quiet time.

However, a public shouting-match between the actor Alan Rickman and the theatre director Jules Wright over their rival bids to run the Riverside Studios arts centre shocked even the hard cases. Three years later, everyone at the Court still remembered the row.

The acrimonious confrontation took place on 28 November 1993, the night of departing Artistic Director Max Stafford-Clark's fund-raising party for his new Out Of Joint theatre company. That well-known character, 'Arfur (Half of) London', had been invited to send Max on his way; all the more amazing, then, that the furious exchange of views between the irate Alan and Jules was never leaked to the outside world.

What Jules now describes as 'a fairly monumental row in which everyone else was extremely entertained' was the culmination of five months of tension and acrimony directed towards Jules Wright.

The so-called 'Rivergate' affair in the summer of 1993 led to a furious campaign in the Press by the supporters of Alan Rickman and the producer Thelma Holt, who headed a starry consortium to take over a dilapidated white elephant in West London's Hammersmith. It was their ambition to turn it into a new Royal National Theatre.

Among the allegations were stories about a missing – perhaps stolen – document that was leaked to the Press, plus the extraordinary sight of Alan Rickman handing a queue of bemused theatre-goers copies of a published letter of support from leading theatre critics. That kind of activism hardly goes with the languid image of a man who likes chaise-lounging around.

The previous year had begun exceptionally well for Rickman's career, but Rima's political ambitions were to be bitterly thwarted. On 26 January 1992, Alan was named Best Actor in the London *Evening Standard* Film Awards for his threefold triumph in *Robin Hood: Prince Of Thieves*, *Close My Eyes* and *Truly Madly Deeply*. For her performance in the latter, his friend Juliet Stevenson deservedly won the Best Actress trophy.

'Now I know it's possible to win an award for over-acting,' quipped Rickman, referring to that witty old slimeball, the Sheriff of Nottingham.

He was busy, busy, busy. Rickman and Ruby Wax had formed their own production company, Raw Produce, to develop ideas that would exploit their shared sense of humour. It was Alan who put a shape to the Ruby Wax phenomenon, bringing her one-woman show into London's West End for a short season in April before a provincial tour. Rickman was turning out to be quite a Svengali with his American Trilby.

At the same time, he was also quietly helping Rima with her General Election campaign. A slightly scowling Rickman could be spotted lurking modestly at the edge of a photograph of Labour candidates and their supporters in the borough of Kensington and Chelsea.

He turned out by her side on polling day, although he was spared the rigours of door-to-door canvassing. Other celebrity Labour supporters recruited by Rima included Lord Longford, Baroness Ewart-Biggs and the novelist, Ken Follett. Yet Rima is very protective of her boyfriend's privacy. 'It wouldn't have been fair on Alan to ask him to canvass for me before. He's got such a famous face,' she told the Tory-supporting *Daily Telegraph*'s Peterborough diary, whose 7 April edition mischievously published the most unflattering picture of a glowering Rickman that it could find. 'I might have produced Alan before if it was more of a marginal seat,' she conceded. 'But he may sway the odd wavering voter on polling day.'

Indeed, four years later she was to explain to the *Daily Mail*'s Nigel Dempster on 3 March 1996: 'Alan is committed to the cause and he gives me a lot of moral support, but he doesn't come face to face with voters. He just delivers leaflets and then leaves. It could be embarrassment which stops him, I don't know. I won't push him. Not everyone enjoys being questioned on policy detail.'

The constituency was split in two for the purposes of the election: Ann Holmes was the Labour candidate for Kensington, standing against Conservative holder Dudley Fishburn, and Rima Horton was up against 58-year-old Sir Nicholas Scott's massive majority in Chelsea – the safest Tory seat in the country with an average of 60 per cent of the vote.

A somewhat strenuous private life had nearly led to Sir Nicholas Scott's deselection. In 1987 he was appointed Minister for the Disabled, but was to leave the post in 1994 after tabling amendments to wreck a Bill of Rights for the handicapped. In the process, the Tory Wet publicly fell out with his Labour-supporting daughter Victoria, a campaigner for the disabled movement, Rights Now, who had exposed the governmental tactics that halted the Disablement Bill.

It seemed as if nothing would unseat the accident-prone Sir Nicholas Scott, who drove a car that crashed and killed a man in 1957. A verdict of accidental death was recorded. In 1995, he ran off when his car shunted another into a toddler's pram; Sir Nicholas was later breath-tested. He was banned from driving for a year and fined £200 with £450 costs.

Rima had become the local Labour Party spokesman on education and town planning and, by 1992, she had become a senior lecturer in economics at the Surrey Polytechnic that is now Kingston University. Although she was the youngest, Rima was the only one of the three Chelsea candidates who coyly failed to give her age – 51-year-old Susan Broidy stood for the Liberal Democrats. Rima's manifesto, published in the *Kensington News*, simply recorded that she was born in Bayswater and had lived in the borough of Kensington and Chelsea for fifteen years. That was the time when she and Alan had first moved into her current flat in Holland Park in 1977.

Her brisk manifesto didn't even mention her marital status, or, rather, the lack of it. This was surprising, given the residual prejudice from some quarters of the electorate against married women standing for office. A single woman without children had and still has a positive advantage; single men had a harder time of it until openly gay Labour candidates began winning seats and thus made marital status irrelevant. The Tories, though, still tend to prefer their candidates with wives attached.

New Labour had sent Rima on the obligatory power-dressing course for the right business-like image, urging her to put her shoulder-pads to the wheel. Lecturing had taught her all about public speaking. Surprising, then, that Peter Barnes says she tells him that she still finds speech-making difficult. She speaks in a husky contralto with a slight lisp that makes her sound not unlike the actress Frances De La Tour; the effect is decidedly sexy. Rima owes her deep, rather thrilling voice to her smoking habit: she can be a bit of a Fag-Ash Lil and has been known to puff away during speeches. In argument, she's forceful but not strident. Of course there's nothing like the line 'when I was talking to my MA students' to impress fellow Kensington & Chelsea councillors . . . those not covertly reading their horoscopes or *Private Eye* or playing with their pocket calculators at the time, as happened during one meeting in the council chamber that I attended.

Alan Rickman is frequently to be found in the public gallery, taking an active interest in Rima's latest pronouncements on pelican crossings or guardrails. Not that this chic and attractive figure with her distinctive dark-brown bob appears to need any moral support. She's incisive and highly articulate, pitching her arguments some way above certain heads in the council chamber who find themselves getting a free lecture on economics.

'She's not rent-a-quote,' said Ian Francis, at the time news editor of the then *Kensington News* when I first contacted him back in 1995. 'She's not on the phone to us straight away about some local issue. She usually waits to be approached, so she doesn't set herself up to be a great local media figure. She tends to stick to what's going on in the council chamber, so she's not a great public person.

'There's no gimmick with her. Perhaps she hasn't mastered the public aspects of local politics – or has chosen not to.'

Certainly Rima is highly sensitive to Alan's phobia about the Press in general and critics in particular. If she were elevated to a political position at a national level, it would make life very difficult for him which is why she has forced herself to be philosophical about election disappointments.

'She's very feisty and no-nonsense: she doesn't suffer fools gladly,' added Ian. Nevertheless, he criticised the Labour Opposition in Kensington & Chelsea for being 'exceptionally inactive. They're active on things like roofs leaking on local estates. But the council tax has just gone up, and there was no outcry whatsoever from the Opposition.'

Certainly it's difficult to avoid the conclusion that the political scene is just a little too cosy in this Royal borough with its cast-iron Conservative majority. With Labour in a minority group there's a limit to what the Opposition can do with its numbers. Certainly Rima, whose politics are Centre Left and whose understated glamour is very much New Labour, is not about to woman the barricades.

'It's a very boring political scene in Kensington & Chelsea,' was Ian Francis' verdict on the Nicholas Scott years. 'Scott will give you a quote, but he won't be proactive.

'Rima strikes me as a bit of a do-gooder. The ambitious ones are on the phone to us all the time; those who are more sanctimonious just get on with their work.'

She's certainly popular with colleagues from both sides of the political fence. She can be glamorous and she has a certain style. She wears chic, expensive-looking clothes, and, unlike many of the other councillors, her official photograph looks as if it was done in a studio

Indeed, the serious-minded Rima is almost a Sharon Stone in comparison with one (male) councillor, whose rugged features have been unkindly likened to a 'Wanted' poster of an escaped convict and who is affectionately known as Magwitch behind his back.

She has a big voice and a glint in her eye, but it has been suggested that she's not a natural politician who maintains eye contact. This might come from being an academic, but she tends to fix on a point on the wall instead and her language can sometimes be a little high-flown.

Most Labour councillors are not exactly gad-about-town figures, but a sophisticated woman of the world like Rima adds a little local colour: she's a great fan of restaurants off the Portobello Road. Even

Tories like her: when I contacted him in 1995, the late Conservative councillor Desmond Harney swooned with old-fashioned gallantry at the mere mention of her name.

Nevertheless, her time had not yet come in 1992: the *Kensington News*' pre-election coverage was forced to conclude that Sir Nicholas Scott remained the firm favourite in the opinion polls for the General Election.

Ruby's show, *Wax Acts*, opened on April Fool's Day, 1992. The Election was held on 9 April, but Kensington and Chelsea, unlike most other constituencies, didn't start counting until 9 a.m. on 10 April. It would be another 24 hours before the results of Rima's bid to become an MP were known.

The public and most of the critics liked Ruby a lot. She had been directed by Alan only once before at the Edinburgh Festival in 1986, but the formula clearly worked for the grander stage of the West End.

Since Rickman and Wax had worked together at Sheffield Crucible in Peter James' production of *As You Like It*, they rehearsed her one-woman show on the Lyric Hammersmith stage where Peter was by then the Artistic Director.

'Alan Rickman was the creator of Ruby Wax,' confirms Peter. 'He suggested a format for her on TV. There was always something unlearned and spontaneous about her thing. Scripted stand-up was not as good for her as the spontaneous stuff.

'Even Ruby doesn't know what she will do when she steps on stage. She starts with a clip-board and nothing else. Her career was greatly shaped by him. Yet there's nothing of the extrovert in Alan. In performance terms, she goes to get 'em while he waits for them to come.'

Alan himself told Valerie Grove in the April 1995 issue of *Harpers & Queen*: 'People assume she just stands at the mike and delivers routines. But she is the most deeply serious person about her work, tussling with very personal material about herself and her parents. It was achingly funny, but you can't be alone on stage for two hours without a sense of structure and lots of bloody hard work.'

Perhaps he allowed her a little too much leeway, according to Anthony Thorneycroft in the *Financial Times*: 'Her show is discreetly directed by Alan Rickman, who might try to sharpen up the first twenty minutes.'

Charles Spencer of the *Daily Telegraph*, however, emerged as a convert: 'I'd only seen her fleetingly on television and approached her one-woman show as an agnostic. After two hours in her company, however, I'm convinced that Ruby Wax is one of the finest comic talents of her generation . . . Constructing wonderful crescendos of fury and indignation . . . She has a splendid way with words, and her sheer vitality breaks down all resistance.'

'Though a virtuous woman may be priced above rubies,' quipped *Evening Standard* reviewer Michael Arditti, 'an outrageous Ruby produces a jewel of a show.'

She did have her detractors. 'I ended the evening pummelled rather than entertained,' moaned Tony Patrick of *The Times*. And Jack Tinker of the *Daily Mail* was coolish, wondering if Ruby's well-developed self-esteem needed any support from him. 'Why do I not fall down and adore her like the rest of her fans?' he asked rhetorically. They were very much in a minority.

Lucky Ruby, unlucky Rima. Nicholas Scott was returned with an overwhelming majority of more than 13,000.

The *Kensington News* reported that Labour candidate Rima Horton, accompanied by her actor friend Alan Rickman, was defiant. She proclaimed that Labour would fight 'again and again' to change the future, echoing a famous speech by Hugh Gaitskell. Labour blamed a hostile Press and 'lies' over its tax plans, and ten days later Rima was still fighting, urging a policy of non-cooperation with the hated Red Routes parking restrictions on main roads.

Rima subsequently made it onto a women-only Labour shortlist for the new seat of Regent's Park and Kensington North, but she lost out to Karen Buck, described rather graphically by the *Kensington News*' chief reporter Jonathan Donald as 'a mighty political machine who fires off press releases'.

In early 1996, Robert Atkinson – Rima's fellow councillor from St Charles Ward – was selected as the Labour Party's prospective parliamentary candidate for the newly named Kensington & Chelsea seat from a shortlist of men and women that did not include Rima.

Rima simply didn't relish facing certain defeat for a second time in a General Election. Sir Nicholas Scott had been reselected for the Tories, only to be followed by the equally controversial Alan Clark on January 25, 1997. Kensington & Chelsea remains staunchly Tory, even after Labour's landslide victory in the 1997

General Election that prompted Alan to growl 'About bloody time too.' Yet Rima won something of a consolation prize in 1995 when she became one of several councillors to write a monthly column on local issues for the *Kensington News* for a few years. 'It's typical of her that she didn't approach us to write it,' said Ian Francis. 'We approached her.'

Alan was profoundly depressed by Labour's 1992 election defeat in general and Rima's in particular, moaning about how unbearable it was, but he was too much in demand to mope around in this country as his Hollywood film career continued apace. *Bob Roberts*, which marked Tim Robbins' directorial début, was a political satire on the rise of a right-wing politician with the unearthly, sanctimonious aura of a religious evangelist (as, indeed, so many right-wing American politicians are).

Robbins played the title role of this smooth paragon and Rickman was his sinister campaign manager, wearing pornographer's brown-tinted glasses that would make even Snow White seem seedy. The movie was a very effective satire on the Svengali-like spin doctors, the sound-bites, the campaign-bus briefings and all the paraphernalia of a modern politician on the move. So true-to-life were these acute observations that *Bob Roberts* seemed more like a documentary than a drama, with the inevitable distancing effect. Never was the audience drawn into Bob Roberts' heart or mind (we assume he had no soul); as for Rickman's character, he was a clever amalgam of all the shifty fixers in the world. So much so that you could swear you'd seen him somewhere before.

Barry Norman's *Film 92* reported on the making of *Bob Roberts*. Its screenwriter Gore Vidal was interviewed, claiming rather shakily, 'It's a bit like *Dr Strangelove*.'

Alan himself said defiantly: 'I hope it will resonate loudly as the scramble for power goes on.' When asked, rather superfluously, if people would say it was a film put together by a bunch of left-wing liberals, he replied with a slight snort of laughter, 'They would be right. That's the kind of mud that will be slung, of course it is.' Robbins and his partner Susan Sarandon, with whom Rickman had become buddies while working on *The January Man*, have long been the most politically active liberal couple in Hollywood. Given Alan's own political leanings, it was only a matter of time before he worked with Robbins as well.

The same mud was slung on what one journalist called the Brown Rice Tour, when Alan joined up with Thelma Holt and the Russian director Robert Sturua to play *Hamlet* at the Riverside Studios in the autumn of 1992 before taking it around the country.

'I'm too old, but what the hell,' shrugged a 46-year-old Alan disarmingly, trying to forestall the critics. He was hardly the oldest Hamlet in history, of course. But Alan still hadn't told the Press his exact age; he let them guess (wrongly). Couples who do not have any children can play Peter Pan indefinitely; there's no hulking teenaged offspring hanging around to betray the years.

Rarely does a Hamlet amount to the sum of his parts, of course; it's such a massive challenge to make the character credible on stage, as opposed to page. Thelma told Valerie Grove in the July 1995 issue of *Harpers & Queen*: 'Darling, I've seen more *Hamlet*s than I've had hot dinners; I spent eighteen months of my life playing Gertrude. I know that play better than any other, and with no disrespect to any of my other Hamlets, Alan Rickman was the Hamlet of my life. He did something rare: he told a story, and it was as if it was a new play.

'People always wonder what will he do with "To be" and "Rogue and peasant slave"; yet I could not have predicted how he would say them. Everything was new.' Well, the producer would say that, wouldn't she?

In the event, she was right. I felt he brought his own unique and angry world-weariness to the role, with the controversial voice the ideal vehicle for delivering that message. His Hamlet looked like the eternal middle-aged student, still studying the meaninglessness of life after all these years. There was a sense of self-disgust that gave the production real tension.

'Inevitably he stresses the dangerous appeal of amorality in Shakespeare's great revenge tragedy. This is a sarcastically amusing Hamlet who can smile and smile and be a villain, taking a lesson from his wicked stepfather Claudius,' I wrote in the *Daily Express* on 16 September.

'There is a harsh erotic energy in his encounters with Julia Ford's sexually repressed Ophelia, who is horizontal within minutes of meeting him. And yet he plays Hamlet as a world-weary, existentialist bookworm, too dangerously fond of Geraldine McEwan's Gertrude and forced to be a hero against his will. It is a fastidiously intelligent reading of the role that confirms Rickman as a leading talent with the power to pull in the crowds.'

I hated the slow production, however, which seemed to have been dressed by an Oxfam shop and made the court of Elsinore look like a refugee centre.

The reviews were decidedly mixed: his performance divided the critics. Alan maintained his usual scornful mien, but was deeply miffed by some of the comments.

'O! What a noble play is here o'erthrown!' declared Clive Hirshhorn in the Sunday Express, calling Rickman's 'not-so-great Dane . . . a posturing, sulky, overgrown schoolboy.'

Clive even picked up on Rickman's speech defect, which can usually be turned to Alan's advantage: 'He swallows some of Shakespeare's most exquisite poetry as though he was ashamed of it. If it is humourless brooding introspection and a total denial of the voice beautiful you want, Rickman delivers in spades.'

If you are forced to conclude that Clive and I saw different shows . . . well, we did. I attended the final preview and he the first night. Perhaps Rickman's stage fright was manifesting itself again. Charles Spencer in the Daily Telegraph wrote of Rickman's 'bad attack of the clinical depression . . . this is a Hamlet who seems to have just returned from Elsinore's psychiatric day centre . . . There is hardly a trace of Hamlet's wit and vitality . . . you feel like giving him a good shake. This is a modishly perverse Hamlet that almost entirely fails to touch the heart.'

Michael Coveney in the Observer, however, found his 'sly and secretive mature student' thrilling in his 'rampant morbidity . . . This sense of standing apart from himself is a quality unique to Rickman's acting.'

On the other hand, Michael Arditti in the Evening Standard thought 'he totally lacks passion' and also talked of Rickman 'swallowing the words . . . he lacks the nobility and pathos of a romantic Hamlet; but he fails to recreate him in his own image'.

Even Michael Billington in the Guardian found himself regretting having urged someone to cast Alan as Hamlet. He hated the way that Elsinore had become a metaphor for the political prisons of the Georgian Sturua's native land, because it imprisoned Rickman within too confining a concept for this most universal of plays. Billington liked Rickman's 'voice, presence and air of ironic melancholy . . . what I miss is any internal tension'.

Likewise, Jack Tinker in the *Daily Mail* was impressed by Rickman but not the rest of the production. 'He seeks refuge in the laconic insolence of a superior intellect . . . the verse superbly spoken with the most extraordinary ability to spring surprises from the most familiar passages . . . However . . . here we must lament a Prince with hardly a hint of Denmark.'

'Rickman's Hamlet is not really Shakespearian. He is too utterly pole-axed by grief,' wrote John Peter in the *Sunday Times*. 'He haunts the stage like the undead . . . Elsinore does not feel like a court, but more like a derelict, urban underpass.' He clearly feels that Rickman's Hamlet is too much of a victim, as opposed to a tragic hero with choices to make and the power to make them. The fashionable phrase would be a disempowered Hamlet, and the Hungarian-born Peter saw his own East European background in the political metaphor about an oppressive state.

Rickman, generous to a fault, will not upstage anyone within an ensemble piece. There seemed an almost inverted snobbery at work here; Hamlet is supposed to be the star of the damn thing, after all. I found Rickman's introspective gloom mesmerising, but there were clearly others who wanted more fireworks . . . or perhaps the Sheriff of Nottingham. Indeed, one critic cruelly remarked that Alan was a natural Claudius.

Still, Rickman should care: the production was critic-proof, selling out for the entire run. Everyone from Rickman to the wardrobe assistant was paid a flat rate of £200 a week as they toured to unusual venues in Bradford, Nottingham, Liverpool and Barrow-in-Furness. It was the old idea of bringing theatre to the people in an unpatronising way.

Barrow's 'stage' was a giant haulage warehouse normally used for storing piles of loo-paper, opposite slag heaps that were known as the Alps of Barrow.

Just as with Ralph Fiennes' glamorous Hamlet at the Hackney Empire in February 1995, the AA signs were out to show theatre-goers the way – such was the attraction of Alan Rickman's name on the billboards.

He evinced a certain pride in taking a low wage with the rest of them. 'Little? Compared to whom?' he haughtily asked Catherine O'Brien in the *Daily Mirror*, challenging her assumptions. 'Compared to Bruce Willis, yes. But compared to people in Barrow who have no job, it's not a pittance. It is pointless comparing it with what I could earn in a film. It is also tasteless. Most actors are subsidising British theatre most of the time. Unless you are working in the West End, the money just isn't there.

'But there is a lot of fun, and that is what counts. I am always wary of actors talking about how difficult their job is. It is mostly a great deal of fun.'

He was thinking of his own father at that point and his mother, who had slaved away in the Post Office to bring up four children on her own. Although he can sometimes sound pompous, at least Rickman avoids luvvie-like preciousness. It helps to have a working-class background. Later, after the director Jude Kelly gushed that he was the best Hamlet she had ever seen, he was to admit that he was 'just relieved to get from one end of the play to another. It is ludicrous in having four soliloquies coming one after another.'

He was talking to the Press in Barrow in order to put the place on the map: with the end of Trident nuclear submarines in sight, thousands of jobs would go with very little local industry to replace them.

Rickman, a past contributor to CND, added: 'I can't say anything but good riddance to Trident. What there must be is fresh investment to stop the community from dying. My political views are pretty well known. We are living in a rotting society, just like Hamlet was 400 years ago.

'Anyone who attempts to play Hamlet has to be a lunatic. I'm too old for it, I've found it completely impossible and it has driven me barmy.' What kept him going was the thought that people who had never seen Shakespeare before might become converts; certainly there were long queues for autographs at every venue. 'That's what it's all about. And it is why I will be back.' In the end Rickman et al emerged smelling of roses from the Andrex factory, with people marvelling as they left that such 'great actors' could come to windy Barrow. 'The cultural epicentre of the Furness peninsula', as Sue Crewe affectionately called its transformation in a *Times* piece on 14 November.

Rickman explained to Michael Owen in the London *Evening Standard* on 22 October 1993: 'By the time we finished, that show had grown into a very different animal and we became an immensely close company. There were problems. We were working with a director who was used to four or five months of rehearsals and we had five weeks.'

Alan found himself having to crack the whip a bit: 'At the end of the first week, we were still on Act 1 Scene 1. That's when I had to say we have to go a bit faster or we'll never finish.'

They took theatre to the people, but it was obvious by now that the people would always take themselves to see Rickman. Thanks to his film profile, he had become a major box-office draw, so much so that in 1993 he was asked to supply the voice-over that introduces all the individual instruments on Mike Oldfield's *Tubular Bells II*. Which was why, when Thelma Holt began thinking of Riverside Studios as a permanent home for her international theatre shows, Alan was an obvious ally in her bid to run it.

West London's Riverside Studios arts centre in Crisp Road, Hammersmith, had just removed its Artistic Director and was advertising in June 1993 for a replacement. The deficit stood at £250,000 and its future was uncertain. This large but tatty white studio space, with its brown-rice food bar, had played host to all kinds of acts from rock bands to theatre groups. It was full of potential . . . as everyone kept saying. Once the dead hippies were scraped off the floor, of course.

Thelma, the ageless godmother of British theatre, saw it as the Roundhouse revisited. Kenneth Branagh had launched his Renaissance Theatre Company at Riverside with his masterly Victorian production of *Twelfth Night*, in which Richard Briers' latent neurosis produced the best, most painfully funny/sad Malvolio seen in years. There was a creative buzz about Riverside once again.

If one felt facetious, one could emblazon 'Ich bin ein West Londoner' upon the Rickman coat of arms. Alan has always felt umbilically tied to the area, despite his peripatetic lifestyle as a movie actor. Thelma lives a few streets away from him in Westbourne Grove, with her loyal right-hand woman Sweetpea nearby. Thelma, whose international productions are backed by some of the biggest names in British theatre, is a vocation and a noble cause for many people. Even the massive black winter cloak she winds round her was a gift from a top Japanese designer. The scene would be a lot less colourful without this influential figure. Small, sandy-haired and forthright, she knows everyone and has a fund of outrageous stories. There was the time when a well-known lesbian tried to seduce her . . . Nothing shocks Thelma.

She and Alan are like-minded free spirits in socialism, as it were. Thelma Mary Bernadette Holt CBE trained at RADA as an actress before founding the Open Space Theatre with Charles Marowitz and playing Shakespearian heroines in the nude. (This was particularly heroic, given the dodgy heating situation.) From 1977 to 1983 she became the Artistic Director of the Roundhouse in North London's Chalk Farm, inheriting that fork-tongued old fraud, Robert Maxwell, as the treasurer.

The circular nineteenth-century engine shed had been converted into a theatre in 1968, becoming associated with such experimental names as the director Peter Brook. Kenneth Tynan's nude revue *Oh! Calcutta!* was staged there. By the late 70s, the unconventional space made a wonderfully atmospheric rock venue, the equivalent of Amsterdam's Milky Way. The Doors made their only British appearance there, with my friend Bob hitching all the way from Wigan to see Jim Morrison before The Lizard King died of an overdose in a Paris bath.

Under Thelma, the Roundhouse really got its theatrical act together for a few brief shining years with such legendary performances as Vanessa Redgrave's *Lady From The Sea* and Helen Mirren's *Duchess Of Malfi*. Reconstructed in 1979, the Roundhouse was forced to call in the receivers four years later. Yet, somehow it staggers on with a mythic reputation and a wonderfully cavernous space that began playing host to the RSC from 2002, when the latter gave up its London home at the Barbican in what many saw as an act of artistic hara-kiri.

Thelma went on to the National Theatre and then became an independent producer. Decorated for her ambassadorial services to theatre, she became a canny chair of the Arts Council's drama panel for several years before resigning on an important point of principle. But there's nothing like your own theatre to immortalise yourself. Like Shakespeare's Cleopatra, Alan and Thelma had immortal longings . . . And the idea of running Riverside vastly appealed to someone as fiendishly organised as he was, even though he intended to be only a creative – as opposed to administrative – force.

He insisted to Michael Owen in the London *Evening Standard* that he had never been the languid dilettante of legend. 'I've always got stuck in. It begins the first time you set foot on a stage and have to start making choices. A lot of other actors are out there doing the same.'

Yet he added revealingly: 'I never saw myself running the place, spending 52 weeks a year there. I thought of it more as a

Steppenwolf operation, like the theatre in Chicago where people come and go.' Which sounded suspiciously like wash-'n'-go theatre. But they were on their way.

10. THAT SINKING FEELING

Jules Wright has a fistful of arty platinum knuckleduster rings and looks you straight in the eye. An Australian boiler-maker's daughter, she was, like Rickman, a late starter in the theatre. They have humour, directness and a working-class background in common. But she freely admits: 'I did have a fiery relationship with Alan when I worked with him.'

It was to get even fierier with the Riverside fiasco. Jules remains convinced that all along Alan Rickman never really intended to get closely involved with running Riverside: his was the name on the marquee, and he caught all the flak. 'The publicity has plagued him ever since,' says Jules, who welcomed the chance to put her side of the Riverside story on record once and for all. Legal constraints prevented her from stating the facts at the time; when I approached her in 1995 for the first edition of this book, it was the first time she had been persuaded to speak.

Her conviction about Alan's true intentions stems from an incautious outburst he made during their 'blazing row' in the Royal Court foyer on 28 November 1993.

'Alan has always been an honourable man, so he would never say something he didn't mean – even in anger,' Jules told me. 'I swear to this day,' she continues with a husky laugh, 'that someone set us up to sit next to each other in the Dress Circle in a packed theatre at Max Stafford-Clark's farewell at the Court.' (This the Court flatly denies, saying that the box office would have processed hundreds of names for a very packed seating plan. But Jules said, 'Thanks a bunch', so Max Stafford-Clark sent her a postcard that thanked her for her support over the years and then added wryly, 'Sorry about the seating arrangements'.)

'I was sitting in my place and Alan came into the Dress Circle. He saw that he would be next to me, so he turned round and walked out. Then he must have had second thoughts, because he turned round and came back in again. I quickly swapped seats with my husband, who sat between us in the end.

'I suppose Alan was expecting us to have a row after Riverside, because I felt incredibly attacked by all the bad publicity. We then had a very, very loud argument later in the foyer afterwards; all the onlookers were extremely entertained. It was a fairly monumental row which ended up as a rather long conversation, as these things tend to do when you both calm down.

'We had spent an hour or so avoiding each other, and then I went up to him and said, "What the hell were you playing at with all the Press coverage? Why the hell didn't you ring me up to get the facts?" I think Rima said something angry at that point and then Alan snapped, "I didn't speak to the Press." I really felt like replying, "But you were spotted handing out photocopies of the critics" letter of support.'

'He also said, "It's about time directors had problems. Actors are always getting stick." But what was curious in the middle of all this was a remark he made when he said: "I'll never lend my name to anything again."

'I can only take his word for it: that he was only lending his name to the project,' concluded Jules.

A close examination of the Rickman camp's proposals for the New Riverside Studios shows just what kind of role Alan envisaged for himself: giving tone to the place as a visiting star with creative input. Thelma would have been the real powerhouse.

'Riverside should not be a platform for an individual ego,' stated the first page of the New Riverside policy document, drafted by the triumvirate of Alan, Thelma and Alan's old RADA contemporary Catherine Bailey. 'Rather, it should seek to embrace the community it stands in whilst sending out beacons to London, Europe and beyond.

'For a long time now Riverside has held a significant place in the loyalties of a very particular group of actors, directors and designers who cannot always exercise their ideas within the national companies,' it commented ... perhaps carrying what might be taken as a faint whiff of paranoia.

Thelma and Alan are mavericks – always have been, always will be. Widely respected for their innovations, but far too individualistic to fit into a big organisation. This was their bid for a rival to the Royal National Theatre on whose stages, incidentally, Rickman had never performed in a National production (his original debut there in Peter Barnes's reworking of *The Devil Is An Ass* had been a transfer).

(Not that there was a sinister reason behind that curious omission. 'I've often considered Alan for roles here, but for a variety of reasons we've never managed to find the right part at the right time. I think he is a wonderfully original actor,' was the view of the National's then Artistic Director Richard Eyre when I contacted him for a comment in 1995. It was to be Trevor Nunn, under whose RSC stewardship Rickman had made his great breakthrough in *Les Liaisons Dangereuses*, who would give him that opportunity in 1998, an opportunity that turned out to be something of a poisoned chalice.)

Their ideas for a genuine mingling of different art forms under one roof make a nonsense of William Hunter's pompous letter in the London *Evening Standard* on 10 August 1993. Hunter, Chair of the Riverside Trust, wrote: 'Most importantly, Riverside Studios is an arts centre, not a theatre. We present a very wide range of art forms. This has been overlooked during the controversy over the [Rickman] consortium's proposal.'

To imply that Rickman and Co. were a narrow-minded bunch of luvvies with only theatre in mind is highly misleading. Their policy document makes it clear that they wanted to create a market place for all kinds of artistic ideas at Riverside ... 'an all-day space, a magnetic place where you can look at a painting or buy and read a book over lunch, have a drink before an evening performance and then supper afterwards'. In other words, a West London alternative to the South Bank arts complex and the Royal National Theatre in particular.

It was always planned as a Steppenwolf operation. 'Actors there have an itinerant but umbilical connection to the company ... We want to actively encourage its use by those performers who do not fit into the mainstream of artistic endeavours.' In other words, a home for talented outsiders.

All very laudable but fatally vague to the dozen trustees on the Board of the Riverside Trust, which included three councillors. The first thing that strikes you on reading the Rickman consortium's New Riverside proposals is that there's no mention whatsoever of their source of finance: i.e. a list of sponsors and their donations. Money makes the bid go around, the bid go around ... It was a glaring omission.

Jules Wright's bid for the Women's Playhouse Trust (WPT) also carried its fair share of stirring rhetoric, but she provided the names of 21 WPT benefactors in her statement such as Coca-Cola, NatWest Bank and Reuters.

Hard-pressed borough councillors are constantly trying to balance the books and figures inevitably speak more loudly than words. The rest is just promises. Or, as Hammersmith & Fulham Council Leader, Iain Coleman, succinctly put it in a letter to me about the Riverside affair: 'a wish-list'.

In times of belt-tightening and general restraint, the average councillor also tends to cut back on syllables as well as money. An encounter with 'palliatives' on page two of the Rickman document might have wasted valuable debating time as they thumbed through the dictionary to see if it had any relevance to more meaningful concepts, such as money, sponsorship and start-up capital. Not that councillors are stupid; but they have to be immensely practical. As for bandying about such expressions as 'community', councillors use the term themselves with so much gay abandon that they're hardly likely to be impressed by the C-word from other people.

And as for the notion of an all-day space, just what does a drop-in centre of artistic excellence do when Johnny Fortycoats or Wandering Mary with her push-pram lurch onto the premises? The streets around Riverside in Crisp Road form a very mixed, partly industrial area, pitted with urban poverty. Most councils would see such a venue as the ideal place for an old folks' day centre or a youth club with table-tennis to prise the disaffected Yoof of Hammersmith off the streets. Those are the tram-lines along which they tend to think.

Catherine Bailey was designated Executive Director of New Riverside, co-ordinating artistic policy and the smooth running of the studios. The artistic policy itself would be 'led' by Alan Rickman (i.e. presumably starring in it), and Thelma Holt was to be the director of it. The proposal promised that these three people would be the key to its success.

Again and again the document invoked the National Theatre plus the RSC's Barbican Theatre, pointing out that Riverside was not far off their scale.

A panel of Associate Artists, of which Rickman was one, would be consulted about programming. The heavyweight names proposed included director Deborah Warner, designers Hildegard Bechtler and Bob Crowley, playwright Christopher Hampton, the actors Fiona Shaw, Mark Rylance, Juliet Stevenson and Richard Wilson, BBC1 Controller Alan Yentob and Dance Umbrella Artistic Director Val Bourne.

Thelma and Catherine's business expertise was obvious in the staffing proposals, which carefully costed everyone down to the part-time cleaners (£10,000 per annum). Ideas for opening the smaller of the two studio spaces to television companies were mooted, with a possible BBC link.

Projects in the pipeline were productions of *Twelfth Night*, directed by Deborah Warner; *The Way Of The World* with Fiona Shaw and Geraldine McEwan, directed by Alan Rickman; Sharman Macdonald's new play *The Winter Guest*; and Deborah Warner's production of *Miss Julie*, with the French film star Isabelle Huppert in the title role alongside Rickman.

Geraldine McEwan did eventually star in a revival of *The Way Of The World*, but at the National Theatre instead in the winter of 1995 (she won Best Actress at the London *Evening Standard* Drama Awards for it). *The Winter Guest* was directed by Rickman to great acclaim at the West Yorkshire Playhouse and London's Almeida Theatre early in 1995. As for Isabelle Huppert, she did indeed come over to London in the spring of 1996 to star in *Mary Stuart* at the National Theatre.

Alongside the glamour projects in the New Riverside manifesto were also laudable ideas for community education and youth theatre, unemployment and summer projects. The potential weekly box-office income and annual budget for both studio theatres were carefully costed. The architect, Sir Richard Rogers, already responsible for the Thames Reach complex next door to Riverside in the Crabtree Estate area of Hammersmith, was approached to redesign the interior; and there were even plans to reopen the bookshop and create a recording studio. But all these good intentions mean nothing without the guarantee of start-up cash.

Confucius say: lack of S-word (sponsorship) lead to F-word. Or some such ancient Chinese proverb.

Grants were envisaged by Rickman's consortium as the core funding for running the building, with starry productions plus the hiring-out of space as the income-generators that would subsidise other activities. All this was placing an immense responsibility on the shoulders of a floating population of stars to pull in the crowds; even Corin and Vanessa Redgrave's Moving Theatre could not work a box-office miracle in a 1995 season at Riverside.

Catherine Bailey's draft concluded on an inspirational note, proposing an arts complex the like of which had never been seen before in this country. There was a clear promise that they would put Riverside once and for all upon the international map.

'At first I thought it was a lunatic plan to get involved in bricks and mortar in these economic times, but when you see the abilities of the group behind it, you know it would work. With the pulling power of the actors in the company, the place would be packed. With names like the ones we have, the money will follow,' enthused Thelma to Michael Owen in the *Evening Standard* on 20 July 1993 well timed to influence the Board.

So what went wrong? The capital's listings magazine, *Time Out*, was the first to break the news that the high-profile Rickman bid had been rejected.

According to *Time Out*, Jules Wright of WPT looked the likely new Artistic Director despite a track record which, according to *TO*, did not begin to compare with Alan and Thelma's starry panel.

The *Evening Standard* picked the story up and made much of the fact that Jules had been on the Board of the Riverside Trust until shortly before her appointment. It even alleged that she had drawn up a job description for the new Artistic Directorship.

Even more ominously, the intermediary to whom Rickman and Co. had submitted their proposal was deemed by *Time Out* and the *Standard* to have delayed handing in their bid until too late for the crucial Riverside Board meeting on 15 July. So why use a go-between? Because a team rather than an individual was applying for the job of Artistic Director, they felt their unorthodox approach needed explanation.

Smoke began to issue from various heads. They smelled conspiracy, or at least incompetence. Six leading theatre critics – the *Guardian*'s Michael Billington, the *Evening Standard*'s Nicholas de Jongh, *The Times*' Benedict Nightingale, the *Daily Telegraph*'s Charles Spencer, the *Independent*'s Paul Taylor and *Time Out*'s James Christopher – felt sufficiently strongly to write a letter of protest to the *Evening Standard* about the conduct of the Riverside Board in selecting Jules Wright as its director-designate.

This thunderous missive, published on 6 August 1993, blamed then councillor and Riverside Board member Jane Hackworth-Young for failing to pass on the Rickman submission to the selection panel until after shortlisted applicants had been interviewed.

'The board's choice as the next director of Riverside was herself on the board of directors until just before the deadline for applications,' they fulminated. 'Miss Wright, Riverside Studios has admitted, helped draw up the job description for the new director. We believe it may be a conflict of interest . . .' They urged the Riverside Board to revoke its decision.

William Hunter, chair of the Riverside Trust, wrote a languid reply to the *Standard* on 10 August: 'It was the Alan Rickman et al consortium's own fault that the application arrived so late – not only after the closing date but after the interviewing panel had completed interviews. The commonsense thing to do would have been to send the proposal straight to Riverside, not use an intermediary. This is what everybody else did.'

Further foot-stamping was to come: 'The reason we did not interview the consortium was that its application was unconvincing administratively, artistically and financially.' Very damaging, if you take William Hunter's artistic credentials seriously (he's a barrister).

Hunter has since refused to talk further about the entire episode, saying pompously: 'It's ancient history.' But Rickman and Co. took their rejection as a Philistine slap in the face for some of London's best-known actors.

Indeed, Nicholas de Jongh wrote in the *Standard* on 12 August: 'Perhaps one should conclude that the Riverside Board has a phobia about stars.'

Catherine Bailey later became convinced that it was a simple case of the turkeys not voting for Christmas. 'The Board interfered all the time: had we got in, the first thing we would have done was to dismiss the Board. It's weak. They knew that, that's why they refused us. The Board is full of councillors wanting to hang on to their honorary positions.

'The idea was to generate our own income from high-profile productions, plus companies and well-known directors from abroad such as Peter Brook and Peter Stein. They were too small-minded to see our vision. Thelma is the only true impresario of our time, a new Lilian Baylis. Thelma and Alan are both such larger-than-life characters. Alan has put a lot back into the business, and people really rate him.'

But such a mythology has grown around 'Rivergate' that someone from outside the Rickman camp even gave me the initial impression that Jane Hackworth-Young was a Tory councillor, as if the scuppering of Rickman's bid was a wicked Conservative plot. Nothing could be further from the truth.

Enter the first Rivergate scapegoat: a neat figure with cropped grey hair and a rather pukka accent. She apologised for that plus the double-barrelled name; people were always leaping to the wrong conclusions about Jane, the Labour councillor for Addison Ward in the borough of Hammersmith and Fulham. She also had a useful background in theatre: 'I worked with Donald Albery, then I was the director of the British Theatre Association for ten years. And I was on the Board of Riverside at the time the bids were invited.

'It happened like this. Jacqueline Abbott, our Mayor, was the original contact for Catherine Bailey. They couldn't get hold of her, so they contacted me instead. I had met Alan originally at the BTA; I liked him enormously. He has a nice sense of humour.'

So far as her left-wing credentials are concerned, she was an impeccably correct contact for the Rickman consortium. A member of Hammersmith and Fulham Miners' Support Group, she had joined protest marches by the Women Against Pit Closures. Jane's family comes from Sedgefield, a former mining community. 'I'm left of centre. I'm not a Blairite.' Until she talked exclusively to me for this book, she had stayed silent on Rivergate, taking the rap at the time because there was grave doubt about whether the council could continue to cough up cash for both Riverside and the Lyric Theatre in Hammersmith.

For this small London borough is unique in having three high-profile theatre venues – the third being the small but innovative Bush Theatre – within a square mile of each other. Keeping them all afloat is a nightmare for any council.

But it seemed there were grounds for paranoia over the decision on who ran Riverside. The reason why Alan Rickman's consortium chose, unlike any of the other bidders, to use a go-between was because, according to Jane Hackworth-Young, they were absolutely convinced that Jules Wright was the favourite for the job of Artistic Director. So they felt they needed, to put it bluntly, some special pleading on their behalf in order to get a fair hearing.

'They thought their bid might not be taken seriously for several reasons,' claims Jane. 'The proposal from a consortium would not answer Riverside's specific job specification. Jules Wright was on the Board, and they believed that the Chair William Hunter supported her very much. Indeed, I had that impression too, and perhaps at the cost of other bids – although I had no objection to

Jules. And Riverside had a deficit of £250,000, a debt they didn't want to take on. So they felt they needed an intermediary to smooth the way and put their case.'

Jane met Alan and Catherine over lunch in a French restaurant in Kensington Park Road on 10 June 1993.

'They showed me their draft. They said they would tidy it up a bit; I made a few suggestions, such as extra figures here and there. It was not absolutely clear at that time that Thelma Holt was committed to the project.

'Time was already very short, because I understood that the shortlist was to be drawn up on 15 July. I said I would take their bid to Iain Coleman, the Leader of the Council, to canvass him on the monetary situation and also because he was quite close to the Chair of the Riverside Trust, William Hunter. That was how it was left.'

What Alan and Co. did not understand were the manifold pressures on councillors with so many causes clamouring for cash. Given that Alan's partner Rima had been a councillor in the neighbouring Kensington & Chelsea for seven years by then, one would have thought she might have advised them. But anyone with any integrity – and Rima prides herself on that – would take care not to get involved with an issue in which there was a personal interest. So she stayed well clear.

'I didn't get the bid document from the Rickman group until 22 June, because I had been away for a long weekend,' says Jane. 'I arranged to see Iain Coleman on 24 June. The main gist of that meeting was on another subject, but I left him the Rickman submission.

'We set up another meeting to discuss the matter on 5 July. To be fair to Iain Coleman, we didn't talk at length about the Rickman bid. I asked him to look at it and hoped that if he considered it worthwhile, he would speak to William Hunter.

'One of my main reasons for seeing him was to sort out whether we were going to be able to fund all three venues for the same year. Both the Lyric and Riverside had a deficit, and we are the smallest London borough after the City.

'I was really deeply concerned that we weren't going to be able to fund both of them. There were rumours every day about what was going to happen. I used my contacts in the theatre to see if there were other options to fund the two of them. The selection process was going on for the next elections; I had to go up north; and I was also writing a paper on the future of the libraries, because I was anxious that we were going to have to cut them.

'I wrote to Derek Spurr, Director of Hammersmith's Leisure and Recreation, on 28 June. I was still scared that the Lyric would have to go. Catherine and Alan thought I was working against them because I was talking to other organisations, but I was trying to explore all the options for both the Riverside and the Lyric.

'At very short notice, Iain cancelled our meeting on 5 July. He's a very busy man. I spoke to his PA because I said all the submissions have to be in and I had to see him.

'The earliest we could set a meeting was for Tuesday 13 July at 6 o'clock. I thought to myself, do I approach Hunter directly? I had previously indicated to him that there might be another bid. I was in a quandary. Then during that week I heard there had been a meeting of the leadership of the Council – and it had been decided not to fund either of the two theatres. I felt I must clarify the situation once and for all with Coleman.

'In the interim Catherine Bailey had confirmed to me that Thelma Holt would be involved, which had not been absolutely certain up to that time. And because of my knowledge of her work, I became even more convinced that the consortium could administer and develop Riverside.

'I saw Iain Coleman on 13 July. He was very candid and confirmed to me that the council could not fund Riverside's deficit. He said "We will definitely be funding only one of the two theatres in the forthcoming year." I pushed him on it and asked if it would be Riverside. He said it would. I tried to ring William Hunter that night, but he wasn't in.'

What appeared odd to Alan Rickman was the legal situation. Jane explains: 'Because both theatres might become insolvent or be liquidated and there were councillors on both boards, there had been concern about councillors renewing their membership of the board. The Council's Legal Services recommended that councillors should resign.

'Subsequently I think that Legal Services rather changed that view, but the important thing about it is that I resigned because the Council suggested I should – not because of any dealings with Alan, Catherine or Thelma.

'Jules Wright was definitely offered the Riverside directorship,' according to Jane Hackworth-Young, 'but my understanding is that she had decided not to go ahead with the financial risk. What was ironic was that she must have known more about the financial risk than anyone else, because she had been a member of the Riverside Board.

'To be fair to William Hunter, he did ask me whether the bid was coming in. He behaved honourably; and when I finally reached him on the morning of the 14th, he agreed that he and members of the Board would meet me before their "shortlisting" meeting the following evening. But I was still aware that he might be biased towards Jules.

'The council officer who was dealing with Riverside also spoke to me on the morning of the 14th, as he had been approached by Catherine Bailey who gave him a copy of the bid. I explained to him what had happened – and about my conversation with William Hunter – and we agreed to go down together to see Hunter and members of the Board. The officer's advice to the members of the Board that evening was that they should consider the Rickman bid, and the members agreed to consult with the Board.

'We were informed that the Board had agreed to consider the bid over the weekend, yet within hours Jules had been approached about running Riverside.

'Iain Coleman had even said to me that he didn't think the Rickman bid was a particularly good one, though I thought it was very businesslike. But I think Iain was terribly busy with the decisions on cuts for the forthcoming year.

'I categorically did not withhold the bid. I passed it on. Alan, Catherine and I had agreed I would take it to Iain Coleman, but I hadn't had dialogue with him. It was not a case of withholding the bid, but of not being able to put their case in good time.'

The timing of the actual decision now seems terribly vague.

'Hunter said the Rickman bid was in late; I said "I thought you were looking at all the bids, not making a final decision," ' says Jane. 'I had opened Rickman's bid on 22 June and passed it on. There were other bids from the Royal Opera house, the Old Vic, Carnival Theatre, Jules Wright's WPT and the English Shakespeare Company.

'I was a bit of a scapegoat because I felt that Iain Coleman didn't support me in processing the bid or subsequently when the matter got to the Press.'

When the public storm broke, Jane was frustrated by the fact that she had to stay silent. 'I could not tell the Press that the council had made a decision to fund only one of the venues. Other funding bodies, such as the Arts Council, would have withdrawn funding from the Lyric, as some funding was dependent on the local authority matching it.

'It would have produced a disastrous domino effect. So I couldn't say a thing publicly without endangering the Lyric. Since that time, the Lyric has launched an appeal which has resulted in attracting funding that has wiped out its deficit.

'I had given the Rickman proposal to Iain immediately I received it. The only reason I had then delayed was because I had understood there would be no funding for theatres at all, which might well not be made public until after people had committed themselves to Riverside.'

In retrospect, Jane could be said to have panicked from the worthiest of intentions. Clearly she didn't wish to lumber Alan's team with a building that carried a deficit of a quarter of a million pounds and had just had its funding withdrawn . . . otherwise she might have been guilty of dropping them in it.

'I think the Rickman application was good; I also think some of the others were good. I didn't think Jules' application was amazing.'

'My sadness was that I wasn't able to explain fully to Alan, Thelma and Catherine what had happened. I did try Catherine's phone and left a message; she never rang me back. She was away on and off during that time.

'The decision by Hammersmith and Fulham to continue funding the Lyric from 1994 to 1995 was taken in the autumn/winter of 1993. The lawyers didn't want me to go to the Press at all, and they wanted me to keep my explanatory letter to Thelma very, very short. It was really just an apology.

'Thelma and Alan rushed to the Press. If only they had held for 12 hours, I felt I could have done something. I wish they had talked to me before they went to the papers.

'In retrospect, I don't know what I would do differently. I don't think it would have had a different outcome if they hadn't used an intermediary. There was nothing anti-Alan about the whole affair at all.'

In fact there was a certain coolness between Jane Hackworth-Young and William Hunter that hardly helped to advance the Rickman cause. A one-time political rivalry meant that she was not, perhaps, the best choice of cleft-stick messenger under the circumstances.

'Hunter was Treasurer and I was Vice-Chair of Hammersmith Labour Party. We both stood for the Chair, and I got it over him.

'Alan's consortium just saw the problem as a threefold one: the deficit, the future funding and the fact that Jules had been on the Board. They had deep concerns about being treated fairly because of that.

'And it was also very strange that the Riverside Board didn't go back to the other original bidders after Jules decided not to go ahead. They offered the directorship to William Burdett-Coutts instead.'

Burdett-Coutts himself was equally mystified. 'I went through a rather strange process with this whole thing,' he admits. 'I went for an interview in July, but I thought that Rickman had got it. Then as soon as they approached me, I phoned up Alan. We must have had three or four meetings about ways in which his team could work together with me, but I never really got a final response on that.

'Thelma did once request both the main studios gratis while I ran the building; they didn't even offer to pay rent. But I would still happily work with Alan. I'll work with anyone; I'm in the business of survival,' added William, valiantly trying to keep his head above water.

Riverside was forced to close for five months from April 1994 for a face-lift under the directorship of Burdett-Coutts, who had made his name by running the Edinburgh Fringe's Assembly Rooms. He moved the entrance from the side to the front and gave it the look of a trendy art gallery instead of the student hang-out it was before. Fingers, not to mention legs, have been crossed ever since.

'It's all fallen flat,' Catherine Bailey later said to me in 1995 with grim satisfaction. Asked to comment on Jane Hackworth-Young's performance in the great drama, she rolled her eyes, and hummed and hawed.

In 1995, Council Leader Iain Coleman confirmed to me the rockiness of the Riverside funding at the time of the Rickman/Holt/Bailey bid. 'It has been public knowledge since 1993 that the support we gave to Riverside would have to be curtailed and eventually abolished. We gave the Trustees of Riverside as much notice as possible of our future intention.'

Hammersmith & Fulham Council combines the positions of Chief Executive and Finance Director in one job that carries the title of Managing Director. There is an odd postscript to the Rivergate story that suggests the Rickman consortium made a second attempt to succeed. On 10 August 1993, the Managing Director of the authority received a letter from Catherine Bailey Limited on behalf of Catherine, Thelma and Alan.

They enclosed a copy of their proposal, which had been rejected by the Riverside Board. In it, they declared that they would only reveal their sources of start-up money – at last, the dreaded S-word – if the Council maintained funding. 'You will note our omission with regard to finance, should the two funding bodies reduce the level of funding, and we wish to state our willingness to reveal our sources of start-up money should the matter proceed.'

In other words, the Rickman consortium appeared to be playing a poker game and keeping their financial cards close to their chest. You show me your willy if I show you mine . . . then we'll see who has the biggest. With cash-strapped councils, however, it doesn't work like that.

'Although we had no direct locus in the matter, the Council's Managing Director did meet with Thelma Holt and Alan Rickman on two occasions,' admits Iain Coleman. 'This was done to have a fallback position if the Riverside Board had to cease trading, in which eventuality the site reverted to the local authority.'

In other words, the council would have to pick up the bill. 'I am advised,' concludes Coleman, 'that the meetings were inconclusive. The proposals continued to be a wish-list of artistic programmes without any of the financial back-up being substantiated.'

So the sticking-point was money all along. The apparent delay in submitting the application had been a red herring which made people suspect a fishy conspiracy. 'Jane did pass on the bid to Iain Coleman because he and William Hunter had worked together as long-standing members of the local Labour Party. But it wasn't passed on to Iain as a formal submission; just as an informal consultative exercise,' says Peter Savage, who was head of the Council Leader's office.

'But the crux of the problem all along was money. One bid was underfunded; the other wasn't. But it was all taken personally, which was a shame. Thelma, Alan and Catherine were given plenty of time to come forward with information about sponsors.

'And they had just the sort of image that we were looking for; so there was absolutely nothing personal. It was a pity that it was interpreted that way.'

Savage explained to me that it's essential to see the colour of the applicant's money first before other funds are forthcoming; it's a delicate balancing-act.

'For instance, we are supporting William Burdett-Coutts in his Lottery bid. That means we would look at practical ways of supporting Riverside, e.g. giving them the freehold or perhaps cash funding. But all this would only happen if he was given money from the National Heritage fund. We wouldn't be able to fund him if the Lottery bid wasn't successful. Our help can only be part of a package.'

Nevertheless, London's artistic community was fired up on Alan and Thelma's behalf, sensing an outrageous and unforgivable snub by the Riverside Board. Frankly, William Hunter's rather rude letter to the *Standard* on 10 August had done nothing to correct that impression.

In his feature published on 12 August, the *Evening Standard*'s chief theatre critic Nicholas de Jongh demanded that Riverside's Board must go as a result of the Rivergate fiasco. He compared Alan's bid with that of Jules Wright, calling the Women's Playhouse Trust proposal 'four pages of pipe-dreams, aspirations and vague platitudes'.

A cut-out of Alan's head was thrust like an Aunt Sally above the parapet. So far as the Press and the general public were concerned, his was the best-known face in the consortium despite the fact that he was only one of the trio who drafted the wording of the bid.

And now to the second scapegoat in the affair.

This is where connections become terribly incestuous in the close-knit world of theatre. The President of Jules Wright's WPT was, paradoxically, Alan's old friend and co-star Geraldine McEwan. Even more strangely, Alan Rickman was among the ten actors credited with a close connection to the WPT as one of those who was approached to lead the teachers' workshops. (Unsurprisingly, he hasn't yet taken up that option.)

Those who did lead the workshops were Kathryn Pogson, Prunella Scales, Timothy West, Anton Rodgers, Neil Pearson, Fidelis Morgan, Janet Suzman, Gary MacDonald and Celia Imrie. So the Riverside row appeared to have bust up a beautiful and fruitful friendship between Jules and Alan that had brought together some of Britain's best-known, most adventurous thespians. No wonder there was a feeling of betrayal and treachery.

Thelma was publicly bitter about Riverside. She told the *Hammersmith and Fulham Post* on 5 August 1993 that the apologies received from the Board and from Jane Hackworth-Young had been completely unsatisfactory.

'It would be difficult to think how a consortium led by Alan Rickman which put forward such ambitious proposals for the Riverside did not even merit an interview.'

However, Jules Wright says: 'As I understand it, no application from the Rickman consortium was submitted before the closing date, before the interviews or before the Board of Riverside and the representatives of the London Arts Board and Hammersmith & Fulham Council had met to decide how to go forward. I don't understand that.'

Alan forced himself to be philosophical to the Press, telling Michael Owen in the *Standard* on 22 October that year: 'There's no point conducting an inquest now, it's so depressing. There was a positive result in the amount of discussion it opened up. I felt we'd started a new wind blowing through the London arts scene. But at the end of the day, I do believe a great opportunity has been lost. It comes down to the stifling, grinding mediocrity we have so much of at home.

'No one is prepared to accept the challenge of making a brave decision, to take a risk on something that might come crashing down or really break through to something new.'

Jules Wright saw things very differently. 'Thelma and I have not spoken since, which is very sad. None of them knew that I spent £5,000 on lawyers . . . and was unable to pursue it because I couldn't afford it. It was just a waste of money.

'I suspect that Alan's group might have thought there was public money around; but they would never have got involved if they had known the state of Riverside's finances. I'm glad the WPT didn't get involved either, in the end.

'It all began when I was pursued non-stop for eighteen months by the then Artistic Director Jonathan Lamede to join the Board of Riverside. I finally did in November 1992.

'But then Jonathan was removed in an extremely brutal Board meeting after a financial crisis. He was asked to leave the room and then William Hunter, the Chair, said, "I think it's time for Jonathan to go."

'I was very suspicious of the way the Riverside accounts were presented – inaccurately, I suspected. There were terrible problems with the whole finances. I spoke to the London Arts Board about this.

'WPT has a freehold building in Islington, and we had money in the bank at the time, too. So I thought we could come to some kind of arrangement to solve the Riverside financial crisis.

'I talked to my WPT Board about it and then resigned from the Riverside Board. I wrote a draft proposal in note form for my Board, which was what ended up being published in the *Evening Standard*.

'I sent the proposal to Riverside; and I and WPT's accountant, Mark Riese of H. W. Fisher & Co, were interviewed by the Riverside Board, the representative from the Hammersmith & Fulham Council and a representative from the London Arts Board. There was no enthusiasm for my proposal in principle from the other side. But by the end of what I thought was a courtesy meeting, we felt they had shifted ground. They subsequently decided to proceed with further discussions between the two charitable trusts.

'I have never understood why the Rickman bid was late. I understood that it was delivered after all the interviews, after the Board meeting at which they had made their decision. Nevertheless, I understand it was seriously reviewed by the Board.

'The next thing I knew was that I got a call from a woman on *Time Out* who said I had been offered the Riverside directorship. I said "Oh no, I haven't." She said "The entire artistic community of London says you have."

'There was just this one draft document to our WPT Board. It was faxed to all those members who had a fax, and a letter was sent to one member who was in New York. Then suddenly it appears in the *Evening Standard*. I still wonder from whom they got it. We can only speculate on this. All I can say is that I know for a fact that none of my Board members or staff was involved.

'In retrospect, I feel I was incredibly attacked in a concerted effort to discredit me; I was Australian and seen as an outsider. On Sunday the *Observer* followed the *Time Out* and *Standard* pieces. The lawyers told me not to talk to anyone. The coverage appeared to imply that I had fixed myself a job. I was never offered a job!' explained Jules. 'It was simply two meetings between two charitable trusts. Our accountants were instructed to carry out a due diligence examination of the Riverside accounts, which went nowhere. Riverside's finances were in a pretty parlous state.

'I never saw a final job description. And I couldn't believe that William Hunter would write a letter to the *Standard* without ringing us up and talking about it: it was impossible to pursue discussions properly thereafter.

'I felt abused,' she says. 'I didn't think Alan was doing this . . . but I dithered about phoning him. Then the extraordinary thing was that I got phone calls from seven actors, saying that Alan had been spotted giving out photocopies of the letter from the critics to the *Standard* in the returns queue at the Almeida Theatre. This was the evening of 6 August; the critics' letter had been published in the *Standard* that day.

'I still think people thought that Riverside was a passport to public money. In actual fact it was one godalmighty headache; I knew it was a financial disaster area because I had been on the Riverside Board.

'So then I went to the solicitors and said "I can't stomach this." Citygate are Press troubleshooters in the City; they came and monitored my calls.

'I have never spoken to William Hunter since. I had met him only three times at board meetings. As for his so-called admiration for me, I was incisive and thoughtful in those three board meetings – maybe William was impressed by that.

'One thing I think the solicitors were right about was that you have got to retain your dignity. I think the whole thing did Alan a lot of damage – but not Thelma, funnily enough.

'I was so wounded by everything. It was reported to me that one theatre director held a dinner party with an exceedingly well-known actor there, and they spent the entire evening slagging me off.

'I have known this director a long time. You never ever discredit or accuse someone without asking "What is the story?" I still can't understand why they didn't contact me directly instead of having all this stuff in the papers. I had launched a rescue bid, not a bid for a job. And I resigned from the Riverside Board long before we opened negotiations for an alliance between Riverside and WPT.

'*Time Out* started it all, and we served legal proceedings on them on 28 September.

'In actual fact,' adds Jules, 'I don't think the Charities Commission would have worn us linking with Riverside. As a registered charity, WPT is not allowed to risk its money.

'The Commission would have thought it too big a financial risk: it would have been hell on earth.

'From the moment that Jonathan resigned, there were rumours that Alan and Thelma were planning to put a bid together. My first meeting with Thelma was one of the great theatrical images of my life. It was after the dissolution of the Roundhouse.

'Thelma walked across one of the biggest spaces I can ever remember entering, and she looked so devastated and sad. It was the end of her dream after the liquidation. They dispensed the money to other charitable trusts, and we had asked for money for our inaugural production, *The Lucky Chance*.

'I think the Rickman bid would have been taken very seriously; they would have been a formidable team to interview. Alan and Thelma are very articulate, talented people. But if you feel that passionately about your cause, speak about it yourself. Why use an intermediary?

'William Hunter's letter in the *Standard* about their bid being unconvincing really upset Alan. But he behaved with dignity. I suspect,' concludes Jules, 'that it got out of hand for all of them.

'Nevertheless, I do hope to work with Alan again; I have done availability checks on him from time to time. The reason there is now this silence is that everybody now knows they got it horribly wrong. As far as I'm concerned, the whole thing has been consigned to the dustbin of history.'

Jules felt particularly upset at what she saw as a personal attack by Nicholas de Jongh in the London *Evening Standard*. She did, however, feel comforted by the support of Ilona Sekacz, the composer of both *The Lucky Chance* and also *Les Liaisons Dangereuses*.

'What you must be going through!' wrote Ilona to Jules on 13 August 1993. 'I just want you to know that I'm thinking of you, and ready to lend a hand in whatever way I can. I've written to the *Evening Standard* to register my protest at the way you're being treated.'

That letter, which was not published by the *Standard*, read as follows:

'I was distressed to read your theatre critic Nicholas de Jongh's articles about the recent appointment at the Riverside Studios. He places a lot of emphasis on the applications submitted by Alan Rickman's consortium and Jules Wright.

'When a panel meets to consider giving jobs or grants, the first thing it notices is the huge diversity in the manner and content of the written applications. But even the most detailed and beautifully presented papers are not necessarily the best. It is whether an applicant can prove that he or she is capable of fulfilling the brief that counts.

'Jules Wright runs the Women's Playhouse Trust impeccably. She commissions and produces a huge volume of new work on a tight budget, and her past record shows she is capable of turning a debt into a profit. She is a tireless and committed worker for women in the theatre, and one of the few people currently fulfilling the taxing dual role of director/manager.

'I know Alan Rickman, Juliet Stevenson and Christopher Hampton, and love and respect their work, but their application to the board of Riverside Studios is not supported by evidence of their managerial skills.

'Jules Wright may be running the WPT single-handed, but this is because the funding the WPT receives is spent on commissions for new work . . . She has always maintained a low profile in the press, preferring to devote her energies to the daily running of a successful company, rather than fighting her battles for funding and recognition in public.

'I know nothing of the rights and wrongs of the Riverside Board's behaviour, but I think it is wrong of your theatre critic to give a false impression of one of our most charismatic and talented theatre directors.'

Thelma Holt's last words on the subject are these: 'I don't think any blame of any kind should be laid at the door of Jules Wright, who was merely after the building like we were. The position of the others involved, though, was, to say the least, a little quaint. In spite of all the criteria we were given to understand were required of us, we were not even considered. There are many opinions as to why this was so, but they are all speculations.

'I'm as confused now as I was then about the rather cavalier, if not uncivil, manner in which Alan, and indeed his colleagues including myself, were treated. Print that if you want to: it is what I feel.'

With the benefit of hindsight, it's clear that Rivergate was a public-relations disaster for the Riverside Trust as well as a major disappointment for the hopes of Alan, Thelma and Catherine. If the nub of the problem was money, why did the trustees not make that clear?

Instead of which, William Hunter's sneering letter in the *Evening Standard* had claimed that the Rickman consortium's application was unconvincing 'administratively, artistically and financially'.

The first two were demonstrably not true; so it was an insulting remark to make. And that was what made the affair so acrimonious. 'You may think William Hunter is a pompous ass,' says one of the people involved. 'I couldn't possibly comment.'

Yet it's likely that Alan would never have spent enough time at Riverside to be a consistent box-office draw, given a rapidly developing film career that took him all over the world. Rima had found the year a tough one, too. After standing as the Labour Party's parliamentary candidate in the safest Tory seat in the country, she had found that even a power-dressing course hadn't helped for reselection.

Rima plodded on, but Alan had moved on to another movie. Anton Mesmer, the man who invented the concept of animal magnetism, was the subject of a Dennis Potter script about to go into production.

In one of those stories that are the much-embellished stuff of Hollywood legend, Alan was handed the script by one of the producers in the back of an LA cab. At last this was to be the first film of his career in which his character was absolutely central. It would capitalise on Rickman's growing reputation as a leading screen actor; and also his astonishing, unorthodox sex appeal. With Anton Mesmer inducing multiple orgasms in society ladies, it couldn't fail.

11. ANIMAL MAGNETISM

Once upon a time there was a fez. Magic acts, however, have come a long way since the days of the homely British comedian Tommy Cooper. This is the age of paranormal TV.

Given the vogue for such glamorous showmen as the Heathcliffian (not to say werewolfian) magician David Copperfield and the slick, sharp-suited hypnotist Paul McKenna, a feature film about the father of modern hypnotism would appear to have a ready-made audience.

Friedrich Anton (otherwise known as Franz) Mesmer, the German physician who invented mesmerism, was born at Iznang, Baden, on 23 May 1733. He graduated in medicine in Vienna, and later dabbled in the use of astrology and electricity in medical treatment. After finding he could obtain results by treating nervous disorders with the aid of a magnet, he developed the notion that an occult magnetic fluid – which exerted a force he called 'animal' magnetism – pervaded the universe and that he alone had a mysterious control over this force. He believed that disease was the result of obstacles in the magnetic fluid's flow through the body, and that they could be overcome by trance states often ending in delirium or convulsions.

In 1766, he published his first work (in Latin) on the influence of the planets upon the human body.

A portrait shows a fat-faced, bland-looking individual. Despite this unprepossessing appearance, he does appear to have achieved a close rapport with his patients and to have alleviated various nervous illnesses. He cured many people by auto-suggestion; but he used much mumbo-jumbo and was pronounced an impostor by his fellow physicians. Expelled from Austria for his unorthodoxy, he became a favourite at Louis XVI's court in pre-revolutionary Paris. Exactly contemporary with the Vicomte de Valmont . . . But in 1784, the French Academy of Medicine and Sciences, whose members included such eminent individuals as Dr Joseph Guillotin and Benjamin Franklin, recognised only that Mesmer's fashionable seances exercised a suggestive influence on his patients and denounced him as a charlatan. In effect, he practised an early form of psychotherapy. Eventually he withdrew from Paris and died in obscurity at Meersbury on 5 March 1815, a man so far ahead of his time that he has almost disappeared into the name he coined.

The early attempts at producing a trance-like state or sleep were a combination of trickery and charlatanism, but the modern scientific study of the process of mesmerism has become better known under the name of hypnotism. Mesmer's consulting-rooms were always dimly lit, hung with mirrors and filled with the scent of burning chemicals. He dressed in the long flowing robes of a magus or necromancer. His methods were inevitably copied by all kinds of swindlers and tricksters, with the result that mesmerism fell into disrepute until it became the subject of scientific study towards the end of the nineteenth century. Hypnotism is an artificially induced state that aims to help people to help themselves, but its effects are notoriously uncertain and even harmful to impressionable people. There's an old canard that says women are more easily hypnotised than men; certainly Mesmer had a preponderance of female patients. His hands-on methods involved bringing them to a delirious state similar to orgasm.

With the right script to flesh out the story, this faith-healer, miracle man, visionary or Svengali (take your pick) is a natural subject for drama; and Rickman had the right footlights appeal. *Mesmer*'s makers, Mayfair Entertainment International, hoped to capitalise on the paradox of such an attractively ugly man. Once again, it was also a period role for which Rickman is peculiarly suited. On this occasion, he elected to stay true to the eighteenth-century fashion for being clean-shaven in order to put as great a distance between Mesmer and Valmont as possible. The project generated enormous interest, especially when David Bowie became an investor. In May 1993, Alan was interviewed about the role at the Cannes Film Festival for Barry Norman's *Film 93* slot on BBC Television. Rickman was banging the drum for *Mesmer* at a Mayfair Films lunch in his honour; yet he was deliberately dressed down in a blue denim jacket and white vest, as if he were trying to look like a roadie.

'Nobody asked me to make movies until a few years ago,' he admitted cheerfully with a face-splitting grin, looking as if he'd spent his day humping equipment and checking sound-levels.

'I said yes to *Mesmer* because of the script. The writers are the least respected people around; they are a service industry. Dennis

Potter is an artist: it's irresistible. You are very glad and lucky to be involved.

'I'm staying on someone's yacht. A driver said, "You come with me, we go to David Bowie's yacht." ' Alan grinned again and thanked David Bowie.

It was easy to see why Dennis Potter had been attracted to the theme of one man's sexual power, transmitted by thought-processes alone, over women. Just the kind of thing over which the crippled Dennis had been fantasising throughout his career. His *Christabel* serial excepted, Dennis did not write substantial roles for women: he saw them as sex objects.

The director Roger Spottiswoode admits the screenplay had been around for quite a time: 'We all came to the project separately; the script was about seven years old.'

Filming took place in Hungary, near the Austrian border. 'The first thing that hit me when I read the script was the erotic charge of it. It's on every page,' Rickman told Michael Owen in a London *Evening Standard* piece in October 1993.

'He has a relationship with a blind girl which certainly goes beyond the usual doctor-patient relationship.

'He touched his patients intimately, we see treatment which borders on love-making, but anyone expecting any romping around on a bed will be disappointed. Not my style, I'm afraid.' (His tune changed for *An Awfully Big Adventure*.)

'Mesmer was a man of moral courage, which always creates a certain aura,' added Rickman somewhat stuffily, clearly psyching himself up to be a serious sexpot. 'He could be selfish and egotistical, but also had great innocence and didn't mind making a fool of himself. I find that quite attractive. He was also close to being an actor. He was very theatrical in his work, used lots of music.'

The minimalist Michael Nyman composed the music, which worked rather better than the film itself. For somewhere along the line, the movie that was to have given Alan Rickman his greatest starring role went so disastrously wrong that it ended up mired in litigation.

Even Rickman was heard complaining to his American agent in a *Late Show* special on his career in November 1994 that his non-naturalistic bits had been cut out of the film, that someone had pointed out you never get to know the enigmatic Mesmer.

Director Roger Spottiswoode was probably the only person happy with the finished product in the end as slanging matches broke out everywhere.

This was the second project within eighteen months on which Rickman, the ultimate control freak, had lost control. A *Mail On Sunday* feature by Paul Nathanson on 12 February 1995 was the first to scent blood, sniff out the scandal and tell part of the story, blaming Alan Rickman for being too prissy and politically correct to play the kind of intellectual sex-machine that Potter had in mind. In other words, it seemed to be accusing Rickman of censorship and bowdlerisation.

Nathanson's piece alleged a behind-the-scenes dispute involving 57 unauthorised and 'substantial' changes that Rickman and Spottiswoode made to Potter's original script.

Mayfair Entertainment International, the majority backers of this £4.5 million movie, also claimed that Rickman's character didn't have the sexual magnetism that Potter intended and withdrew their £3.2 million contribution.

'The 57 changes are substantial and were made without any consultation with us,' Mayfair's joint managing director Ian Scorer told Nathanson, complaining that Rickman had turned Mesmer into a distant, inaccessible figure rather than a hot-blooded sensualist.

Mesmer's new owners, Film Finances, disagreed, defending Rickman's script changes. 'Obviously he was very proactive as the lead actor. He did have input,' James Shirras, director of legal and business affairs, told me.

'One of Mayfair's complaints was that Rickman's performance was not sufficiently erotic. But if he wasn't then that's the way he chose to play it.'

Mayfair go further, alleging that Rickman refused to lick the eyelids of a young blind female patient because he was concerned that it would make him look like a lecher. And Scorer also alleged that at a private screening of *Mesmer* in Los Angeles in February 1994, Rickman had wanted to make the ending more political. 'Instead of the final scene between Mesmer and the blind girl being played to piano music, he wanted the sounds of gunfire and helicopter engines from Sarajevo.

'He thought it needed some really punchy, violent noise rather than the lyrical, touching finale. It was meant to make it more politically correct, but people said, "Whaaat? Mesmer was in Paris in 1780, not in present-day Bosnia!" '

Co-producer Lance Reynolds also rent his garments in anguish at the memory, claiming he had spent five years developing and nursing the project with Potter. 'The changes were very much done by the director and Alan Rickman, and I was not consulted,' he told Nathanson. 'I would see the rushes, call a meeting with the three other producers and express my concern, but it would be forgotten. I was jumping up and down and saying "This is not the film!"

'I was upset as I adored Dennis Potter. That was the point of working all those years on it – and not to have people rewriting his work.'

It sounds heart-rending as well as garment-rending, and certainly makes a good story, but it's not the complete picture. Rickman was portrayed as a killjoy Dave Spart whose starring role had gone to his head and who was just the kind of humourless lout that would (like the Hackney headmistress Jane Brown) denounce *Romeo And Juliet* for being 'heterosexist'. It was enormously damaging, and Scorer and Reynolds sounded very convincing.

It was felt at the time that Mayfair seized on an opportunity to validate pulling out of the film. They therefore criticised alterations to the script, which had been made without that much collaboration with Dennis Potter because he was too ill.

James Shirras of Film Finances Services Ltd, the new owners of *Mesmer*, was also acerbic in the spectacular way that only lawyers can be when they cast off the legal jargon, let their wig down and tell you what they really think.

'You've been on my conscience,' he admitted when I contacted him for a second time to try to arrange a talk about the *Mesmer* fiasco. 'Fascinating is not the word for *Mesmer*. You need to be resilient to stick with it to the end.

'Mayfair said Rickman was not sexy enough, which is ridiculous. This is a man who has more fans turning up to see him than Hugh Grant at the première of *An Awfully Big Adventure*, which I attended. Rickman has a big following.

'There were certainly cash-flow difficulties at the beginning, during the first few weeks of filming. Neither Rickman nor Roger Spottiswoode were paid properly until the fifth week. However, the suggestion disseminated in certain quarters that money which should have been available to meet production expenses on *Mesmer* was diverted elsewhere is without foundation.

'The major cash-flow problems at the beginning meant it was difficult for the producers to get their ducks in a row. That caused discontent on the set. Roger and Alan were implored to keep on working; they were extremely good about it.

'To some extent, they blamed Mayfair for the difficulties. But they had to be kept sweet, and I understand it was not always easy to do that.'

The budget for *Mesmer* was eight-and-a-half million dollars. There were quite a lot of deferments for what's known as the 'Talent', standard moviespeak for the director, producer and stars. The deferments for Rickman and Spottiswoode were six-figure sums in dollars. The cash budget of approximately six million dollars made it eight-and-a-half million dollars in total for the production.

'Film Finances now has the rights of distribution, which Mayfair were supposed to acquire,' says Shirras. 'We have now appointed a sales agent and sales are now being made. You would think there would be a lot of interest in one of Dennis Potter's last scripts, but . . .

'Our misfortune was that Mayfair ever agreed to finance the film based on that script. They prepared a legal case based on the divergences between the film as delivered and the original script. The discrepancies are very, very minor. It doesn't amount to a row of beans. They put their case to arbitrators, and the arbitrators believed them, to many people's amazement. I was very surprised.

'We knew the script was very, very odd. Mayfair were saying that it had been turned into a doctor-patient relationship as opposed to a man and his lover, but that assertion is so unverifiable,' says Shirras with exasperation.

'Alan had apparently been impressed by the script, though; I think he had found more in it, frankly, than most people did.' Indeed, one friend says: 'Alan found it terribly significant.'

The originating producer, Lance Reynolds, has been smarting about it all for years. 'I worked for five and a half to six years on *Mesmer* and it was such a bitter experience,' he squeaks. 'I would like to gracefully decline about commenting on working with Alan Rickman. Dennis Potter was very important to me and I was very close to him.'

When I spoke to him in the autumn of 1995, Reynolds alleged: 'I have not even been paid for *Mesmer*.'

This was disputed by James Shirras, whom I contacted at around the same time. 'It was not true that Lance Reynolds was not paid,' he insists. 'And if he felt things were going wrong, why didn't he do something about it? He was there for the whole shoot. I think it's fair to say that his relationship with the other producers was not all it might have been.

'We at Film Finances tend to get involved in these things when a producer needs to borrow money from a bank. They started shooting in September 1993. We were contacted about providing a completion guarantee. We look at the project and the individuals involved and decide whether they can do it. We were familiar with the Hungarian-Canadian producer Andras Hamori, so we were happy with him. Frankly, he was the reason why we got involved in the first place.

'Lance Reynolds was the originator of the project. He got some money for *Mesmer* from Bowie's business manager Robert Goodale. Goodale had nothing to do with the making of the film; he simply lent some of Bowie's money to the project for development.

'Another producer was Wieland Schulz-Keil, who had recently done John Schlesinger's *The Innocent* . . . which I believe was a problematic production. Schulz-Keil brought in the German film studio Babelsberg in Berlin, so it became a British-German-Canadian co-production.

'Andras Hamori was the hands-on producer, responsible for managing the production. Schulz-Keil and Reynolds had less clearly defined roles, but were supposed to be around. Someone at Mayfair must have said at the sight of the finished product, "How the hell are we going to get our money back out of this?"

'So they cited the script changes as a reason for pulling out of their contract. Most distributors who want a long-term future in the business would be extremely reluctant to do this.

'We lost the arbitration and paid the money back to the bank, so we are now trying to dispose of the territories from Mayfair that we inherited. Selling films is not really our business.

'This kind of arbitration is in fact extremely unusual,' points out Shirras. 'The Mayfair case was so preposterous, to say that this was not the film they wanted delivered. I thought they were trying it on. We didn't agree that the film didn't conform to the script. Their case was utter nonsense, but it had the virtue of simplicity and clarity. They must have been incredibly surprised when they won; and the arbitrators did say that Mayfair should consider themselves fortunate.

'The arbitration was essentially about who was going to pay the bank off ... Mayfair or Film Finances. It should have been between Mayfair and the producers, but if the producers lost the case, we would have had to pick up the tab. We could have called in the producers as witnesses, but we formed the impression – mistaken, as it turned out – that the arbitrators didn't want the producers to appear.

'Roger Spottiswoode and Alan Rickman both appeared as witnesses. They said it was nonsense about many changes, that film is always a collaborative thing. Roger had in fact been in touch with Dennis Potter, who said "You will just have to work it all out on the floor."

'The arbitrators' decision is really very difficult to understand, except on the basis of a very narrow and legalistic construction of the relevant contracts,' he concludes with a shrug. 'I felt from the very beginning that it would have been better in front of a High Court judge. But it was written into the contracts that we should go to arbitration if any difficulties developed, the reason being that arbitrators are appointed by the disputing parties for their knowledge and understanding of the film industry. I suspect that if we had been able to go to the High Court, Mayfair would not have gone ahead with the action.'

There are some who question the good taste of a peculiar feature of the film. Director Roger Spottiswoode, of course, sees things differently. 'You can play mad, but there are people who are severely subnormal who still look normal. We did bring some asylum patients out of Bratislava for a couple of days of filming. There are a limited number of things one can do; these people didn't really know what a film is, for example.

'But they seemed happy. You have to be careful not to exploit them, but there are precedents for using real patients: they did that in *One Flew Over The Cuckoo's Nest.*'

Spottiswoode stands by the film he made. 'The arbitration was an attempt to get out of paying for the film,' he alleges. 'Obviously it succeeded. None of that was to do with Alan or myself.

'The main concern was that Dennis had written a very dark script about a very dark character, and the financiers had thought it would be a light, airy, sexy romp. It's about a character who's ambiguous. They wanted something simpler, nicer, hopefully more commercial.'

As for Mayfair's allegations that Alan tried to turn the film into a metaphor for Bosnia with the sound of gunfire and Sarajevan helicopters, Spottiswoode admits: 'Alan did have an idea that there should be a more modern sound at the end to show people the contemporary relevance. I tried it and I didn't think it would work in the cinema. It's very theatrical. It was hitting the nail on the head too much. But with no ideas around, a film is dead. One discards the bad ideas.

'Alan is a man of strong ideas; you have to work them out with him. He doesn't like to be a tool. The same has been said of Gene Hackman,' he adds diplomatically.

'Mesmer was a very difficult, prickly, complex character, and Alan had great courage to play him. Mesmer was compelling and brilliant, but also extremely difficult and unpleasant. Both ludicrous and expressive. There is a tension there: Mesmer is impenetrable. He's endlessly pompous and arrogant: he married a woman for her wealth and then paid no attention to her. He was quite contrary.

'The movie was not a big blockbuster. It's a small, interesting, dark film. Alan won the Best Actor award in Montreal when it was screened there. But it probably won't make him a big star, it's not that kind of film.

'Clearly Mesmer was quite erotic and strange. When he strokes Maria Theresa's breasts in the first scene, we played it as if the characters didn't quite understand what they were doing . . . we didn't want to give a twentieth-century consciousness to a pre-Freudian time. I could have made the film more explicit, but that would have been wrong. Sexuality was repressed then.

'Our medical ethics are recently come by. Cartoons of the time showed Mesmer's group therapy as orgasm, or what we would call primal scream therapy. It was all about the discovery of the unconscious.

'Mesmer disappeared back into the tragedy of history. So did the girl in this film, Maria Theresa. She was supposed to have regained her sight for a few days after meeting Mesmer, but she died blind.

'All this was just around the time of the French Revolution, with the growth of new ideas. It was at the end of the Dark Ages, in a way. There had been almost no medical progress until then. And a man who dared to suggest that the mind and body might be connected was considered a fool. Mesmer was very much ahead of his time; would that great geniuses were nice people, too. I don't think he was.'

Spottiswoode is as angry as Shirras over the result of the arbitration.

According to Mayfair's allegations, Alan Rickman had a hands-on approach to Dennis Potter's script and a hands-off approach to the sexy side of Mesmer. In fact, a valuable insight into the way he works on a film set was provided by his friend Catherine Bailey's *Late Show* profile on BBC 2 in November 1994.

Alan is everywhere on the set, as omnipresent as Woody Allen's Zelig even for the shooting of scenes that he's not in.

Spottiswoode is overheard muttering about how long it's taking as Alan paces up and down in front of the camera, talking about options. Rickman is obviously desperate to direct.

'It's difficult to make it specific in that dress without making it obscene,' he worries after a scene with his leading lady, a *décolleté* Amanda Ooms who is prone on top of a piano. He consults with the director and bites his nail nervously (a Rickman habit well established in *Robin Hood: Prince Of Thieves*). 'It's getting a bit blurry,' he says querulously of the way he wants to play it in his mind's eye.

Rickman admits to Bailey that he asks questions not because he's trying to be difficult, but in order to be 'clearer. So you know where to place this peculiar energy called being an actor. I enjoy the corporate thing. I would never get involved in a one-man show . . . I don't know what that's for.'

As for his famous deliberation over parts: 'The yeses and the noes are all to do with the script . . . you either want to say those lines or you don't. One is constantly asked, "Just be yourself." ' He thinks for a few moments, waiting several perfectly timed beats before his answer, and smiles mirthlessly. 'Whoever that is.'

Rickman is filmed opening the car-door for the Hungarian chauffeur on location, absolutely unheard-of behaviour from the star of a film. But then Alan always wants to be thought of as the good guy. 'It could be a heap of shit,' he says fatalistically with a nervous grin, discussing the outcome of *Mesmer*. He takes care to introduce Catherine's camerawoman to members of the cast – Gillian Barge, Simon McBurney and Amanda Ooms – plus even the makeup man.

As for his notorious perfectionism, he admits: 'Maybe it's just tenacity or something . . . never wanting to let go. Maybe one should let go more often. But the work could achieve so much; and so little is asked of it most of the time.' There speaks a frustrated director whom life has cast as a great actor instead. He did indeed throw his weight around in one way. *Mesmer* cast-member Simon McBurney, the Artistic Director of the avant-garde troupe Theatre De Complicité, recalls being roughly handled by Rickman on set. 'Mesmer married a widow with a son by her first marriage; I play that son, Franz. Franz is a skulker and tells on Mesmer to his mother, who suspects Mesmer of having sex with his patients. *Au contraire*, it's Mesmer who throws Franz down the stairs for trying to rape a girl.

'So I have a very volatile relationship with him: several days of being thrown back against a wall by Alan Rickman! He really gets into his part and doesn't hold anything back.

'But it was a very happy and enjoyable show. It was difficult because Potter could have no part of it; he was dying at the time. The actors – Alan and Amanda Ooms and Gillian Barge and myself – formed a strong bond together.

'It was the first experience I had had of working with Alan, and I now consider him one of my friends. I was really impressed by his astonishing courtesy. He's polite to everybody. He was genuinely thoughtful about the extras in Hungary, who were paid a pittance and didn't even have a hot meal. He wouldn't work until they had been fed.'

Spottiswoode, however, has a plausible explanation for the great Extras' Lunch Saga: 'Our extras were treated the same as they are on every film. They get boxed lunches prepared in the hotels, while the main cast get hot meals because they have far more work to do and have to be on the set longer.

'But Alan becomes very passionate about causes; it happens with many actors. He is quixotic: it's a sweet side to him. Sometimes he's right – and sometimes he's wrong.'

'When he starts to work, he's very precise and incisive,' says Simon McBurney. 'He's very intelligent and doesn't suffer fools gladly. His concern was always with trying to achieve the best possible scene. He's fantastically rigorous on every level: I found that extremely endearing.

'But he's not difficult in an unconstructive, childish, pointless way. Jeremy Irons was pulling everything his way in the movie *Kafka*. Alan doesn't do that.

'The number of film actors who misbehave on set makes Alan's own position more remarkable. He was always concerned with such things as whether people had a lift to and from the set. On the majority of film sets, it's *de rigueur* for leading actors to misbehave. It's mistaken for egomania, but in fact it's a monstrous insecurity. This is a preposterously insecure profession because you go down as quickly as you come up. These things don't last for ever. So it makes his attitude all the more remarkable.

'He was a supporter of my and many people's work, he makes it his business to see other people's work. He's one of the few actors at the peak of his profession who does that. We got on well. We shared a love of rollercoasters, and we went to the park in Vienna where they shot *The Third Man*, the Prater Park. We got on the rollercoasters and screamed our heads off. There was one horrendous one that pushed you up backwards.

'But every time I thought I knew what Alan was like, I found he had changed. He's a very enigmatic and surprising person. He's a giggler, but he's quite imposing. I didn't know where I was with him at first.

'He was very terrifying and scary on set, working with such intensity. Acting is such a strange and curious thing to be doing, it's a very weird job. Everyone has their own methods. Gillian Barge is not an improviser, she learns her lines until she's word-perfect. With Alan, it was much more introspective. He wouldn't necessarily always communicate it, you would have to intuit it. But compared with taking a theatre company round the world, being on a film set was like a holiday. I felt like a dog let off a leash.

'Alan and I went out to the wine district for one day, and we also went on some incredible walks. I have a lot of friends in Vienna, so Alan and I were hanging around in cafés and cooking meals with them. He was very sweet. He was helping an Austrian friend of mine with his role as the father in my production of *Lucie Cabrol*. He's considerate that way.

'He has a seriousness, not an aloofness. When the project was conceived, it was conceived with his name attached to it. He's the principal actor holding the whole thing together, and he would spend a lot of time behind the camera as well as in front of it.

'I think that kind of thing can be quite intimidating; but Roger is not a tyrant director like Coppola, his style is much more collaborative. Alan brings his own allure to the film. He treated the entire script with enormous respect. He was concerned to portray the complexity of Mesmer as a man who was out of his time. To portray him as a sexual philanderer is not true to the intentions of Potter. Mesmer came to the conclusions that only Freud came to a hundred years later.

'Medicine was enormously politically dominated: it was divided between healing and surgery, and surgery won. Mesmer was stumbling upon an early psychotherapy, and this was illuminated by a confrontation with sexuality. The ambivalence of that is what's fascinating.

'There is a very strong sense of the loneliness of this man, and there were some very mesmeric sexual moments in the film . . . a simmering sexuality there. Potter brought out a lot of the wry humour and humanity, and we almost revolve inside Mesmer's head. It's a very internal drama – a man trying to make sense of the world. He develops an unspoken sexual relationship with Amanda Ooms as a patient who has been sexually abused by her father. There's an ambivalence about her character, and my spying on her sessions with Mesmer adds to that.

'We filmed in a wonderful castle at Fertod in Hungary, a sort of Versailles in semi-ruins. It's now up for sale. We also filmed in a medieval town called Sopron. I enjoyed myself terrifically.

'I think the finance people in films are sometimes psychopathic,' is Simon's final verdict. 'It's just a great great shame that *Mesmer* was never followed through. Having so many co-producers didn't help; they were always turning up on the set.'

So what of the movie itself? The cinematography has a luscious integrity, perfectly in keeping with the period; and all begins well as two dainty eighteenth-century clockwork figures revolve on a music-box to the lush sounds of a Michael Nyman composition in unusually romantic mode. The image could be taken as a metaphor for the way so many competing interests chased each other round in ever-decreasing circles.

The whiskerless Rickman looks youthful and vulnerable in the role. His theories of animal magnetism are mocked by the surgeons from the Royal Society of Medicine, which has summoned a special assembly to examine his claims. One can't help thinking of the Inquisition. They question him about his visit to a lunatic asylum with a sympathetic fellow doctor. 'We walked through the pillars of misery and Dr Mesmer wept. I saw him take away a seizure,' testifies the colleague. A dropsical leg has also been cured. Mesmer has persuaded people that a cure lies in their own hands, can be part of their own experience.

We see a flashback of a girl having fits. Mesmer strokes her face and chest, encouraging another sceptical physician to follow suit. She raises herself up after what looks like a faith-healing session. The other doctor disputes the cure and insists on bleeding her instead. 'Open up one of her veins.' He thinks Mesmer's methods are pure superstition. 'Passion and medicine do not mix. The moon is a symbol of lunatics.'

Rickman's Mesmer, moving around as if in a dream or trance, insists: 'I have made a discovery that will lift pain and misery.' In the role of his wife, Gillian Barge conveys a most ambivalent attitude towards her man: she jeers at him, yet boasts of him to others: 'My husband has an original mind.' Nevertheless, she describes him as 'the son of a shitarse gamekeeper. Don't I pay the bills and give you some sort of entry into a better society?' And she calls him 'a genius living on his wife's charity'. His only defence is sarcasm, referring to her 'generous spirit, tact, charm and missing back teeth'.

Most of the time he seems in a world of his own, and the interior life of Mesmer is never satisfactorily explored by the script. The man is little more than a romantic ideal, despite all Rickman's efforts to give this sketch some depth.

He tells a shallow woman on a balcony: 'We could hear the music of the heavenly spheres if only we strained to listen.' He also informs her, in one of the script's more stunning *non sequiturs*, that man is the only animal to know it will ultimately die.

The next scene shows a blind girl in a veil, playing the piano. She then has a fit, writhing on the floor as if in the grip of a grand mal. She is Maria Theresa, played by the extravagantly beautiful Amanda Ooms. Mesmer watches, transfixed. The surgeons are about to bleed her when Mesmer rises and says: 'This young woman is in urgent need of the attention of Franz Anton Mesmer.' He shoves them unceremoniously aside. 'They should never cover such an exquisite face.' A distressing tendency to refer to himself in the third person is the first sign of Mesmer madness.

Ooms lies moaning on the piano; Rickman raises his hands like a conductor. When he places his hands on her face and body, she screams. He runs his fingers down her bodice. His nostrils dilate and he flings his head back as she goes quiet.

He mumbles about the sun being a magnet that draws us out. 'There's an unseen force . . . an animal magnetism moving from me to you,' he whispers. 'You can feel it, you can feel it. Here is your patient. She has not been harmed.' Then he stalks away.

As is his wont, Rickman wears no wig; he dislikes too much artifice. His hair is swept back from his face, and he reeks of repressed sensuality. Everything in the film conspires to turn him into an enchanted figure, the focus for all female eyes but not quite in touch with his own urges. There's an air of wonderment about the character, who seems to be working out the plot as he goes along. Of course he's ridiculously idealised. We hear the music of magical prisms from a chandelier in his study where he holds court, a Copernican globe in the background.

As his colleague applies an instrument of torture to a weeping Maria Theresa's sightless eyes, we see a flashback to the girl being sexually assaulted by her father. 'If only you knew my ache,' he says, his hands on her breasts, 'you can have anything you want.' She asks to be taken to Mesmer. In a glib piece of camerawork, Mesmer's face dissolves into a shot of the moon.

The journey back to childhood, where the watching, waiting, eavesdropping child is the father of the man, is integral to a Dennis Potter screenplay. The film shows us the young Mesmer, perched on a rock and listening to the beat of the universe. The adult Mesmer is still haunted by him.

A pretty waif adores Mesmer and tells him outside his door that she loves him. 'You think you do,' he says gently. When Maria Theresa is brought by her father to Mesmer's house, they walk in the garden and the besotted waif watches jealously from her window as she plays her music box. This is Francesca, the young cousin of Mesmer's wife.

'I can hear the turn of the world,' says Maria Theresa. 'And can you hear the human heart?' Mesmer asks her whimsically. 'When I was a boy, I too could hear the turn of the world.' There follows a very intense scene in which he strokes her lower arm and holds her hand, telling her that she would never want to see for herself the contamination of the world.

There is a mob at the gate: the rabble invade the house and Mesmer meets them on the stairs, saying like the man of destiny he is: 'I'm the one you seek.' They have all come for healing. The halt and the lame follow Mesmer down stone steps for an experiment in electrical impulses. He tells the crowd to join hands in a charmed circle: this is the scene that used real inmates from an asylum.

'You poor people,' he says compassionately. 'Poor, sick, pitiless world. Where shall we end the abuse and cruelty?' He goes round the circle, strengthening the force between them. 'This force needs pain, and pain will resist.' There is much agonised crying and lamentation when he uses the cane as a kind of lightning rod. They break the circle and all have fits. He hugs some of them, trying to pass on his energy. They quieten down. 'The storm has passed over you. Each of you has gone some little way towards harmony,' he says; perfectly on cue, we hear the music of the spheres.

Then the clamour begins again: they berate him, because their illnesses are still there. 'You have to look in,' he says defensively, but he is assailed by self-doubt.

Back in his study, Mesmer encourages Maria Theresa to be tactile. He clasps her face and asks her to breathe, his lips very close to hers. His wife bursts in, as wives tend to do, and accuses him of kissing his patient. This is a moment of pure farce, clumsily introduced. It's a pity that we see so little of the volatile home life of the Mesmers, apart from the laying on of threatening hands around her neck as he says sarcastically, 'Light of my life, leave us.'

The sexual tension is almost tangible as he meets Maria Theresa in the gardens for a Braille version of sex. Her fingers travel over the prominent Rickman lips, getting to know him. Back in his study, he runs his hand along her neck; she (and by now presumably half the audience) is almost brought to orgasm. 'No, father,' she suddenly blurts . . . and her secret is out. Her father has been molesting her.

'Don't be ashamed,' he whispers, hugging her. Mesmer shows tremendous restraint, but it's clear that he's overpoweringly attracted to her. He runs a silk scarf across her throat in an intimate gesture and then blindfolds her with it.

Days later Mesmer takes off Maria Theresa's silk bandages; she still insists that she sees only darkness. 'What is to be is out of our hands,' he insists. 'We make our own lives.' He is trying to make her assert her will-power.

A lucky fall, somewhat unconvincingly choreographed, restores her vision. The pains in her head have gone. 'Now my head sings instead.'

There follows a scene of extraordinary erotic intensity, all the more powerful for the way in which Rickman carefully reins himself in. 'I knew before I met you,' he says, as if this is their destiny, and their kiss creates the most exquisite frisson. He has awakened every one of her senses. Mesmer knows he is falling in love, but the erotic pull of the universe is irresistible. 'Oh let it go, let the arrow fly,' he says testily to a stone Cupid with its bow poised to strike at human hearts.

The character is instinctively gallant, which must be a first for Dennis Potter. Seeing Francesca molested at a window by his sly stepson Franz, Mesmer rushes up the stairs in order to fling Franz down them. As he explains venomously to his wife, 'I'm cleaning the house.' But alas, it's chucking-out time all round. The action moves forward to his expulsion from Vienna, when Mesmer and his baggage are flung out of a coach. 'You know the orders . . . keep out of the city.'

'This is a day of infamy and outrage that shall long be remembered,' says an outraged Alan Rickman, his moon face so caked in mud that he looks like a B-movie monster from a very black lagoon. It's a great moment of unintentional hilarity which rather undermines all the self-conscious Romanticism that has gone before.

And so on to Versailles in the Dennis Potter time-machine, where Mesmer has developed a reputation for curing paralytic fits. An over-ripe beauty asks him to cure her backache. She says that it hurts 'at certain times'. 'Your nerves are out of alignment,' he says smoothly, extricating himself subtly from a tricky situation.

He asks a group of ladies to form a circle. 'The force in me comes flowing into your flesh, your nerves, your bones.' They are asked to clasp a series of rods suspended over a large barrel of water. There is a chorus of ladylike moans as he puts his hands on naked shoulders, telling them to place the rods upon whatever part of the body ails them most. 'It surges,' he says, and the group groan. 'Your body is now a battlefield.' There is a cacophony of orgasmic shrieks.

This is the infamous scene of mass hysteria, straight out of Ken Russell. One woman writhes on the floor in a fit, while another's head plops foolishly into the barrel of water. It's absurd and grotesque. Are we supposed to assume Mesmer, the misunderstood idealist, has now become a cynical charlatan? The film sends out conflicting signals, unable to make up its mind.

'I cure the sick because I can reach into their souls . . . This is just play-acting,' he tells his friend Charles. 'One day we shall come to acknowledge that our emotions and our bodies are not separate.'

There are sounds of civil insurrection outside, presaged by that film-maker's cliché: a runaway horse. 'When society is sick, all its members are too,' Mesmer says to the medical assembly that is about to denounce him.

'Gentlemen, you are in the veriest danger of losing your lives,' continues Mesmer, who appears to have extraordinary extra-sensory perception, aware that the mob are approaching with their lighted tapers. Is this the first stirring of the French Revolution? We are never told.

Maria Theresa has lost her faith and is back in the darkness again. 'You abandoned me,' she says. 'I cannot see.' 'Do you want to see?' he asks her rhetorically.

Mesmer dreamily relives his boyhood; Potter is forever rewinding the tape of life. 'When I was a boy, I could see from one horizon to another. Everything was in harmony, in balance, except human beings. And I could not bear to do nothing about it.'

The last shot shows Mesmer and Maria Theresa, side by side but apart, in an abandoned hall from which everyone else – horse, mob, fellow physicians – has vanished. On balance, even anachronistic Sarajevan helicopters might have helped.

No wonder the project ended in frustration for all concerned. It's a fragment, a tantalising might-have-been that provides little more than a sumptuous showcase for Rickman's sexuality.

Nevertheless, Alan Rickman's performance as Mesmer did win him the Best Actor award at the 1994 Montreal Film Festival. And at Dennis Potter's memorial service in November of that year, Alan kept faith with the writer's memory by reading from the script of *Mesmer*. It seemed as dead now as Dennis.

12. 'GOD DIDN'T MEAN HIM TO PLAY SMALL ROLES'

The celebrity of an actor, hired to recite other people's words, is a source of agonised embarrassment to Alan Rickman. Not only does he long to direct more, but he is acutely aware that the writers don't get the credit that the performers do. Actors should be the servants of the writers, as he once put it, but they get promoted over the heads of the playwrights instead. As Peter Barnes wryly remarks, 'A lot of people haven't grasped that actors are not making up the words as they go along.'

Stephen Davis once told me how Alan had stood up at an awards ceremony while dishing out the acting prizes and said, 'Can we please spare some thought for the writers?' Davis added: 'It is extraordinary that we are such a visualising culture that we are now living in the cult of the actor. In Hollywood, they are the ultimate royalty; and Alan is embarrassed at the amount of publicity given to actors. I think he is very conscious that he is an actor who profits greatly by success and fame and charisma but who is very careful that he doesn't use people as a grandstand for his career, because he's a man of very high principles. But it does cut both ways: you create a tremendous amount of mystique by being Garboesque. It's a win-win situation to be in.'

Alan Rickman routinely rejects so many roles that Ruby Wax says she feels sick every morning at the thought of the amount of money her purist friend is turning down every single day. Dusty Hughes' story of the ceiling-high piles of script in Rickman's flat suggests a crazy paper factory. No wonder Alan has to be fanatically tidy. He is famously faddy and principled, but that doesn't stop him being offered first choice on countless projects. Perhaps that hard-to-get quality simply whets producers' appetites: they know he's not to be bought for any price. Indeed, you could dine out for years on revelations about the major roles that Alan Rickman has declined. Nevertheless, he is contrary enough to moan about the parts he doesn't get.

When he reached 50, Alan Rickman found himself at a crossroads whose three-fingered signpost behaved like a demented weathervane according to mood. One direction pointed to continuing film stardom, another to heavyweight theatrical roles and the last to directing.

He risked typecasting in the first, he was often too busy to pursue the second and he was a relative newcomer so far as the third option is concerned. No wonder he was frustrated. He had never been more in demand for major movies; yet Alan Rickman faced a quiet mid-career crisis.

Before the Rivergate controversy drove a wedge between Rickman and his old colleague Jules Wright in 1993, he complained to her one day that nobody asked him to go on stage anymore. 'The problem is that people become inhibited about asking him and assume that he's not available. Maybe Alan is lost to the theatre now, like Gary Oldman,' said Jules to me in 1995.

This exasperates all those who would like to see more of Rickman in what they say is his natural habitat on stage: 'He is the most complete man of the theatre I know,' insists his old RADA contemporary Stephen Crossley.

'I ask Alan Rickman every year to rejoin the RSC; I ask him to name his parts,' Adrian Noble told me in 1995. 'But it's difficult when you enter the film game to find the time; with film, it's not only the actual filming that takes time, but the hanging around beforehand while they find the money.

'Once you move into film seriously, it's very hard to carve out the time to do more theatre. It's much more risky – you stand to lose more.'

Peter Barnes agrees. 'It's difficult to return after you leave the theatre, because theatre is hard. And you get more exposure in movies, so theatre becomes something you do only for yourself. I have always done movies to finance my theatre work. With theatre for actors, it's very much a case of working for yourself.

'He's obsessed about not playing villains. I can understand why he doesn't want to do them, but for a long career it's pretty good to have a stand-by like that. You will never be too old to become a villain. He's more a character star than a star star. And Gene Hackman doesn't go out of fashion.

'Alan turned down the Lytton Strachey role in *Carrington* before Jonathan Pryce was offered it. He's since moaned to me about turning that down plus the role of the baddie Scar in Disney's *The Lion King*, which then went to Jeremy Irons. He had second thoughts, but it was too late. He was too proud to admit it, when he should have done it.'

Indeed, it's tempting to conclude that Alan had his regrets only after Pryce and Irons were seen to have made such tremendous successes of Strachey and Scar; a dog-in-the-manger attitude is only human, after all. After much humming and haaing, Sir Anthony Hopkins finally agreed to play Richard Nixon on film only after director Oliver Stone craftily asked him what he thought of Gary Oldman for the role. 'I think Alan is much better than Tony Hopkins, who has never been the same since he gave up drinking,' is Peter's opinion. 'One doesn't wish for artists to self-destruct, but in giving up one must be brutal and say they lose something.'

'I certainly discussed the role of Lytton Strachey with him,' says Christopher Hampton, writer and director of *Carrington*. 'When he came with me to the screening, I think Alan was upset that he hadn't taken it. He said, "Oh my God, what have I done!" '

'He was also offered the role of Peron opposite Madonna in the movie version of *Evita*, which then went to Jonathan Pryce,' says Barnes. At this rate, Pryce – yet another friend of Rickman's – will be learning to read Alan's fingerprint profile on every script he's sent.

'Alan was also told that he was second on the list after Anthony Hopkins to play Hannibal Lecter in *Silence Of The Lambs*. If Hopkins had decided not to do it, then Alan was the next choice,' explains Peter.

'The funny thing is, Alan said that that one couldn't be turned down, that it would make him the biggest and most powerful star in Hollywood. It would have been a stellar leap. I think Alan would have been extraordinary, though I can't understand why it didn't go to Brian Cox – who played Hannibal Lecter originally in the film *Manhunter*.'

Silence Of The Lambs did finally make Hopkins a British superstar in Hollywood. He won the Oscar for Best Actor and was also awarded a knighthood, though many felt that the Queen's honours system should not have rewarded an actor for playing a serial killer who disposed of the bodies by eating them.

Still, it was a testament to the sheer size of the part, which Hopkins seized with tremendous relish. 'But it was a one-note performance,' said one film critic in exasperation. One can only sadly speculate on the insidious power of Alan Rickman in the role.

'I think Alan is much better than Tony Hopkins, who has never been the same since he gave up drinking,' is Peter's opinion. 'One doesn't wish for artists to self-destruct, but in giving up one must be brutal and say they lose something.'

Some of the stories about the scripts on which Rickman has first refusal are almost farcical, though not particularly funny, of course, for the actors that unwittingly took his leavings. 'In *The Last Action Hero*, the villain was played by Charles Dance. He agreed to it after seeing an early script. Then he happened to see a later script with the words "Alan Rickman" in brackets after the name of his character . . . !

'Alan takes endless time to decide about which scripts to accept, goes through the whole Hamlet routine and cogitates for ever about whether to take a part,' adds Barnes fondly. 'He often rings up friends. He rang me up about playing Colonel Brandon in Emma Thompson's film of *Sense And Sensibility* – he said to me, "The thing has got Hugh Grant in it."

'I think he was worried at the time about all the attention on Hugh Grant. Plus I have the impression they didn't get on in *An Awfully Big Adventure*.'

The director Mike Newell was a modestly successful film-maker who unexpectedly hit the jackpot with the low-budget British movie *Four Weddings And A Funeral*. It became the biggest-grossing UK film of all time and turned Hugh Grant into an international star, charmingly knock-kneed and sweetly stammering. The over-grown-boy-next-door image was, of course, far too good to be true. An over-tired Hugh sullied his escutcheon when his idea of in-car entertainment at the seedier end of Sunset Boulevard excited the prurient attention of the Los Angeles Police Department. The rest is mugshot history.

Grant was signed up for Newell's follow-up project, a screen version of Beryl Bainbridge's story of a post-war Liverpool repertory theatre company and its struggles to stage a production of *Peter Pan*. The title, *An Awfully Big Adventure*, was a quote from a poignant line in J. M. Barrie's play about the little boy who didn't want to grow up: 'To die will be an awfully big adventure.'

By general critical consensus, the lightweight Grant was disas-trously miscast as the manipulative and vitriolic theatre director with whom the naïve young heroine falls in love without realising that he is homosexual. (The word is not in her ken.)

Not many people know, however, that Alan Rickman was offered the role of the waspish, cold-hearted Meredith first. The casting would have made a great deal of sense. 'I asked Alan's agent if it was the case that Alan doesn't want to play villains,' remembers Newell. 'He said yes, that was the case, but that Alan would like to play the part of P. L. O'Hara instead.'

O'Hara is the film's equivalent of the cavalry, riding to the rescue of the heroine (and the movie itself) on an old Norton motorbike. Just when you feel the story couldn't get more leaden, along comes Rickman to wake things up. The result is a broken-backed piece of work that is fascinating only for a few well-observed cameos and for yet another of Alan Rickman's scene-stealing performances.

'He is not a chameleon actor, because he is very noticeable,' says Peter James, principal of the London drama school LAMDA. 'It seemed to me that *Mesmer* was the next logical step for him. You can't cast him in absolutely anything, although he's managed to cover a surprising breadth of roles. But it would be very difficult for him to play a plumber. He looks so elegant, so aristocratic.' As opposed to Kenneth Branagh, who is forever being told (despite the kings he has played) that he looks like a plumber. Both Ken and Alan come from similar backgrounds – if anything, Branagh's origins are more bourgeois – yet you would never associate Rickman with the tradesman's entrance.

'God didn't mean him to play small roles,' is Newell's classic observation. 'But I don't agree that he couldn't play a plumber; he would just make you feel that the plumber was a leading part.

'In theatrical terms, he's absolutely a star. But on film he's a leading actor, a great big leading actor who graces any film he's in. He's financially very useful because people feel easier about investing in a film he makes.

'Alan feels he's a leading actor; in the theatre, he's allowed to play a huge range of parts. In Hollywood he played villains before heroes, thus he has been typecast in villainy. That way he's going to have a boring time; it limits him.

'His villains are in fact warped tragic heroes. But he's very canny, and doesn't get that across in a wrong-headed way as some actors do. It's difficult to get actors to play motiveless malignity; they want the devil to be understood, at least. On the contrary, I want to be satisfied in my villains, not for them to be understood!

'Alan *is* pernickety sometimes; but then famous old actors like Ralph Richardson and Laurence Olivier were also pernickety about getting something absolutely right and pat. There is a sense of rhythm and fitness and being in the right place at the right time. But I had a harmonious relationship with him.

'Affection is important to him,' adds Newell. 'He wants to have the sort of authority where people take advice from him. He's a guru.'

Newell denies the rumour that there was a rancorous atmosphere between Rickman and Grant on *An Awfully Big Adventure*; Hugh's encounter with the prostitute Divine Brown was to occur later, duly recorded by Emma Thompson's *Diary* (' "All right for some," I thought') on the filming of *Sense And Sensibility*.

Rickman and Grant are, however, completely different types, though Newell insists, 'There was no coolness. But Alan does have a bit of Eeyore in him, though he would be puzzled if you pointed that out. It doesn't strike him that he's pessimistic.'

The one thing Grant and Rickman indisputably do have in common, of course, is their invaluable early dramatic experience as Old Latymerians. Hugh was also taught English and Drama by Alan's old mentor, Colin Turner, and appeared in many school productions during the 70s. In 2001, Latymer Upper's Head of Middle School Chris Hammond was invited to a party at Mel Smith's London house where he found Alan Rickman and Hugh Grant reminiscing together about their days at Latymer, all rivalry between the first choice and second choice for the male lead in *An Awfully Big Adventure* apparently long forgotten.

Given his aversion to yet more screen villainy, it's rather amusing to see Rickman briefly donning the mantle of a black-hearted fiend when P.L. O'Hara plays Captain Hook in *Peter Pan* with Hugh Grant's Meredith taking over after O'Hara is drowned. There is no comparison between the two performances. O'Hara is also an intriguing mixture of hero and villain in his own right, befriending and sexually awakening the heroine without realising – until the devastating finale – that he is in fact seducing his own long-lost daughter. Both Meredith and O'Hara are seducers of the young and innocent; and when O'Hara tries to upbraid Meredith for his treatment of a youth, he is fatally compromised by his own cavalier behaviour.

'There was a big difference in the two voices for Captain Hook,' Newell admits. 'Hugh had a thin tenor and Alan a great booming, baritone voice. It's the difference between a film actor and a stage actor, because Alan is very much a theatre animal.

'Alan is very ambiguous and enigmatic, very powerful. He stands still, which reinforces the enigma. He's a calm actor rather than a tumultuous one; everything seems to come from a very deep and solid place. You are constantly invited further and further in, so you find yourself suckered in.

'He's what is known as a backfoot actor, with tremendous weight and talent. He would have been fairly obvious casting as Meredith; he would have been magnificent. He's very difficult to miscast, because he hides everything.

'I do regret not being able to go into O'Hara's previous history before he was presented in the film. I wished I had actually shown his failed life as an actor, his cramped Maida Vale flat.' In the event, however, the sad cast of Rickman's haggard face said it all.

'It was a great moment of revelation for Alan at the end of the film when O'Hara realises that he's the father of Stella, the girl he's seduced. He played the version without words; we had two versions. He said to me, "I know what you're going to ask me, to do it without words." And of course he had this amazing eloquence without words.

'We used a Norton motorbike – the biggest bike we could get hold of, 450 cc or 500 cc. I wanted something truly huge, but this was the biggest, meanest bike the English made in those days. He rode the machine for 20 to 30 yards, then a stuntman took over. You are not supposed to notice the join.

'An old bike like that is a cranky thing, and I was concerned about Alan breaking bones. I was very unhappy about him half-learning to ride it. I remember one time that it wasn't quite in control. But he was very game.

'As for the death scene, he fell just nine inches into the water; we showed the cast-iron wheel hitting his head, but in fact it was foam rubber. The sound effects did the rest.'

An Awfully Big Adventure contained Rickman's first film sex scene, with P. L. O'Hara and Georgina Cates's Stella both naked from the waist up for an unusually delicate and tenderly erotic deflowering of a virgin. We see a back view of Rickman, bending over her in bed: he might have been her tutor.

He certainly fitted Bainbridge's description of O'Hara in the original novel: 'in profile, the man appeared haughty, contemptuous almost.' O'Hara clings to the rags and tatters of a thing he once called integrity, but the character is so tarnished by his equivocal relationship with Stella – partly paternalistic, partly predatory –

that only Rickman's strong and complex presence ensures he retains our sympathy. O'Hara's doubts and misgivings are evident throughout.

Charles Wood's screenplay was far too episodic to maintain a strong narrative, and most viewers will have been either bored or confused or both. *An Awfully Big Adventure* was a cinematic flop, going quickly to video.

So much for the dream team of Newell and Grant, with only Rickman and a few other stalwarts – Alun Armstrong as Stella's uncle, Prunella Scales, Nicola Pagett and Carol Drinkwater – emerging with much credibility.

Mike Newell says, rather cruelly under the circumstances, that for the supporting cast of *An Awfully Big Adventure*, 'I wanted people who were over the hill or about to be over the hill'. And Alan himself admitted in a location interview on Barry Norman's *Film 95*: 'It's a strange film to be doing in a way, a bit like being a vulture on your own flesh . . . we have actors playing actors, using a stage for a film set and using our own lives as raw material. Georgina is remarkable . . . she claims to be seventeen but I'm going to put it out that she's forty-three.'

He reminisced about his own days in rep: 'I had to haul up my own cross because I was Inquisitor and ASM at the same time for a production of Shaw's *St Joan*. And then I had to put the kettle on. Everyone's memories of rep have that kind of mixture – pleasure and pain.'

There is precious little pleasure in *An Awfully Big Adventure*, compared with much pain and cynical back-biting, led by a hard-boiled Nicola Pagett and a jaded Carol Drinkwater.

The theme of lost innocence – pace Peter Pan – is brusquely handled in a relentlessly downbeat and depressing setting that should at least dissuade a few cross-eyed daughters of Mrs Worthington from following a hard life on the wicked stage.

It's hard to care about anyone, not least the coldly self-contained young heroine Stella. Little wonder that *An Awfully Big Adventure* failed to catch fire at the box office, with most people attracted only by the names of Hugh Grant and Alan Rickman.

Variety magazine loathed it, calling the film 'a dour, anti-sentimental coming-of-age story . . . a rather disagreeable look at the irresponsible and corrupting behaviour of adults toward youthful protégés'. Austerity Britain, indeed.

Rickman's character was a misfit in more ways than one: he looked anachronistically modern, with a blond bob that inspired a catty story in the London *Evening Standard* about shipments of hair gel to the location in Dublin (there wasn't enough of pre-war Liverpool left to shoot there).

This unglamorous evocation of his theatrical beginnings fired him up to go back to the stage with a long-held ambition. After one or two forays as a director, he wanted to flex his controlling muscles again. Ruby's one-woman show had been really a matter of editing.

Rickman wanted to join the grown-ups and direct a proper drama, specifically Sharman Macdonald's *The Winter Guest* – a project that had been thwarted by the failure of his Riverside bid. Even so, for someone who gives the impression of being the epitome of self-control, he was still oddly uncertain about his own capabilities. 'When he wasn't sure if he could do *The Winter Guest*, he asked me to look at it with a view to me doing it,' says Richard Wilson. 'And while he was directing it, he said to me, "Your name is mentioned often."

'But you always felt Alan should become a director – I'm surprised it took him so long. Alan is always being sought after for his advice. He gives it freely. I have asked him things too; he is a sort of guru.

'He does go along to an enormous number of productions. He's very supportive of friends who haven't worked for a while, giving encouragement to them during bad spells. Now he's a movie star, it doesn't prevent him going to Fringe shows. And there's no reason why it should.

'My feeling is he would want to do both: act and direct. It's nice to be able to think about your role and forget everyone else as an actor, because directing is tough. But I would be surprised if he ever left the theatre.'

For a Fringe salary of less than £200 a week, Rickman premièred *The Winter Guest* at West Yorkshire Playhouse in January 1995. A co-production with London's fashionable Almeida Theatre, it starred Emma Thompson's actress mother Phyllida Law. The play had come about through conversations between Alan and his old *Les Liaisons* co-star Lindsay Duncan. Back in the late 80s, Lindsay would visit her mother, a widow who had become seriously ill with Alzheimer's disease, in a seaside town on the west coast of

Scotland. Not that it was all gloom and doom: when they got together, there was much laughter and mutual comfort. From Duncan's stories, Rickman gradually realised there was the genesis of a mother–daughter play in this; and who better than his old discovery to depict that most intense of all family relationships? Poignantly, Duncan's mother, to whom the film was dedicated, died while Sharman was writing the play whose very title referred to winter's most reliable visitor: Death.

At Leeds, the *Guardian*'s Michael Billington called it 'a haunting, elliptical play about unresolved lives, beautifully directed by Alan Rickman'. Alastair Macaulay of the *Financial Times* thought 'Rickman shows considerable skill as a director, not least in pacing. Nothing rings false'.

Charles Spencer in the *Daily Telegraph* felt: 'Macdonald's great gift is the ability to persuade an audience that it isn't watching a play but rather the random, remarkable flow of life itself . . . beautifully drawn characters have come to seem like familiar friends by the end of Alan Rickman's superbly acted production.'

The design was so effective at creating an icy seaside-town setting on the West Coast of Scotland that it took me back to marrow-freezing childhood holidays on bleak pebbly beaches in Montrose . . . as Mark Twain said of a summer in San Francisco, 'the coldest winter I ever spent'. Rickman and his designer Robin Don communicated wordlessly by sending each other sketches.

When it opened in London two months later in March, my *Daily Express* review praised 'the beautifully fluid production that dips in and out of four different couples' lives in an almost cinematic way'. Jack Tinker in the *Daily Mail* wrote: 'Alan Rickman directs with an unerring sense of place and occasion . . . An evening of magnetic and haunting charm.' And Clive Hirshhorn of the *Sunday Express* called 'this nostalgic tone poem . . . an unflashy little gem'.

Benedict Nightingale's *Times* review was equally impressed: 'This is a funny, touching, rather beautiful play: in the most literal sense, a haunting piece of writing.' Yes, we were all beautifully spooked and transported.

Poor Rickman then sat and waited for the directing offers to pour in, as opposed to the acting offers that must have given his postman Repetitive Strain Injury from the weight of the scripts. 'We were having lunch at my usual table at the Café Pelican in St Martin's Lane and Alan was moaning that no one had asked him to direct again after *The Winter Guest*,' remembers Peter Barnes. 'I said, "Alan, don't you realise that people have pigeon-holed you as an actor? They want to see you in front of the camera, not behind it!"' Barnes adds, with some sympathy, 'It's very difficult for actors to become directors; I can think of only three or four who have pulled it off in the past.' Yet he can see only too clearly why Rickman longs to do more directing in order to be in greater control of his career. 'As an actor, you can only do what you're offered. And one of the big dilemmas for any actor working in the movies is, do you actually make every film that's offered to you if you're free and the script doesn't actually offend you, or do you select the scripts?' says Peter. 'Both decisions bring with them certain drawbacks: either you become a hack or, if you select, there are great gaps in your career. And there's never any guarantee that a film is going to be good; you are in the hands of the director and the cast and a script that may seem good but which goes down the tubes suddenly. The problem is that you might have good instincts about a script, but there's an awful long gap between the written word and the realisation on screen. Alan is intuitively good at selecting, but no one ever knows how things will work out. It's a dilemma for intelligent actors.'

'If Alan wanted to direct more, he could,' insists Adrian Noble. 'I don't think he's pining to be a director at all.' And he recalls his 1985 RSC production of *As You Like It*, with Alan so perfectly cast as the Forest of Arden's dandified drop-out Jaques. 'You can't be a Jaques type as a director, you have got to be Duke Senior. You have to say "We have to leave the forest today." You don't dally with being a director.'

Perhaps, then, there really is a hint of Jaques the intellectual dilettante about Alan Rickman. He finds it hard to stay in one place for long: he once told the journalist Valerie Grove in *Harpers & Queen* magazine that he liked to present 'a moving target'. Hence all the obsessive travel, never happier than when on trains and boats and planes, from one film location to another.

'Alan has a terrific visual sense; he gets cross about designs sometimes. He endlessly goes on about design not happening till rehearsals begin,' adds Noble. 'In fact that happened with our design for *As You Like It*, which didn't materialise until six weeks after rehearsals started. And it was awful.

'He is a fantastic collaborator: he has a peculiar blend of terrific analytical skill plus improvisational or group effort. He has a strong visual sense, and a sense of the function of theatre. But being pernickety is an actor's prerogative, of an intelligent human being. Alan is careful.'

Rickman even hoped that he could turn *The Winter Guest* into a movie, perhaps encouraged by the critical use of the word 'cinematic'. His big ambition was to direct on screen, and he had talks in Los Angeles with his old friend Niki Marvin over possible ideas.

But the general consensus on *The Winter Guest* was that this was a fragile tone poem unsuited to the wide sweep of cinema. That didn't stop him from directing a film version in late 1996, however, with Phyllida Law and Emma Thompson.

He certainly loved the change of pace in directing on stage. 'He has a wicked sense of humour, and he had a brilliant relationship with the younger members of cast,' says an Almeida Theatre worker. 'He behaves like a born father; I'm surprised he hasn't got children of his own. But he's not into small talk. He's not frightening exactly, though he could be. He knows exactly what he wants.

'When I first saw him, I was surprised that he hadn't done anything about his teeth . . . But so many women are fascinated by him, my mother included.'

Directing *The Winter Guest* was an obvious move, given his Riverside ambitions to spread the scope of his talent. He told Michael Owen in the London *Evening Standard* on 10 March 1995: 'It's been like bringing the two disciplines of art school and drama school – which were both my background – together for the first time. A complete pleasure, until you come to that moment when, as it should be, the play passes into the hands of the actors. Then I feel a bit of an intruder, the guy with the coffee cup who keeps interfering.'

'It was a very important thing for him – even more than winning the BAFTA awards,' says Stephen Poliakoff.

When producer Niki Marvin's film *The Shawshank Redemption* was nominated for eight awards in the 1995 Oscars, her mother Blanche asked Alan whether he was going to escort Niki to the ceremony in Los Angeles. He smiled but politely declined: 'I'll go when it's my Oscar,' he said with some determination.

The pull of acting, however, was still too strong. Emma Thompson had just finished a screenplay for Jane Austen's *Sense And Sensibility*, commissioned four years earlier after the film producer Lindsay Doran had seen a comedy sketch about two sexually unawakened Victorian ladies from Emma's BBC TV series *Thompson*. At the time, Doran was working with Emma and her then husband Kenneth Branagh on the latter's film noir *Dead Again*.

It just so happened that Rickman had made another interesting little film noir called *Murder, Obliquely* for a 1993 American TV anthology under the series title of *Fallen Angels*. The play was eventually shown on British television's BBC2 in 1995.

One of the producers of *Murder, Obliquely* was Lindsay Doran; and the executive producer was the veteran Sydney Pollack. In a passably languid American accent, Rickman had played the part of the wealthy and enigmatic Dwight Billings, over whom Laura Dern's heroine nearly lost her reason. Despite the knowing voice-over and the retro costumes, this stylish exercise was just the right side of camp; and Rickman also gave it a weird kind of rumpled integrity. He looked like a human being, not an idealised eligible bachelor with a dark secret.

There was a hint of Scott Fitzgerald's *The Last Tycoon* about the melancholy anti-hero of Cornell Woolrich's short story, set in the 40s (though, as usual, Alan Rickman's hair lived in a different decade).

Cleverly, the role added a sinister overlay to the familiar Rickman quality of sexual danger. There is a moment when the light hits Rickman's left eye (the right one is coyly hidden behind a door), giving it a translucent, X-ray quality. Only then does it suddenly seem feasible that this likeable, vulnerable man, who has been valiantly trying to piece together the fragments of his heart, might have murdered the bosomy trollop who broke it. And who called him Billie, to add insult to injury. The puckered lips, the tight smile, the abject eyes of a man who is a prisoner to jealousy . . . he plays, with some subtlety, a pitiable victim turned aggressor. There is a sting in this tale.

And you realise he might just be asking Laura Dern to marry him at long last, after she's given him more shameless encouragement than is strictly decent in a good girl, in order to provide himself with an alibi. Or just to kill her too, having acquired a taste for it. Even his butler Luther was slightly creepy.

For their next project, Doran and Pollack wanted the same 'brooding romanticism' that they had also seen him deliver in *Truly Madly Deeply*.

Sense And Sensibility controversially cast Alan Rickman as a doormat: the chivalrous, kindly and thoughtful middle-aged Colonel Brandon. It was dangerously close to playing a nonentity. Rickman was there to add gravitas to a cast led by Hugh Grant again, Thompson herself, rent-a-beau actor Greg Wise and newcomer Kate Winslet.

Brandon is almost a feminine role in the traditional mode, in that he must sit back and possess himself in patience while he waits for Marianne, the flighty young girl of his dreams, to grow up and see sense. Eventually he gets his chance to play the hero when he leaps on his horse for a secret mission whose outcome drives the narrative along; but most of the time he's lurking discreetly in the background like the proverbial good deed in a naughty world. If he were a woman, he would be knitting and doing good works; here he stoically cleans his gun as if his life depends on it. (Very Freudian.)

To make a personality like this more than just a gentlemanly wimp represents a considerable challenge for an actor with edge; and no one has more edge than Alan Rickman.

In the novel, Brandon is a rather shadowy figure; Jane Austen's men exist only in relation to her women. In the Taiwanese director Ang Lee's film, Rickman gave Brandon the intensity of a soul in torment.

'He accepts the relationship between Marianne and Willoughby with great grace and dignity,' said Rickman later, explaining his take on the man. 'He doesn't ever assume that Marianne will return his feelings, and he behaves like a perfect gentleman even while watching the woman he loves fall in love with another man.

'Brandon carries a fair amount of mystery with him, because of a long-ago love affair that went very wrong. And he hasn't formed any close relationships since. Brandon is a very compassionate and feeling person. He becomes Marianne's anchor, allowing her to mature from a creature of many moods to a wise young woman. So my job, really, is to present a very steadfast image, the opposite of the more mercurial Willoughby.'

Steadfast on screen, steadfast in life. What the screenplay doesn't say – and Ang Lee ruthlessly cut out a melodramatic scene in which Brandon visits a fallen woman he once loved – Rickman expresses with his eloquent eyes. His face is puffy, middle-aged; at the age of 49, he's playing a man that Thompson's script says is 40 and Jane Austen described as 35. In truth, it gives him an extra dimension of vulnerability; and he immediately wins the sympathy vote.

Austen baldly described Brandon as 'the most eligible bachelor in the county ... though his face was not handsome, his countenance was sensible'. At first Rickman seems distinctly uncomfortable in passive mode as the lovesick Brandon, magnetically drawn to Marianne.

The film makes overt what the understated Austen style made covert. And the unfortunate goblin hat in outdoor scenes hardly helps: there are times when he's in danger of looking like a nineteenth-century Diddyman.

For the first time in his movie career, Rickman was having to sell simple virtue without making it sanctimonious or boring, although it was not the first time that he had played a victim. He couldn't even take refuge in the kind of scathing humour shown by the satirically-minded ghost Jamie in *Truly Madly Deeply*. And he met his directorial Waterloo in Ang Lee, who is a great believer in the dictatorship of the director (as opposed to the proletariat).

'He likes to participate in the movie-making process, does Alan,' says Stephen Poliakoff. 'He sees himself as a participant.' Alan picked holes in the direction, as is his wont. Do birds fly? Do fish swim? There were reports that Lee immediately warned Rickman not to overact (he also told Emma Thompson not to look so old and Hugh Grant not to be nerdy). And it was back to school for the entire cast as they were set 75-page essays to write on the motivation of their characters. Why I think Colonel Brandon is one of the good guys ... by Alan Rickman. Or words to that effect.

There were dark mutterings of mutiny from Rickman, the most experienced film actor of all the principals, but nevertheless he picked up Ang Lee's Best Director Golden Bear award for him at the Berlin Film Festival in February 1996. Clearly there were no hard feelings.

Yet Colonel Brandon is such an insubstantial part on the page that anyone, frankly, would succumb to the temptation to overact in order to bring him to life. Rickman duly absorbed Ang Lee's t'ai chi philosophy of less is more and settled into the rhythm of the strong-and-silent act with grace and authority.

'It's true that I asked Alan to write an essay on his character,' Ang Lee told me. 'Alan was able to bring out the tragic depth and hidden righteousness of Colonel Brandon to make him an attractive character.

'I wouldn't say that I "warned" Alan not to overact; one doesn't "warn" British actors not to overact,' he added humorously. 'Instead I encouraged him to act less and make Colonel Brandon a genuine man. Alan Rickman is a brilliant performer. His portrayal of life as an actor is maybe too good to be true to modern life, yet brilliant is brilliant.

'His voice possesses a musical quality that produces a lyrical line-delivery. He can read off a telephone book and make each entry sound important, special and attractive.

'He possesses an outstanding look. His presence is so impressive, and so unlike the character portrayed in the novel, that at first I thought casting him would be a risk,' the director admits. 'Alan, however, downplayed the inherent passive and unattractive characteristics of the character, as suggested by the novel, to make his Colonel Brandon an attractive man; in essence, he gave a real boost to Austen's character.'

Neither was Rickman's own directing experience an issue, according to Ang Lee. 'Alan's directing experience on stage has nothing to do with his performance as an actor,' he explains. 'Acting and directing aren't related. As a director, you watch people. As an actor, you are watched. Though the two may co-exist in one person, they are definitely two different, separate creatures. I only know him as an actor.'

In one of the most prolonged pieces of foreplay between an actor and the audience in the history of the cinema, it seems an age before Rickman's slow-burn Brandon makes his move and eventually gets the girl. 'He's the sort of man that everyone speaks well of, and no one remembers to talk to,' sneers Greg Wise as Brandon's spiteful rival Willoughby at one point. That's the one line which doesn't ring true with this casting: on the contrary, Rickman's Brandon has far too much presence to be ignored.

Brandon's air of mystery is second nature to Rickman; and he can also make the memory of grief still seem raw. 'As Alan puts it,' wrote Emma Thompson in *Sense & Sensibility: The Diaries* (published by Bloomsbury) on the making of the film, 'it's about a man thawing out after having been in a fridge for twenty years. The movement of blood and warmth back into unaccustomed veins is extremely painful.'

Nevertheless, there are still flashes of Alan's old asperity (i.e. attitude) here and there. Brandon stirs himself out of his lovesick reverie when he stares challengingly at Willoughby, with that curdled look of jealousy which Rickman does so well. There is also one early scene in which Brandon immediately endears himself to his lady love's young sister by satisfying her curiosity about the mysteries of the East Indies. In the kind of intimate gesture that is peculiar to Rickman, he leans forward and whispers sibilantly 'The air is full of spices' with one of his hot hisses. It's a variation on the technique he uses to intimidate a screen enemy: far from being coldly aloof, he's the ultimate in-your-face actor.

Rickman's on-set composure even discombobulated Emma Thompson, as her *Diaries* records. 'Sometimes Alan reminds me of the owl in Beatrix Potter's *Squirrel Nutkin*. If you took too many liberties with him, I'm sure he'd have your tail off in a trice.' Since Old Brown the owl held the impertinent rodent by the tail in order to skin him alive, that's quite a menacing role-model. You can even see a distinct physical resemblance to Rickman in Potter's illustration of Old Brown's narrow amber eyes.

It was a remarkably apt analogy. She drew it after a sopping-wet Greg Wise had 'bounded up to Alan and asked, with all his usual ebullience, how he was. Long pause, as Alan surveyed him through half-closed eyes from beneath a huge golfing umbrella. Then, "I'm dry." ' Indeed, 'dry' just about sums him up.

Thompson's description of her own character Elinor – 'a witty, Byronic control-freak' – in fact fits Alan exactly. If you want romantic gravity, you reach for Rickman. As Emma gushed in a BBC2 documentary *Sense And Sensibility: Behind The Scenes*, 'Colonel Brandon is the man of all our dreams: the wounded older man who's a river of compassion and love and strength and honour and decency.' For Ang Lee, 'Colonel Brandon was the only solid man, the real man in the movie.'

Thompson's *Diaries* recalls how she and Alan talked seriously about the rigours of theatre over lunch in his trailer: 'He was as much put off by two years in *Les Liaisons* as I was by fifteen months in *Me And My Girl*.'

But much of the time on set, he earned his keep as the king of the wry one-liners. When Thompson's co-star Kate Winslet complained, 'Oh God, my knickers have gone up my arse,' Alan's reply was: 'Ah: feminine mystique again.'

ET was consequently much impressed by Rickman's mature mixture of gallantry and irony. 'He was splendid, charming and virile . . . (At) the party on Saturday, Alan nearly killed me, whirling me about the place.' (As with many big men, he doesn't always realise his own size and strength.)

'Alan's very moving,' she later recorded. 'He's played Machiavellian types so effectively that it's a thrill to see him expose the extraordinary sweetness in his nature. Sad, vulnerable but weighty presence. Brandon is the real hero of this piece, but he has to grow on the audience as he grows on Marianne . . . Finish scene with Alan. Me: Oh! I've just ovulated. Alan (long pause): Thank you for that.' She marvelled later about how 'Alan manages to bring such a depth of pain' to what is, in effect, the plot of a penny dreadful.

But the old tartness, thank God, was never far away. It's a relief, in the middle of all these eulogies, to read his reaction to a trespassing moggie.

'Very nice lady served us drinks in hotel and was followed in by a cat,' Emma's journal chronicled. 'We all crooned at it. Alan to cat (very low and meaning it) "Fuck off." The nice lady didn't turn a hair. The cat looked slightly embarrassed but stayed.' Perhaps he was under strain from being so nice all the time . . .

The chance to play against type was a huge relief for Rickman. *Sense And Sensibility* also reunited him with an old mate, the actress Harriet Walter, who was on brilliantly malignant form as the snobbish Fanny Dashwood, the nearest that Jane Austen got to a traditional wicked step-sister.

After Brandon's nuptials to Marianne, he follows the custom of throwing a handful of coins in the air. One hits the frightful Fanny, and the film ends with a glimpse of her backwards collapse into a bush, a piece of comic business she and Rickman invented.

'We are the envy of other countries because we have the identification with the theatre. It's a heartbeat. In America they really envy it. And for me, Alan is one of the forces of gravity in theatre,' says Harriet.

'It's not to do with throwing a lot of parties. He had that effect on people long before he was famous. He has high standards and he takes you seriously – you feel elevated, you think that someone out there is looking out for you. He manages to keep that interest in other people going.

'You endow people like this with power, but of course you need to be critical yourself. It's up to you to be grown-up. I don't always agree with him, but we are aiming at the same centre. He has pretty tough standards, and I might rebel for a day or two.

'But he's a very good listener. He takes you seriously, you feel encouraged. That's why we have kept up as friends for so long.'

Movie-making is a schizophrenia-inducing business, however, and Colonel Brandon remains one of Alan Rickman's least interesting parts even though he did his damnedest with it. He went straight from playing the nice guy to portraying that practitioner of the political black arts, Eamon de Valera, the man who is popularly supposed to have ordered the assassination on a lonely country road of one of the great Irish heroes. The career of Eamon de Valera forms a direct trajectory to the career of the current Sinn Fein president, Gerry Adams.

13. ROCKET TO THE MOON

By 1995, Rickman's old friend Peter Barnes was telling me: 'Alan is now on a rocket to the moon – we are just waving to him from the launch pad. He has risen into the stratosphere.'

And talking of space-travel, the role of Dr Who could have been tailor-made for Rickman. Even as late as early 1996, there were recurring rumours that Steven Spielberg still wanted him for the part. Mind you, they said the same thing about Eric Idle.

The truth is that Alan Rickman's name is flung into the ring whenever a producer wants to add tone to his project. It's rather like the story of the drama critic who, when asked why his newspaper employed someone to write play-reviews, replied: 'To add tone to the paper.'

In fact the American enthusiasm for making a television movie about the eccentric British hero with two hearts, thirteen lives and a virginal girl companion came from Philip Segal, a self-confessed Dr Who nut and Steven Spielberg's head of production at his former company Amblin. Eventually Paul McGann assumed the Einstein hairstyle and Regency dress sense of the latest Time Lord incarnation in 1996.

On the advice of his agent, Rickman is wary of cutting himself down to size for the small screen: it seems a retrograde step. He did, however, make two exceptions for American television. The production values of Murder, Obliquely had been particularly high; and Rasputin was premièred on American television in March 1996, although its makers Home Box Office also hoped the film would have a theatrical release in the cinema when they sold the distribution rights. So far as British television is concerned, however, Rickman remains aloof, much to the chagrin of Jonathan Powell and other moguls at home. He was even suggested for the new incarnation of the dandified John Steed in a remake of the ultimate secret-agent spoof, The Avengers, but bowler hats don't exactly become him. As his former co-star Sheridan Fitzgerald says, 'The face is its own statement.' In retrospect, it was just as well that he didn't play John Steed; despite Ralph Fiennes in the role, the big-screen version of The Avengers was a flop.

'I had the impression Alan won't do television at the moment because his agent thinks he should be available for film,' says the playwright Dusty Hughes. To Dusty, this is a shame.

'Maybe it's because I'm writing more and more for TV these days. But the situation is changing: the status of TV is going up in America, with series like *ER*. Quentin Tarantino directed one episode: there's much more kudos about television out there now.

'I absolutely adore the theatre, have done since I was fourteen. Alan is the same. I think he'll always do theatre and also directing, if he can: he loves it all. I think he wants to direct films.

'But one of the dangers with people who do stop being actors pure and simple is that they might completely stop acting one day.'

With Rickman in so much demand, there seems little chance of that. There's so much he has not done that one suspects the best is still to come. His Hamlet and Antony were very belated assaults upon the great Shakespearian roles, though he did briefly consider taking the offer of Oberon, king of the fairies, in a film version of *A Midsummer Night's Dream*.

Just as he was never one of life's Romeos, so he would not make an ideal Henry V. On the other hand, he would surely make a magnificent Macbeth; and, of course, Prospero. His maverick talent is best suited to slightly off-centre parts.

The real truth is that this fascinating oddity is a natural Iago, the second-in-command who steals the limelight from Othello. Or a Cassius, upstaging Brutus. He is the hidden agenda who surprises us all, who emerges from the shadows. There is a lot of sense in what Peter Barnes says about villains being good stand-bys if you want a long career, a canny piece of advice that seems even cannier after Alan's doomed attempt at playing ageing heroism in the National Theatre's *Antony and Cleopatra* in 1998. But Dusty Hughes argues: 'He can do the villains standing on his head – and probably yours too. Knowing Alan, he'll always try to do the things that aren't easy.'

The year 1995 was another exceptionally busy year for Rickman. He went straight from the *Sense And Sensibility* set to Dublin for director Neil Jordan's new picture *Michael Collins*, shot that summer.

Liam Neeson played the martyred Republican hero Michael Collins, 'The Big Fella', with Rickman cast as his calculating adversary Eamon de Valera. At least, that's the simplistic view.

Rickman reverted to type, yet he still retains that ability to startle us out of our seats.

The myth of Collins is that he was the bluffly heroic reincarnation of Finn MacCool, Cuchulain and other legendary Irish supermales. The Big Fella was a shrewd manipulator of men, with the devious silver tongue of an Irish Lloyd George. And Collins came up against that other Celtic smoothie when he entered into negotiations with Lloyd George over the establishment of the Irish Free State.

Wily and ruthless though Collins certainly was, he cultivated a hail-fellow-well-met persona that made him an immensely popular folk-hero.

By comparison, Eamon de Valera seemed a cold, charismatically-challenged figure; but Alan Rickman was determined to find the latent passions in this rather clinical, fastidious character. De Valera was a paradox, not only in having dual nationality – he had a Spanish-American father and an Irish mother – but in being an almost frigid intellectual among the poets and playwrights of the early republican leaders. He was a mathematician with ecclesiastical ambitions who involved himself in the passions of a nationalist uprising. He even dressed like a clergyman, with his long coat and hat. His lengthy tenure of office had as much to do with the clerical control of Ireland as the very priests themselves: he became the church-in-state. Historically, he was the Robespierre and Collins the Danton of Ireland. De Valera escaped the firing-squad after being condemned to death for taking part in the Easter Uprising; the British reprieved him, for devious reasons that have never been fully explored. He became the spokesman for the republican movement, just as Gerry Adams is today. De Valera made a speciality of touring America, whipping up support, holding out the fund-raising begging-bowl and meeting statesmen. Here, then, was an inscrutable strategist with a curiously contemporary appeal who cloaked himself in mystery; Rickman was in his element.

Casting director Susie Figgis had already worked with Rickman on *An Awfully Big Adventure* and was later to cast him as Severus Snape in the *Harry Potter* films. 'The indisputable thing about Alan Rickman is that he has strength. You notice him if he walks into a room: that's what makes him a leading actor,' she says.

'I cast him in *Michael Collins* because we needed someone who had real weight, an intelligent political figure. He has to still a crowd of 2,000 people: Alan was the man to do it, without shouting.

'He's a big fish in a rather pathetic little British film pond. I can remember him in *Les Liaisons*; he's one of only five and a half people or so in this country who can get a film on the road to finance . . . They are what's known as The Money.

'Alan's certainly not the lavender thespian type. He went through a stage of not wanting to be a smooth villain, anyway. He brings intelligence to the role.

'As de Valera, he was concerned to make the man multi-dimensional with a point of view. He's very astute that the character should be brought forward. The first script was rather underwritten. He is the villain of the piece, but Alan would be anxious to play him not as a villain but as de Valera would have seen himself. With his own passionate beliefs and delusions.

'His height helped too: de Valera was six foot two in real life. He was the really Big Fella of the two. Although he and Collins were originally brothers-in-arms, the main theory is that de Valera shafted him.'

In 1922, during the Irish Civil War, Collins was ambushed by waiting gunmen on a country road eighteen miles outside Cork. Some think the British ordered the killing; but the finger of suspicion still points at de Valera. With his ascetic, bony face and aquiline nose, Rickman even looked like the man.

As for the role of Rasputin that followed, what took such an ideal candidate for the Siberian Holy Devil so long? A delay by America's Home Box Office in getting the wherewithal together. Yet from Mesmer to Rasputin was an obvious progression: both were highly charismatic, much demonised and much misunderstood characters who exercised an extraordinary power over women. By November 1995, Rickman was knee-deep in snow on location in St Petersburg. Greta Scacchi took the role of the Tsarina Alexandra, whose fanatical beliefs in Rasputin's mystical powers contributed to the fall of Russia's Imperial family. Ian McKellen was rather astutely cast as the ill-starred last Tsar, with Uli Edel of Tyson fame directing a production bolstered up by fine British character actors.

The role of Rasputin was just the sort of part Rickman had been avoiding for years, but there are times when it is necessary to give in gracefully to one's destiny. It was too good to miss.

Most people's hazy notion of the Mad Monk is of a long-haired, heavily-bearded orgiast with the most sinister powers of persuasion

– in short, the Charles Manson of his day. Photographs show an altogether more sensitive-looking individual garbed in the robes of a wandering holy man, of the dubious kind that were two-a-penny in Imperialist Russia.

Rasputin had become a member of the Khlisti, a strange, sex-based religious sect whose name means 'whippers' or 'flagellants' in Russian. Their leader kept a harem of thirteen women, whom he liked to pleasure *en masse*. As there are so many Greek words in the Russian vocabulary, it is possible that the Khlisti were also millenarians who believed Jesus Christ would return to earth and reign for a thousand years in the midst of his saints. Whatever, Rasputin certainly had a Christ-complex, strongly reflected in Peter Pruce's screenplay and Alan Rickman's impassioned performance.

Obscurantism reigned at all levels in the benighted society of turn-of-the-century Russia, particularly among the ruling Romanovs who were in-bred and not very intelligent. There was every opportunity to make a glorious career out of charlatanism.

The monk Rasputin was a self-styled mystic whose influence was based on his personal magnetism and alleged power as a healer; he had alleviated the sufferings of the haemophiliac Tsarevitch, the Crown Prince Alexei, hence the royal favour. Shades of Mesmer, indeed. Rasputin's drunkenness, debauchery – said by their enemies to have involved the Tsarina herself – and shameless nepotism in promoting friends to high office produced more than the usual crop of foes. Some even convinced themselves that he and the Tsarina acted as secret agents for the Germans in the First World War, such were the hysterical stories surrounding him.

Rickman approached the role with his usual analytical zeal, very much concerned to be more than just a pair of mad staring eyes and a matted beard. Rasputin is too complex, too controversial, indeed too poignant an historical figure to be played – in the style of the Sheriff of Nottingham – as a manic cartoon. Tempting though it must be. The murder of Grigori Efimovich Rasputin in peculiarly horrible circumstances by a group of noblemen was taken as a fatal omen, since he himself had made the prophecy: 'If I die, the Emperor will soon after lose his Crown.' And so it proved. Moreover, Rasputin's legend was considerably enhanced by the fact that it took him an inordinately long time to die. He survived a large dose of cyanide before being buggered, then shot and slashed to death. Since his curse came true with the subsequent assassination of the royal family in a cellar, Rasputin could be said to have possessed an almost vampire-like vitality. Alan Rickman is one of the few actors who can suggest that kind of power from beyond the grave without resorting to the risible excesses of Hammer Horror. Rickman's performance as Rasputin makes one long for his eagerly-awaited Aleister Crowley – if writer Snoo Wilson can ever get the go-ahead to make the film. And Rasputin also won him three Best Actor awards: an Emmy in 1996 and a Golden Globe and a SAG Award in 1997.

The film opens in a Siberian forest in 1991, where the bones of the Romanovs are being disinterred. The Crown Prince Alexei is the narrator, apparently speaking from the tomb. 'He was my saviour, my wizard. Father Grigori was magic,' pipes the boy.

Pruce's script concentrates on the mystical side of Rasputin's story, more or less ignoring the complexities of the political dimension. Rickman responds with an old-fashioned star perform- ance that keeps Rasputin's mystique intact. There is no fashionable deconstruction here to strip away the myths, just Rickman hypnotising the camera, and most of the cast, with his strange, kohl-rimmed, Siamese-cat eyes.

He is first glimpsed on the snowy steppes of the Siberian lowlands, pulling a cart as if he were Bertolt Brecht's Mother Courage – as ambiguous a figure as Rasputin in her way.

Rickman looks authentically Asiatic. He is whipped by jeering horsemen who say that he has lost his soothsaying gift, but he doesn't crouch down like a beaten dog for long.

For Rasputin has attitude. Hearing a heavenly sound, he raises his arms to the skies in a self-consciously messianic way. The 'felonious monk', as Variety magazine wittily called him, has the striking, silvery pallor of a consumptive, or an elegantly wasted rock star with too much Gothic makeup. With his mossy brown beard and moustache, Rickman lurks under more facial hair than a hobbit, but those burning orbs and hawkish nose make him instantly recognisable.

As usual, he refused to wear a wig; his blond mop was darkened and bobbed in a shorter, scruffier style than the Yogi-like Rasputin of history. In truth, Rickman's Rasputin looked rather like a hot-headed revolutionary on a bad-hair day – an effect heightened by the Maoist-style collarless jackets of Russian tradition. It was an inspired image for the religious and political ferment of the period.

In her book about her father, Maria Rasputin wrote of Grigori's 'potent animal magnetism . . . an almost aphrodisiac aura'. Edel's film shows remarkable restraint in the sex-scenes; instead, it's the man's alluring personality that Rickman projects. He begins by spiritually seducing Peter Jeffrey's Bishop, who falls down and worships this tatterdemalion scarecrow from nowhere.

All the great risk-taking actors can give florid performances that verge on the vulgar. Sometimes Rickman's thick Russian accent is comic, particularly when Rasputin is ingratiating himself with the ailing Alexei. The man is part mountebank, part mystic; and not quite in control of his gift. The oily richness of his voice luxuriates in such lush lines as 'her voice blooms like a kiss in my ear'. He's talking of the Virgin Mary at the time, but it could, of course, be any woman. He has an hypnotic effect upon Greta Scacchi's Tsarina at their very first meeting. It is a soft-focus, discreet attraction that provides a marked contrast to the gross peasant appetites he displays elsewhere. If Rasputin really did entice the Tsarina into ways of wickedness, the director and screenwriter are certainly not going to tell us about them.

Rickman's Rasputin is no common lecher; there is a strangely playful, childlike innocence about his greedy sensuality. The character feels helplessly dominated by his senses, something with which the highly sexed Rickman strongly identified and which attracted him to the role in the first place. 'God blast desire! The lust of my flesh has tormented me,' shouts a drunken Rasputin as he goes wenching late at night. It's as if he is possessed by a demon of lust. But he can't resist a dangerous flirtation with the royal princesses, asking them: 'What do you know about love?' as they walk in the grounds of the palace.

There is a naïvety as well as a native cunning in this holy devil. 'The soul may belong to God, the flesh belongs to us,' he announces to the Romanovs over dinner.

He slurps his soup, handles the potatoes and starts to tell such a dirty-schoolboy story about two homosexual monks that he is expelled from the table by Ian McKellen's shocked Tsar, who appears to have led a very sheltered life of monogamous marital bliss. For if Rasputin is depicted as the innocent victim of destiny, so too are the Romanovs.

'I didn't choose to be a holy papa . . . it frightens me too,' explains Rasputin as if he were a guileless child visited by God, an unworthy vessel into which is poured a divine power. It is his sheer force of will that appears to send Alexei's illness into remission, though David Warner's royal doctor explains in utter exasperation that the rogue is simply slowing down the flow of blood by hypnotising the boy.

We have been kept waiting a long time for evidence of Rasputin's notorious orgiastic endeavours, which begin halfway through the film when he is treated as a marriage-guidance counsellor by a comely woman whose husband is failing in his marital duty. Rasputin woos her with honeyed words, but one never feels that the man is cynically faking his ardour. Rickman's performance has the fervour of one who genuinely wishes to make a convert to the doctrine of free love.

'The greatest gift in the world is love . . . only then can we enter the gates of heaven. The greatest sin of pride is chastity. Before we repent, we have to sin,' he tells her throatily, his voice thick with desire.

He takes her in his arms and demands she kisses him, then indulges in an orgy of china-smashing to show off his passionate Russian temperament. 'I would cut these wrists if it would give you a single moment of happiness. Think of God, my angel . . . he gave us this pleasure.'

He lifts up her long skirts and whispers to her. Moments later, he's kissing her neck on the bed. 'God is love.' He fumbles at his lower clothing and two prurient gentlemen in the building opposite raise their binoculars to catch sight of her legs wrapped round Rasputin's neck. The next scene shows him besieged in his apartment by respectable ladies who all want to 'come' closer to God . . . the rest is left to our imagination. As ever, Rickman is flirting most of all with the camera . . . a gloriously old-fashioned seducer who understands the art of dalliance and knows how to take his time. No wonder so many women are intrigued by him.

He goes further in a restaurant scene, where he is dancing wildly in a red shirt like a revolutionary who has unexpectedly won the election. Rasputin is as drunk as a skunk; yet Rickman skips lightly and deftly in his black boots, Fred Astaire at last.

Here is the latent exhibitionism that is integral to the passive-aggressive syndrome. He sees the sex-starved woman whom he serviced so expertly and kisses her violently in front of her astounded husband. Rasputin is asked to leave (without the patronage of the Romanovs, he would have been challenged to a duel) and he roars, 'The Empress kisses my hand ... I'm her saviour and angel.'

The Tsarina's handsome young nephew Prince Feliks Feliksovich Yussupov rises angrily to his feet in the restaurant. Rasputin puts his face close to his and says provocatively, 'Very pretty ... but I prefer women.' Maria Rasputin's highly coloured account of her father's rise and fall portrays the married Feliks as an aggressive homosexual who is mortified by Rasputin's rejection of his advances. There is no such suggestion here in this sanitised account, but Feliks is to prove Rasputin's Nemesis none the less.

'I'm a great man,' shouts Rasputin, climbing on a table and exposing himself in order to prove it. Not that we actually see the Rickman genitals – the camera cuts away just as Rickman is loosening his trouser-band.

Rickman is hypnotising the viewer all the time with Rasputin's wild mood-swings. He hurls furniture around, rips at his clothes in a frenzy as if tormented by what orthodox Jews call a dybbuk. 'We will all drown in blood ... oceans of tears ... death is behind me,' he shouts at Ian McKellen's decent, mild-mannered, permanently perplexed Tsar. 'Why was I chosen? I don't know, but I am Russia. I have your pain.' He's a cross between a manic-depressive Jesus Christ and that wild New Testament drop-out, John the Baptist. Rivetting. And yet more momentous forces are at work; the heir to the Austrian Empire is assassinated by a Serb at Sarajevo, and one wonders just how much Rasputin is involved in the gunning down of the Russian Prime Minister Stolypin at the opera (apart from that, how did you enjoy the show, Mrs Stolypin?) 'Death was behind him, just as Father Grigori said,' relates Crown Prince Alexei with grisly relish.

Rasputin has predicted both the First World War and the Russian Revolution, but he is demonised by the popular pamphlets for causing the deaths of ill-armed Russians facing the might of the Prussian machine-guns. He is the scapegoat that everyone needs now that the superstitious Tsarina's support is falling away with the return of Alexei's chronic haemophilia. Even Rasputin is beset by self-doubt: 'The Holy Mother won't answer my prayers ... she has turned her back on me.'

The final trap is laid for Rasputin, summoned to heal Feliks' sickly wife. Rickman's pallor is ghastly. Rasputin's excesses have caught up with him. He registers a flicker of suspicion, but he's so arrogant that he regards himself as impregnable. A man who can't control his appetites, he greedily eats the cyanide cakes that Feliks has prepared for him. Yet they have no effect and the indestructible Rasputin grows drunker by the minute as a barrel organ cranks out a popular war-time song: 'Goodbyeee . . . don't cryeee . . .' Even when Feliks shoots him in the chest, he is still hypnotised by Rasputin's closed eyelids until a hand suddenly shoots out to clamp Feliks' neck in a stranglehold. The legend seems to be true: Rasputin is the vampire they can't kill.

The film makes no attempt to dispel the myths. In reality, Feliks was probably a lousy shot, and Rasputin was heavily padded by his clothing and his sheer bulk. But Rickman's interpretation, while never sentimental, gives itself over to romantic myth-making on an epic scale. We are invited to suspend our incredulity. Or, maybe, it is simply Rasputin's sexy electricity that survives, the sheer force of character that can make one feel a long-dead person's presence in a room.

He escapes across the snow and the palace guards shoot at him. Finally a bullet from Feliks finishes him off as he scales the gates, staring up at the sky before he slithers down and dies. He seems to be offering up his soul to the moon.

Students of the Russian Revolution will find the film a fatuous piece of highly partial history, but it's Rickman's show. Again. Rasputin's body is thrown in the River Neva, but he bequeathes a poisoned legacy. He has left the Tsarina a letter with a premonition of his own death and a warning of worse to come: 'You will all be killed by the Russian people.'

As if by thought-transference, the Tsar finds a mystique within himself that awes the soldiers who have come to arrest him as an enemy of the people. He and his family last for another eighteen months after the death of 'Father Grigori' before they are shot in a cellar; yet, Alexei appears to survive the mayhem. 'Sometimes we have to believe in magic,' says the voice of this boy narrator. A member of the execution squad lifts a pistol as if to finish him off; the film tells us that Alexei's remains have never been recovered. Did he escape with a charmed life like his mentor Rasputin? The latter's influence lingers tantalisingly on.

Rickman may have complained that the final editing of *Mesmer* made the character too enigmatic, but all his own instincts conspire to create a mystery around the men he plays. Rickman's Rasputin took his secrets to the grave, an endlessly fascinating riddle.

14. THE BLEAK MID-WINTER

After finishing *Rasputin*, Alan needed a rest from the business, even though his three awards for *Rasputin* were to make him more in demand than ever. In his case, there were very personal reasons for dropping out of circulation for a while: his octogenarian mother had been unwell since 1995, so he began to spend more time in London.

Just before making *Rasputin* he had also fitted in a blink-and-you've-missed-him performance in *Lumière and Company*, a short documentary to mark the centennial of those pioneering film-makers the Lumière Brothers, with François Mitterand, Isabelle Huppert and Liam Neeson among the cast and David Lynch and Spike Lee among the directors. At the beginning of 1996, he told friends that he was taking a long-delayed break for a few months before beginning work on the film of *The Winter Guest*. When Huppert came over from Paris to prepare for her role in Schiller's *Mary Stuart* at London's National Theatre, Rickman acted as escort and squired her round town, throwing parties to introduce her to people. Back in 1993, when his consortium made its bid for Riverside, he was to have played opposite Huppert in Strindberg's *Miss Julie*, a much-postponed pet project.

While he was beginning pre-production work on the film version of *The Winter Guest*, Margaret Rickman became increasingly poorly. Alan was acutely aware that his peripatetic career had kept them apart for long periods. Later, while ostensibly talking about *The Winter Guest*'s central mother-daughter relationship, he was to give away clues to that difficult time in his life: 'It's a moment that comes to many of us, that point when the roles switch and the child must become the parent. You either accept the responsibility and look after your parents or you don't.'

When Emma Thompson came on board to play her own mother's daughter in the film, Rickman had signed the Oscar-winner who would guarantee the finances. As he explained to the *Los Angeles Times* in 1997, 'Whenever the film version came up, it was sort of automatically assumed that Emma would do it too. She helped finance the project,' he admitted, 'but it's also a great part for her as well as being a great gift to her mother.' Alan felt a particular affinity with Phyllida Law, who had, he pointed out, been widowed young like his own mother. Margaret had brought up four children on her own, while Phyllida raised Emma and her younger sister Sophie after the death of their father Eric Thompson. As he acknowledged, the casting of a real-life mother and daughter 'could have been a nightmare, they might have been horribly competitive or their real-life relationship might have been incredibly complicated to shake off'. But their complementary acting styles and the 'bonus' of their physical resemblance turned them into a dream-team.

Yet, in order to cast Emma, Rickman had to drop the Welsh actress Sian Thomas who had played her role on stage to great acclaim. He hated cutting Sian out of the equation, but it had to be; though he was tired of playing screen villains, Rickman was to discover the hard way that sometimes a director has to play the bad guy for the good of the film. 'It was tough for her and me and it was a difficult thing to cope with in one's head; we'll do something else [together] down the line and I just hope that somehow makes up for it,' he said.

Despite the beautiful performances, however, the film is curiously inert, at times too reminiscent of a studio-bound television play. You may find yourself wondering why there are no frosty gusts of breath issuing from the mouths of the characters, who spend much of their time talking outdoors in the frozen wastes of a Scottish mid-winter, but that was because Rickman shot the film in a string of Fife fishing villages from October to December 1996 with the art department supplying the ice and snow that hadn't arrived in real life. The frozen sea was created in the computer; what a pity they didn't muster up ice-cubes for the actors to suck to make the setting look cold enough. A location like Iceland, Rickman explained, would have been 'too cold – and you won't get the insurance to put your actors on the ice'.

By filming a story with such a wintry setting, no one could say that he made things easy on himself as a first-time director; but would we expect anything else? 'It was a great experience, but sometimes it was just awful,' Rickman admitted. As he told the *Boston Globe*, 'My friend Bob Hoskins says film-making is like being pecked to death by pigeons; I would use a more violent bird. I suppose I saw it as a challenge – why not take it on?'

Why, indeed? In early 1997, while he was in the middle of editing *The Winter Guest*, Margaret Rickman died. 'He got very in on himself in that period when his mother died; he was very close to her,' recalls Peter Barnes. 'The film didn't help; that subject matter is not a barrel of laughs at the best of times.' Even Alan himself admitted that for him, the winter guest of the title was 'a moment in the life of everyone when you have to grow up quickly'. It certainly was the ultimate maturing experience, that moment when the middle-aged man finally became an orphan and lost the one person who had always continued to indulge him on some level as a child. And for those who don't have their own children, the sense of bereavement is even bleaker.

But Alan doesn't rant and rail and beat his breast; instead he retreats crablike into his shell (also a very manlike reaction, of course). He was determined not to allow himself to wallow in despair, either on or off screen. Yet despite changing the original tragic ending of the stage version and stubbornly describing the film as 'a hymn to life', Alan's wanly delicate directorial debut seemed mired in gloom – though without being Bergman. Some viewers felt, and audiences seemed to agree, that the film was rather precious – in the wrong sense; although it had its admirers among the critics and it won three awards (including the prestigious Golden Lion at the 1997 Venice Film Festival), the lack of narrative drive hardly set the art-house box-office on fire.

The same charge was levelled at Rickman's next two projects that same year, with Alan returning to acting for the movies *Dark Harbor* and *Judas Kiss*. Rickman justified jumping back on the performing treadmill again by saying rather defensively to the *Boston Globe*, 'Acting is not something I'll stop doing. I can't see how.' He was anxious to reassure himself, after the loss in his own life, that it was business as usual; hardly ideal circumstances under which to make fully focused choices. Yet both movies were offbeat projects that carried the adrenaline-producing element of risk to which Rickman always responded. *Dark Harbor*, he hoped, would turn out to be 'another strange love story in the vein of *The Crying Game*'. He played the husband, his first spousal role since *Close My Eyes*, in an arctic marriage that ices up even further with the arrival of a mysterious and good-looking stranger. The latter comes into the lives of a couple when they rescue him after an accident in which he nearly became roadkill. Playing the wife was Polly

Walker, star of Peter Barnes's Oscar-nominated *Enchanted April*, with newcomer Norman Reedus completing the triangle as the stranger to unsettling effect. Despite good reviews for the performances – and in particular, a role that astutely deployed the Rickman quality of tumultuous mystery – this wannabe Hitchcock was pulled from its US theatrical release and went straight to video.

From *Dark Harbor*'s location in Maine, he flew straight to Pasadena to film the quirky *Judas Kiss*, which was also pulled from theatrical release and subsequently premiered on Cinemax cable TV in 1999. Though some critics detected the influences of Pedro Almodóvar and Quentin Tarantino in the film, it was by general consensus filed under 'cult' – always a useful way of hedging bets. But it did reunite Alan with Emma Thompson for the third time, one of the reasons why he had agreed to do it. As soul-mates in socialism with the same facetious sense of humour, they had become good friends. And, in the roles of an alcoholic police detective and an FBI agent respectively, Rickman and Thompson proved to be dryly amusing in what *Variety* magazine called 'a wannabe film noir that's badly in need of a rewrite.' It gave Emma a gun-toting peach of a part, and it also cast her new partner Greg Wise, whom she had met on the set of *Sense and Sensibility*. Alan, by now permanently on the run from screen villainy, saw the chance to escape into lugubrious black comedy in this efficiently plotted but unsparkling script by a first-time writer-director who had been working as a Columbia TV stagehand until just before his metamorphosis into a would-be Raymond Chandler.

To compound the problems, Alan's old knee injury from *Die Hard* began playing up during the middle of filming *Judas Kiss* and left him in so much pain that he had to see a doctor. There was to be no let-up, though, because his next film project was due to start shooting in Memphis in February 1998. Rickman was cast as an angel with attitude in *Dogma* – the latest project from Kevin Smith, the loquacious, self-indulgent writer-director who might one day be a genius if only he allowed himself a tougher editor.

Before arriving in Memphis, however, Rickman paid a flying visit to London to deliver a speech at the National Film Theatre that attacked his old alma mater, the Royal Shakespeare Company, and conclusively showed that the old campaigner in him had not been de-fanged by celebrity success. It's difficult to think of any other actor with his international reputation who gets stuck into the politics of the British arts scene in this way, but Alan is as much a maverick as the parts he plays. He had discovered two remarkable schoolboy actors, Douglas Murphy and Sean Biggerstaff, for the cast of *The Winter Guest*, he remains heavily involved in fund-raising for his old drama school RADA and he takes his growing reputation as a mentor for young people seriously. Impulsiveness is not a quality you immediately associate with Alan, but when he feels deeply about something, as Jules Wright discovered, he doesn't hesitate to give it plenty of welly.

Word had reached Rickman of some RSC company members' unhappiness. Never having forgotten his own bad experiences there as a young actor, he called the organisation 'a factory'. 'It's all about product endlessly churned out – and not sufficiently about process,' claimed Rickman. 'They don't look after the young actors. There are a lot of people who slip through the net. People are dropping like flies.' The RSC hit back by accusing Rickman of being 'out of touch', pointing out that the RSC was 'one of the few companies actively concerned about nurturing and developing young talent'. Yet their subsequent troubles at the beginning of the 21st century – widespread opposition eventually engulfed Artistic Director Adrian Noble, leading to his decision to stand down after he had dared to make radical changes to the RSC – were to show that the prescient Rickman could claim to have had his ear to the ground two years earlier.

One of the reasons why Rickman manages to stay in touch with what's hip, why he is considered so cool by people half his age, is that he always takes care to listen to and talk to the younger generation, something he calls 'passing on the baton'. He drags friends along to see such eclectic theatrical innovators as Pina Bausch and the stand-up comic surrealist Eddie Izzard, who has since followed Alan into acting – including a much-admired West End performance in a revival of Peter Nichols' *A Day In The Death Of Joe Egg*.

'Alan is still very much in touch with the whole simplicity of the process; he stays in touch with the basic elements,' explains Peter James, who persuaded Rickman to give talks to his LAMDA students. 'Fame and money came later to him; it's always a better way for it to happen than for young actors who have it too soon. He has astonishing leadership and spokesman qualities and he has passionate views on subjects and issues: training, the subsidy of theatre, new young actors.' As the RSC found out.

Rickman went on to send himself up alongside a young cast by playing Metatron, a black-clad, spiky-haired angel or 'seraphim' without genitals – as Rickman takes pains to show Linda Fiorentino in the film – but with a hotline to God in the cosmic conspiracy-theory movie *Dogma*. Kevin Smith had written the script while he was still shooting the film that made his name: the award-winning *Clerks*. Rickman first appears in Linda Fiorentino's bedroom in a blaze of flames put out only by a fire extinguisher: 'Sweet Jesus, do you have to use the whole can?' he screeched. There are those – particularly the self-styled Rickmaniacs on one of Alan's many websites – who argue that he overdid the black eyeliner and sooty hair, which were to be revisited later in Harry Potter. But he got forgiven when this crotchety angel discovered his inner cherub and walked on water to comfort Fiorentino in a wonderful example of Rickman's ability to switch from sour to sweet instantaneously. As *Mesmer* had revealed, films are collaborative experiences; the gourmandising side of Metatron, who demonstrated his superhuman powers by whisking everyone to a ritzy restaurant, was suggested by the bon viveur in Rickman.

Rickman followed up *Dogma* with more self-mockery in the film *Galaxy Quest* by creating the perfect parody of a self-obsessive Shakespearean actor reaching his career nadir by playing an alien in a long-running sci-fi series and then getting so locked into that character that a bunch of genuine visiting aliens mistook him for the real thing. If he had been a more limited actor, it could be said that he risked cannibalising himself – as Mike Newell's so-called 'over-the-hill' cast were sometimes in danger of doing on *An Awfully Big Adventure*. Interestingly, *Galaxy Quest*'s star, the comedian Tim Allen, seems uncannily like a younger version of Alan Rickman with the same feral looks, though Rickman would never be seen mugging as shamelessly as Allen can do. 'How did I come to this? I played Richard III with five curtain calls; I was an actor once,' gloomed Alan's character, staring at his alien reflection in the make-up mirror. And indeed he might stare, with Rickman resplendent in a sort of fossilised ram's head that turned his character into a distant relative of Mr Spock from *Star Trek*.

Galaxy Quest was a cunning, well-sustained romp, with lots of subtle jokes about show business along the way, such as: how do you tell the difference between aliens and obsessive fans? It's so marginal sometimes ... Of course, for an alien species to be so inspired by a sci-fi show that it bases its entire culture on *Galaxy Quest* was the ultimate accolade for anyone's acting talents. On top of which, Alan got to do the first punch-up in his movie career with Allen's vain leading man. So much for those who say he never mixes it; that he's too aloof; inside that glacial English exterior, there is an Irish-Welsh bruiser.

Such a diverse trio of roles one after the other had established a satisfying distance between Alan and the screen villainy that made his name. But then, out of the blue, came the great Asp Disaster in October 1998 that would, for a while at least, blight his stage career and expose a speech impediment which had never once been apparent in the films that liberated him. Yet, to be fair to Rickman, it had never been so apparent on stage either until his ill-starred *Antony and Cleopatra*. With someone like Alan, who always takes aeons to decide what he will do, one wonders why on earth he decided, on the turn of a sixpence, to take on such a major role as Antony on the cruelly exposed Olivier stage in a production by Sean Mathias, a hot young director who had made his mark in the West End with a sex-drenched production of Noël Coward's already sexy troilism play *Design For Living*, but who had never directed Shakespeare before.

Perhaps the fates were against it from the outset, for Rickman took over from Alan Bates who had been contracted to play Antony for some time but then pleaded a knee injury. Not that taking another man's leavings would worry Rickman – he certainly has an ego, but not to that extent. And the profession is full of stories of people who took on roles almost by default, only to triumph; from *42nd Street* onwards, it's the stuff of show business legend.

Nevertheless it was a big decision to make in a hurry. 'It's a mystery why Alan Rickman did Antony,' says an exasperated Peter Barnes. 'He had once played a very small part in a production of *Antony and Cleopatra* by Peter Brook, so maybe that's why he wanted to do the lead part all these years later. But I said to him, "Why the hell did you decide to do it with that director?" '

The truth is that actors are often attracted to a project because of the other names in the cast. Helen Mirren was already on board as Queen of the Nile so Rickman did the gallant thing and leaped into the breach left by Bates to play opposite one of the world's great performers. Not only was Mirren an international name from playing Jane Tennison in Lynda La Plante's ground-breaking detective series *Prime Suspect*, but also a heavyweight classical actress with a most un-English sensuality that had earned her the nickname of the RSC sexpot in her early stage career. She was no less sexy in her 50s, deciding to go topless in Cleopatra's death scene. The stage coupling of Rickman and Mirren was widely seen as a dream-team, and it set the box-office on fire, selling out the production long before the reviews were published.

Yet Tim Hatley's cumbersome and clunking stage design overwhelmed the actors and the all-important intimacy of the play, which would have been better served in the Cottesloe studio theatre – always the actors' choice – than the problematic Olivier. His voice already muffled slightly by a short moustache and beard grown for the part, Alan retreated into himself and often became inaudible – a problem compounded night after night as the impact of the bad reviews gathered momentum. Most were excruciating, with the headline writers having a field day, though some damned with faint praise instead. 'The grand fall of the great warrior becomes more of a drunken stagger into disillusionment and despair,' wrote the *Stage*'s Tara Conlan, while acknowledging that Rickman 'does bring out Antony's common humanity and his war-weariness – when you can hear him.'

So much for the one original idea in Mathias's production – that the battle-weary Antony should, very plausibly, be an alcoholic. It seemed to have fallen as flat as the rest of the evening, with Mathias lacking the experience in Shakespeare to articulate his theme.

But Rickman was never going to be the ideal man of action; more the ideal man of inaction. With his last Shakespearean role, Hamlet, still lingering in his mind, Alan's Antony was in truth more middle-aged Prince of Denmark than decorated hero of old Rome – as Michael Coveney's perceptive review alone suggested. 'Rickman's Mark Antony is a spineless poet of a warrior, caught with tragic splendour.' Coveney did add that 'his articulation could be sharper. But in his case, what else is new? He cuts a marvellously shambolic and charismatic figure.' But with the production failing to make clear its governing idea that Rickman's slurred diction was deliberately imitating an alcoholic, it was an unforgivable bodge that left the hapless actor in the role of the fall guy. Yet it was always going to be a tremendous risk for someone with a speech impediment to make his voice more slurred than usual, and many of the critics simply made the assumption that he couldn't speak the verse.

Nearly three years later, when the dust had settled, Rickman tried to defend the production in a BBC News 24 interview: 'I was playing somebody who was basically an alcoholic. And I think people got very upset that they weren't seeing a great hero. The point about the play, to me, is that you see these childlike people who were once great and they're now reduced to being drunk, rowing, throwing things at each other . . . It's the most extraordinary deconstruction of a great duo, and they're presented as little children.' He was to take the same theme later that year and deconstruct Noël Coward's spoiled Elyot and Amanda in *Private Lives*; but with Mark Antony, it was a deconstruction too far in trying to turn elements of the play into a Shakespearean *Who's Afraid Of Virginia Woolf?* Particularly when some of the most peerless poetry in the English language had to be delivered in the middle of their spats.

Some elements of the media, scenting blood and detecting a lack of on-stage chemistry between the two leads, stirred things up and tried to make a crisis out of a drama by citing alleged bad karma between Rickman and Mirren as a reason for the fiasco in the first place. But with reviews like the ones the production was receiving, the alleged lack of chemistry would become a self-fulfilling prophecy. 'I hadn't heard that they fell out, but it's easy to fall out if you are in a desperate production,' says Barnes. 'You get to the point where you hate going on stage.'

Stories of difficult rehearsals, where the lack of communication between the director and at least one of the leading members of the cast was apparent, had indeed seeped out. Sheridan Morley hit the mark in his *Spectator* review, when he wrote of an Alan Rickman 'so patently exhausted and dispirited, presumably from rehearsals, that his defeat at the hands of the Romans and Cleopatra herself . . . also came as no surprise. Whether Alan Bates would have survived any better is debatable.'

Rickman angrily refuted the charge that Cleopatra and her Antony were not getting on: 'I've never been closer to an actress on stage than I was in that production. And off-stage the greatest of friends . . . People wanted to create some kind of furore off-stage as well as on.'

Just as well that *Antony and Cleopatra* had been planned as a limited season of only 54 performances, for careers can be damaged by a long run in such a critically savaged production.

There are, of course, exceptions: Peter O'Toole's much-panned *Macbeth* became a must-see, rather like an on-stage car crash, and it merely confirmed him as a maverick steer.

Although Alan was later to tell the BBC that *Antony and Cleopatra* was a success by virtue of being a sell-out (in the box-office sense), at the time he was so devastated by the adverse reaction that he told his producer friend Paddy Wilson that he doubted whether he would ever go on stage again. And this at a time when American movie stars were already forming long orderly queues to prove their serious acting credentials by appearing on the ultimate live arena, the London stage. But as Paddy knew only too well from their days in rep, when the passive-aggressive Rickman is seriously unhappy with a production, he digs his heels in and retreats into himself – with the inevitable result of an underpowered, muffled performance.

Yet the great shock, of course, was that he had first made his name on stage as a character who was a byword for vicious power and control. Suddenly, it seemed that Alan Rickman had lost it.

15. SHRIEKS ACROSS THE ATLANTIC

One June evening in the year 2000, Alan Rickman clumped on to the main stage of London's Royal Court with Doc Marten boots, bicycle clips and a bad attitude. Mention to anyone that Rickman was taking part in a benefit for the restoration of Burmese democracy, and they would have expected yards of high-minded worthiness from him as he deployed that cawing voice to its most thrilling extent in a speech or a reading that concentrated minds on great causes. Instead he was performing a Victoria Wood sketch about a stroppy tour guide who had parked his bike in the Brontë Museum before dragging visitors round the place in a take-it-or-leave-it way. The whole thing came complete with a Yorkshire accent – which no one had realised he could do – and the kind of cosmic disgruntlement which men from that part of the world regard as their divine right. He could strop for Britain.

To add to the party atmosphere the assembled actors were all seated at tables on stage while waiting their turn to perform. They couldn't believe how funny and northern he was (the two are not necessarily synonymous). Especially that working-class icon Miriam Karlin, a legend in her own picket line with a long history of radical theatre, the distinction of being one of the first funny ladies on British television and with no film profile to be tainted by.

The legend goes that it took Alan Rickman three years to get his confidence back on stage after the disaster of *Antony and Cleopatra*. Not so. Nearly two years after the serpent of Old Nile had apparently done for Alan's grand theatrical ambitions, he screwed his courage to the sticking-place and went back on stage in a deliberately low-key way for two one-off events: the benefit for the Burma UK campaign, in which he performed the Wood monologue in those black bovver boots, and a masterclass at the Theatre Royal Haymarket three months later in September. His triumph in *Private Lives* in 2001 was the high-profile return to the stage that rehabilitated him in the headlines, but it was the first two events that really broke the curse and reassured him that he could still cut the mustard.

Rickman had been contacted early in 2000 by Glenys Kinnock, the wife of the former Labour leader Neil Kinnock but prominent in her own right as a Member of the European Parliament. The Kinnocks were theatre buffs and had long since become friends with Rickman, a kindred spirit in socialism; Alan is also heavily involved in the charity One World Action, of which Glenys is the president. As organiser of a fund-raising benefit in support of Burma's imprisoned pro-democracy Opposition leader Aung San Suu Kyi, Glenys had asked Alan if he would join a celebrity cast for the show at the Royal Court in June that year.

Philip Hedley, Artistic Director of the Theatre Royal Stratford East, had a long record in directing such events. He, after all, was the man who had once persuaded the great Peggy Ashcroft to make her entrance by riding a bike on stage while John Gielgud was delivering Prospero's final speech from *The Tempest*: 'Our revels now are ended'. She was, Philip recalls, all of 73 at the time. Ashcroft had rushed from the theatre named after her in Guildford, Surrey, where she was doing a one-woman show, to reach the Court for the final minutes of a fund-raiser for The George Devine Award; Hedley suggested a bike as a prop to make a joke of her mad dash. That was an historic occasion, and not just because Peggy got on her bike; Laurence Olivier shared the same stage as Ashcroft and Gielgud that night.

Yet many people on that same stage for the Burma UK benefit in 2000 came from, as Hedley puts it, 'a different world' to him and wouldn't have known that Philip the Radical could also direct these mega-starry evenings with aplomb.

Both he and Alan found themselves in the same boat on this occasion: each had been stereotyped by their peers, some of whom didn't know how much either man was capable of. 'I know Alan and Richard [Wilson] from various fundraising theatrical dos and dinners with the usual suspects,' says Hedley, 'and they happened to be standing together and talking to me after the Burma benefit and saying to me, "That was really good." And they're not naturally effusive people. There was a sense of "I didn't know you could do that" – and yet Alan was getting the same reaction as well from his fellow actors. He seemed so secure in the character. And people there like Miriam Karlin were very impressed by that, because they hadn't known that it was part of his range.'

'Although Alan is very chatty and agreeable when you meet him, I had the cliché in my mind of the highly serious actor,' admits Philip. 'He had phoned me up about the choice of material before the show: he gave me, as director, a choice of three pieces – and the other two were much more serious. He actually auditioned over the phone, going through each piece. I very much liked the idea of the Brontë guide being wonderfully pompous and unknowledgeable about the Brontës, saying "Mind the bike" when visitors were tripping over it while trying to get round the museum. The character was wonderfully ungracious without meaning to be rude; he was down-to-earth, he didn't know how crass he was being. So I was attracted by the idea of Alan doing that.

'I can claim no credit at all for how good it was, because he just did it; there wasn't a run-through. We were not aware he could play a working-class character. This was a very unimaginative man, worthy of a Mike Leigh play; and Alan could do that difficult thing of playing the character genuinely, not patronising him, but also being enormously funny and adept at the same time. He pressed all the right buttons.

'If you had a play with that character in it, you wouldn't have thought of approaching Alan to play it. That's why it was brave: he wasn't using the tools you could fall back on when you're lazy. He obviously went back to his working-class roots in some way; he would have known that kind of man. But,' Philip adds tellingly, 'how many people in any position of power know he can do that?'

How many, indeed? Rickman has fought against typecasting all his life; and it would seem that he had reinvented himself just a little too successfully all those years ago at Latymer Upper. With a background like his, this was the ultimate paradox.

But with so many film offers coming his way, he didn't have time to brood for long about making a proper return to the stage. Invariably he opted for character roles in indie movies, in which he wouldn't be dictated to by a major studio and where his name – that real-life Robin Hood tendency again – could help to raise the finance for struggling film-makers. In a transformation that recalled Michael Douglas's turn as a bespectacled ordinary Joe in *Falling Down*, Rickman was almost unrecognisable in menacing horn-rimmed glasses and pinstripes for the role of a burnt-out, but still fully fanged, executive in the corporate comedy *The Search For John Gissing*, which co-starred Juliet Stevenson and which won the Critics' Choice Award for Best Feature at the 2002 Sarasota Film Festival. Actor/director Mike Binder played an American businessman who arrived in London with his wife, played by Janeane

Garofalo, to take over final negotiations for a big merger with a German firm. He was replacing chief negotiator John Gissing, played by Rickman with all the venom and passive aggression of one passed over for the job and determined to sabotage his successor at every stage of the game. It was the kind of satire on the corporate ethic, or lack of ethic, that American film-makers do particularly well.

He followed it with *Blow Dry*, which, according to the end credits, was curiously only 'based on' a screenplay by the acclaimed writer of *The Full Monty*, Simon Beaufoy. Rickman played an equally burnt-out, but by no means extinct, hairdresser. The Yorkshire accent was deployed again, with Rickman getting top billing in this uneasy and uneven tragi-comedy about a crimping contest. It was the second time Alan had played a cuckold, here losing his wife Natasha Richardson to an over-the-top Rachel Griffiths in one of the least convincing lesbian relationships portrayed on film. Talk about subverting stereotypes: the hair-dresser was the straight guy for a change. Even for a Yorkshireman in a backstreet barber's shop who charges £2 extra 'if it wants washing', Rickman seemed unusually dour in the role and, though he acquitted himself with panache in the final scissor-sharpening moments, the film was not his finest hour. All one can say with conviction is that at least he had the hair for it. Rickman defended the film to the *Irish Times*, revealing that he had wanted to work with the director Paddy Breathnach after watching his sublimely funny gangster film *I Went Down*. Paddy was a loquacious Kevin Smith, only funnier – except, unfortunately, in *Blow Dry*.

Funniest of all was Alan's voiceover for a power-crazed pilot fish in the animated feature *Help! I'm A Fish*, which Rickman imbued with his insinuating brand of cartoon menace. Rickman's pilot fish drank a potion that gave him a human voice and an overweening desire to rule the ocean, which is how he managed to upstage the great white shark in his territorial ambitions. It is left to three child heroes, who have been turned into fish by the same magic potion, to defeat him and save the day. More than one reviewer remarked on how the pilot fish's newly acquired vocals resembled the sinister tones of Rickman's Sheriff of Nottingham, who had been some-thing of a cartoon character himself in human shape; here Rickman was really letting rip and enjoying himself in an animated feature whose sophisticated visuals, as *The Times* observed, paid tribute to

Busby Berkeley, Fritz Lang's *Metropolis* and even the Beatles' psychedelic period. But there was no doubt who was the star: as the *Guardian* pointed out, *Help! I'm A Fish* 'flags a bit when Rickman's superbly wicked character isn't on.'

Strangest of all was the part of Man in the twenty-minute *Play*, that reunited Rickman with Anthony Minghella, the writer-director of *Truly Madly Deeply*, for one of Channel 4's most ambitious commissions: all nineteen of Beckett's plays to be screened between 2001 and 2002.

The sight of a landscape populated entirely by despairing talking heads in pots, with the camera focusing on the front row of pots, could have been designed by Hieronymus Bosch in one of his visions of an adulterers' hell. Trapped in an eternal triangle, Rickman, Juliet Stevenson and the lovely Kristin Scott-Thomas were buried up to their necks in gigantic urns with mud-caked faces as grey as the vessels they had been poured into. There was to be no sitting or slouching and slacking in these pots, as Beckett's religiously followed stage directions make absolutely clear. Despite a fleeting resemblance to the unfortunate, mud-covered Mesmer after he had been tipped from his coach, Rickman was oddly compelling and hypnotic as he and his women chanted the tale of their *ménage à trois* from their earthenware prisons in just fifteen bleak minutes. John Hurt had already made an acclaimed West End comeback in *Krapp's Last Tape* before filming it for the Channel 4 season; getting Alan Rickman to stand upright in a pot with a face smothered in muck was an equal coup.

Yet there was a perception in some quarters that *Antony and Cleopatra* had, for a short time, created a blip, a bit of a career-falter; and the media abhors a vacuum, longing to fill it. Somehow the rumour spread that Rickman, long since tired of playing the villains that kept resurfacing in endless television reruns of *Die Hard* and *Robin Hood: Prince of Thieves*, might want to play the would-be good guy in real life and put his money where his socialist mouth was by following a political career instead.

Neither would the edge that Alan Rickman brought to everything disqualify him. When the spin doctor Peter Mandelson was asked who he would like to portray him in a film of his life, he famously replied, 'Alan Rickman – because he is not afraid to play the hard guy.' Being a Labour politician didn't necessarily mean being a softie, as Mandelson, that alarming charmer credited with turning the Labour Party into a ruthless, election-winning machine, had proved only too conclusively.

Because he is a political animal with strong views and a good grasp of policy debate, some of Alan's friends had long speculated about whether he would enter politics. Others pooh-poohed the idea. 'Rima is a very substantial intelligence, but I think there are too many lies and too much dissembling that has to go on in politics for Alan to enter it himself,' Peter James told me back in 1995. Maybe Rickman is just not diplomatic enough.

But an opportunity for the rumour-mongers suddenly presented itself when Michael Portillo was mooted as one of the candidates for the safest Tory seat in the country, Kensington and Chelsea, after the sudden death of Nicholas Scott's successor Alan Clark. With the blow-waved Portillo still giving all the Tory ladies a thrill even after (or, some mischief-makers suggested, because of) revelations in *The Times* about his homosexual experimentation at university, it was reasonable to speculate that Labour needed an equally glamorous 'star' – or at least one with just as much hair. Speculation about Rickman turned into a story in the *Sunday Times*, followed by a furious rebuttal from Rima Horton on the front page of the local *Kensington And Chelsea News* in September 1999. 'Why on earth,' a sarcastic Rima was quoted as saying, 'would Alan give up his highly paid and extremely highly respected career as an actor for the unglamorous and frankly hopeless job as a candidate?' Well, if she must put it that way – quite. 'At first Alan was bemused and then perturbed by the sudden interest in this,' she added, 'but he now treats the whole affair as something of a joke.'

The *Sunday Times* had pointed the finger of suspicion at Margaret McDonagh, then the General Secretary of the Labour Party, for wanting to sprinkle some show business stardust at the Party conference that year. The story claimed that discussions were believed to have been held at the highest levels in the party between McDonagh and Alastair Campbell, though the paper acknowledged that Alan had already proved somewhat off-message as a 'renegade' Labour supporter by joining Tam Dalyell, to protest against Government action on Iraq, and Vanessa Redgrave in sending messages of support to the newly formed Emergency Committee on Iraq.

But it still seemed a long leap to make from the undeniable facts: that Alan's partner had parliamentary ambitions and that Rickman had been a guest at a Number 10 Downing Street party held by the chancellor Gordon Brown shortly after the election, along with Rickman's old mates Bob Hoskins and Richard Wilson and the actress Helena Bonham-Carter. He was also a guest at the election night party held at the Chalk Farm home of the QC Helena Kennedy to celebrate Labour's 1997 landslide victory, but so what? That didn't necessarily make him MP material; it just meant that Helena Kennedy knew a lot of actors. Despite Rima's emphatic denial that the story had any substance, some people remained convinced that there had been loose talk at Labour's Millbank HQ. In August 2002, I phoned Margaret McDonagh at home to ask her to put on record for the first time the truth about her alleged involvement in wanting Rickman to run for Parliament. The story was, she told me, absolutely not true, and she remains as puzzled as anyone over how the rumour started. 'I had no discussions whatsoever with Alastair [Campbell] about the Chelsea by-election,' McDonagh told me. 'I've never known Alan to articulate that he wanted to be an MP. Besides,' she added, 'unless there's some problem, it's up to the local party to choose its candidate.'

Two years after the story had first run and had been rubbished by Rima, Alan finally denied it formally in an interview with Tim Sebastian of BBC News 24. 'I think they tried it on,' he said, not naming names, 'because somebody in a press office somewhere thought they're not going to let Portillo have all the publicity without any challenge. I have no political ambitions in that way anyway, so it was complete nonsense.'

Yet his social conscience had not been allowed to rust; it simply manifested itself in other ways. In September 2000, he agreed to do his pastoral bit for his profession by holding a Masterclass, a well-established annual event at London's Theatre Royal Haymarket in which prominent playwrights, actors and directors share the secrets of their trade for free with an audience of drama students and schoolchildren. Rickman remains one of the biggest names ever to commit to Masterclass. Although, unlike some of the other Masters, he refused to allow his contribution to be filmed for television, he honoured his commitment despite still being fogbound from a dose of flu caught while filming the first Harry Potter film, The Philosopher's Stone, in Durham Cathedral. Dressed down in his trademark black for the Masterclass, Alan perched on a Dave Allen chair on stage (later one irreverent student was to characterise the afternoon in almost Beckettian terms as 'a man on an uncomfortable chair') and established an immediate rapport with the front stalls for what he saw as a conversation rather than a Masterclass, unhindered by ego. Once again, he had stepped out on stage without visible nerves, though he was to admit that the problem of stage fright gets worse, rather than better, with age.

Later that year there was also a further development from the Burma UK benefit in June. That had made public the mutual admiration society between Alan Rickman and Victoria Wood; and Wood, who likes to use actors in funny roles rather than comedians in order to shake up our expectations, asked him to be a guest star in a costume-drama spoof alongside Michael Gambon, Richard E. Grant and Robert Lindsay in her BBC1 Christmas Day comedy *Victoria Wood with all the Trimmings*.

So much for Rickman not doing any television these days; he certainly does parachute in for the odd guest appearance. But for an actor at a certain level in his career, film and theatre remain the most prestigious art-forms; in Hollywood, there's a snobbery about television which means that A-listers rarely do more than the odd guest spot, such as Brad Pitt dropping in on an episode of *Friends* to have a screen spat with his real-life wife Jennifer Aniston.

And Alan wanted to go back to the theatre, where, despite his fear of that nightly ordeal, he could prove himself as an actor more than in any other arena. Once a play opens, the show belongs to the actors to improve or impair it. Film is a director's medium in which the actors are pawns to be spliced and sliced in the editing suite, as Rickman discovered on *Robin Hood: Prince of Thieves* and even on *Harry Potter and the Philosopher's Stone*.

Plans were brewing among West End producers for the perfect project for Rickman's theatrical comeback: an RSC Class of 85 reunion – of Rickman, his *Les Liaisons* co-star and old friend Lindsay Duncan and their director Howard Davies. Yet they were taking risks with the *Antony and Cleopatra* jinx, by using the same designer, Tim Hatley. The plan was for a revival of Noël Coward's *Private Lives*, which would, like *Les Liaisons*, rely upon the sexual chemistry between the two leads – with rather less fatal results. And Alan himself was suffering from cold feet about even being in a Coward, as he was later to admit on American TV in *The Charlie*

Rose Show: he might be a mannered actor in some people's eyes, but he wasn't *that* mannered.

In the event, Hatley's perspective-defying sets were as imaginative and daring as the production and the performances proved to be; everything came together. It opened at London's Albery Theatre on 4 October 2001 to ecstatic reviews. An immensely confident and radical reading of the play it rescued Coward from the usual stylised archness and dwelt very specifically on the excitement of sexual violence between two sparring partners; Alan's early years of work with Peter Barnes, in tapping into those dangerous but undeniable undercurrents in the chaos of human behaviour, had not been wasted. Rickman and Duncan told the *New York Times* that Davies – who made a point of saying he had never read *Private Lives* until he got the job of directing it – wanted them to say the lines 'without any of the usual stuff that comes with Noël Coward, to make these people real'.

As a result, the smack Rickman gave a hysterical Duncan was only too audible, the passion behind it only too believable as they fought each other on the sofa, unable to live with or without each other. Rickman's Elyot, after all, is the man who declares at one point, 'Women should be struck regularly like gongs', a line greeted with a collective intake of breath from the audience at the matinée I attended. Rickman delivered it scornfully, implying that it shouldn't be taken seriously, that this was just Elyot's bullshittery in the battle of wills with an imperious dominatrix, but he certainly followed the threat up in the struggle with Duncan. They were evenly matched and she gave as good as she got, but Rickman also had the wit to capture the needy uncertainty, the neurotic vulnerability and, most importantly, the self-awareness that gave his Elyot unexpected depth.

There were those – Peter Barnes among them – who thought Rickman was robbed when he lost out as Best Actor in the Tony Awards (to Alan Bates for his role as Zuzovkin in the Turgenev play *Fortune's Fool*) after *Private Lives* had transferred triumphantly to Broadway in April 2002, though the production itself won a Tony and Lindsay Duncan was named Best Actress. 'She was sexy, but so was he – and funny as well,' argues Peter. Nevertheless the critics went mad for both of them, with Clive Barnes writing in the *New York Post* of 'a surprising, electric *Private Lives* done jungle-style; this Elyot and Amanda have the heady scent of an entire zoo of predators ... Rickman feral and unsatiated'. As with the Vicomte de Valmont, he was the wild animal in the boudoir, the man who put the kick into Coward, defying expectations and playing against type once again.

His old friend Peter Barnes had been pretty creative himself, this time on the family front by becoming a first-time father at the age of 69 – his daughter Leela was born in the year 2000. 'I did things back-to-front,' admits a sheepish Peter, who then found two years later that his wife Christie was expecting triplets in November 2002 – the same month that the second *Harry Potter* film was released. 'My friends can't imagine me being a father, they just think of me as a writing machine. A producer friend of mine went to see Alan in *Private Lives* on Broadway in the summer of 2002. I told him to tell Alan about the triplets but, when he arrived backstage and said he was bearing the latest news from Peter Barnes, Alan said to him, "Don't tell me, I already know," and started roaring with laughter. His reaction was very similar to lots of people's, and you could almost hear his shrieks of laughter across the Atlantic. I don't know who told him, but he knows everybody, he's so gregarious; sometimes I wonder how he gets the time to do it, but he always has been like that.'

Far from belonging to the W.C. Fields school of thought – that would like to see little people lightly fried – Rickman, despite his sometimes daunting presence, is a child-friendly man.

Barnes was particularly impressed that Rickman made time to come along to his little girl's second birthday party in May 2002. 'Alan is tall and that can be a little intimidating for tiny tots, so Leela was slightly intimidated by him at first. But actors usually get on with kids because they can express fantasy. He brought her a present of an animal alphabet, which she has over her cot; she loves it. It's a big silkworm with lots of pockets containing a letter of the alphabet and an animal.'

Stephen Davis, who has often had Alan's nieces Claire and Amy to stay at his home in the Cotswolds, regards Rickman as a 'virtual godfather to my children Natalie and Zoë. Over the years we raised them in company with Alan and Rima; Ruby Wax and her husband Ed have raised their three children in his company, too. The reason he's not an official godfather is that Rima told us we needed Roman Catholics as godparents because my wife Jane is Roman Catholic. But I've always been sorry,' adds Stephen, 'that I didn't go against the Pope on that one. Alan would have made a great dad; I suspect the reason he and Rima don't have children themselves is that they came late to the idea of parenthood because of career reasons.'

To those who know Rickman well, it came as no surprise that he agreed to do the *Harry Potter* movies – which meant filming one a year – after having read the books first. Being a 'virtual' godfather is one thing, but the childless Alan Rickman was to discover another way of enjoying those childhood pleasures vicariously by joining an all-star cast for the big-screen realisation of the most successful children's stories ever written.

16. THE SLITHERY SLOPE TO SNAPE

Thanks to the success of *Private Lives* on both sides of the Atlantic, Alan Rickman had proved he was back in action as a leading man. And Hollywood was watching; movie producers are always looking in the shop window of Broadway, which is how Alfred Molina landed the role of a lifetime as Frida Kahlo's painter husband Diego Rivera in the film *Frida* after starring in the New York transfer of *Art*.

Yet, because of Rickman's commitment to projects by independents and his reluctance to sell his soul back to the major studios, his film career had taken a decidedly eccentric turn by the beginning of the 21st century. He not only dreamed of directing again, but also of becoming a producer in order to develop scripts himself. Having arrived at his mid-50s, he was learning to conquer his neuroses and owning up to his control-freak tendencies: 'I suppose it's the director in me,' he admitted disarmingly to a group of drama students before adding: 'But I'm getting better at letting it be.'

At the Brussels Film Festival in 1998, he had argued that 'there have always been actors who have become directors. You only have to think of Orson Welles, Robert Redford, Dennis Hopper . . . I think that we simply want to "write". Working as an actor in many films allows you to observe directors. It's like taking a film-school course.' Or, as he put it much more trenchantly on another occasion to a group of students: 'You learn fastest if, on the second day of filming, you realise, "It's another idiot."' No wonder some directors fear him. Yet, despite this nagging ambition to take over the show, he will never give up performing. 'Acting is a compulsion,' as he puts it.

'Tides of banality and callowness have washed over society over the last ten years, and Alan has not budged a bloody inch,' said the writer Stephen Davis, making his friend sound like some cranky old sea-god when I invited him to reassess Rickman in the summer of 2002. 'His livelihood is in the celebrity business, but his integrity towards personal publicity and promotion in this New Labour age of cult celebrity and superficiality is an absolute bloody beacon. Of all the people I know who come from a generation where we were highly idealistic and optimistic, he, along with some of my old college contemporaries, has not wavered or diluted his values. Even when he does Noël Coward . . .

'He doesn't take himself as seriously as other people think he does. Above all, he doesn't confuse the illusion with the reality in what has become a virtual reality society. He's aware there's something more significant. He's not looking for the quick payday, the smash-and-grab raid on the BAFTA awards; he doesn't care. He is indifferent to those things, and I think that's fantastic. He's a Bronze Age standing stone,' adds Stephen, who in 2001 became the first person in a century to discover such a stone. Part of a pagan worship site, the 4,000-year-old, 6-foot-high stone was 300 yards away from Stephen's house in his back garden. (He hasn't yet decided whether to nickname it Alan – even though it's the same height.)

Considering that Rickman fears the ageism of the business more than most because he made his name relatively late, his incorruptibility shows no little strength of character. He knows what he's up against as a middle-aged actor: 'You are on a shelf with a sell-by date on your forehead. You are in a profession where you are constantly judged.' Yet he has joined the ranks of the movie immortals, celebrating his 57th birthday in February 2003 in the knowledge that he has now become a household name to millions of children around the world for his role in the *Harry Potter* films. And that meant getting into bed with a major movie studio again.

As with Steven Spielberg's *Indiana Jones* series, the first two *Harry Potter* films, *The Philosopher's Stone* (known in America as *The Sorcerer's Stone*) and *The Chamber of Secrets*, reverted to that sure-fire formula for success of going back to the future, with movies that recreated the old-fashioned excitement of movieland's melodramatic past but repackaged it for modern audiences with the cutting-edge special effects of today. After all, that was the whole point of the books themselves, the secret of their success. And the movie realisation was exactly the kind of project that suited Rickman's retro appeal, which harked back so effectively to a more glamorous age where silken villains prided themselves on a deadly wit and chutzpah.

Yet some argued that Alan had not been showcased to his best advantage in *Harry Potter*, since he had to share screen space not just with Dame Maggie Smith, Richard Harris, Robbie Coltrane and

Zoë Wanamaker but also myriad special effects of the kind that can blow a mere actor away. He had feared the same with his very first movie, *Die Hard*, but at least that had no fire-breathing dragons or hobgoblins hogging the limelight – only Bruce Willis.

'There was no place for the actors to expand in the first *Harry Potter* film,' complains Peter Barnes. 'I thought they were terribly restricted. I gather that a lot of scenes had been cut, and it certainly gives that impression – particularly with Alan's scenes. But that's formula film-making at its peak, I suppose,' he concludes, shrugging. 'Painting by numbers.' There's no help for it, then, but to wait and see it as a series, judging the performances across all seven films.

Other friends feared that, with the role of Severus Snape, Rickman had fallen into the trap of villainy again after years of resistance. But, as all fans of *Harry Potter* know, Snape, the Professor of Potions and head of Slytherin House at Hogwarts, is a classic red herring: a neurotic, irritable schoolmaster capable of petulance and viciousness but not, as it turns out, a malignant baddie. In other words, he's not as black as his hair is painted, even though he does a very good job of putting the filmic frighteners on. Even so, Rickman had deliberated 'for ever', he later confided, about doing the film – until everyone he knew insisted that he 'must' do it. Why? Because it was an event, a phenomenon. Had he played that old vampire Voldemort, of course, he would have been locked into villainy forever.

Yet, as soon as you see Snape on screen, the logic of Rickman playing him becomes apparent with the unmistakeable influence of an earlier incarnation of Rickmanesque deviousness: Obadiah Slope from *The Barchester Chronicles*, Alan's first big success. The pasty face, the clerical look, the flapping black cloak, the sulky lips: it's all there, bar the obvious contrast between Snape's lank and sooty hair and Slope's swept-back blond quiff. And how Slope-like are such lines as 'I can teach you how to bewitch the mind and ensnare the senses', delivered with Rickman's usual menacing sibilance.

From the very beginning, Rickman catches Snape's vulnerability, despite the fact that the camera is up to its old tricks with him by shooting him up the nostrils in order to depict him at his most sinister. Snape seems frightened and uneasy in the presence of Harry, which puts him on the defensive: a classic passive-aggressive reaction. 'I think at heart Snape is basically quite an insecure person,' Alan later admitted. 'He's always longing to be something else that people will really respect, like a black magician – not just a schoolmaster. That's why he envies the more popular and successful boys like Harry.'

Snape, of course, does have the secret ambition to be a Professor of the Dark Arts, the source of all the dramatic tension in his character. And in Potter he enviously recognises the real thing: a genuine wizard garbed in grubby schoolboy attire. The legion of adult fans of Harry Potter will appreciate such nuances, but Rickman took care to put on a grandstand show for the tots as well. As J.K. Rowling described him, Snape had 'greasy black hair, a hooked nose and sallow skin'. In other words, a pantomime villain on the page, but, with Rickman's performance, a supercilious class act on screen; you certainly wouldn't want to be kept in detention by him.

That was not his only contribution; such is the collaborative medium of movie-making that everyone is encouraged to chip in with ideas, and Alan had not forgotten his art-school training. The thirteenth-century Lacock Abbey in Wiltshire was used by the design team as location interiors for Hogwarts, but other shots of the boarding school for young wizards bore a distinct resemblance to Woodchester Mansion in Gloucestershire as well. It was not a coincidence: Woodchester Mansion happens to be a special conservation project for Rickman's old friend, the Cotswolds-based Stephen Davis, who has now persuaded the Prince of Wales to become its patron. 'The *Harry Potter* people worked very hard to make the location of Hogwarts resemble our conservation project, which looks like a cliché of an abandoned Gothic mansion,' confirms Davis.

Despite his early misgivings and the fact that some of his scenes were cut, Rickman was firmly on board the *Harry Potter* roller-coaster. After finishing the Broadway run of *Private Lives* in September 2002, he went off to film the third *Potter* movie.

In the meantime, Rickman had also kept up his commitment to indie film-making by starring alongside Michael Gambon and the model-turned-actress Sophie Dahl in a fifteen-minute silent film about theatre queues, *Standing Room Only*, which was released in 2002. But he was more in demand than ever, and yet another biggie beckoned: the latest romantic comedy from the award-winning Richard Curtis.

The *Four Weddings and a Funeral* screenwriter was making his directing debut with *Love, Actually* and taking no chances with his casting. Hugh Grant, Colin Firth, Rowan Atkinson and Liam Neeson were joined by Emma Thompson (reunited with Rickman to play his wife), Sharman Macdonald's talented actress daughter Keira Knightley and that inveterate scene-stealer Bill Nighy for a shoot that began in September 2002.

By 2002, Rickman had also formed a production company with the Australian actor Hugh Jackman, whom he had first met at the National Theatre back in 1998. Jackman, best known to movie-goers for his role in *X-Men*, had won over British audiences as a personable Curly in Trevor Nunn's hit revival of *Oklahoma!*, while Rickman was starring in repertoire in the asp disaster on the same Olivier stage. The two men got on so well that when Jackman's actress wife Deborra-Lee Furness made her directorial debut four years later with *Standing Room Only*, there was a part in it for Rickman as well as Jackman. Even the names seemed made for each other.

Somerset Maugham's *The Moon And Sixpence* was intended to be one of Rickman and Jackman's first projects as co-producers, with a screenplay and direction by Christopher Hampton. It was planned that Rickman should take the lead in Maugham's story of a stockbroker who deserted wife and country to become a painter in the South Seas. But, although Hampton was enthusiastically telling me in late 2002 that he thought the part was a potentially great one for Alan, the team found themselves bogged down in tortuous negotiations for the rights from the Maugham estate. The dual role of an actor–producer can be an immensely draining one, though it's a route that more and more actors are opting to take. Yet, as Alan's old friend Jenny Topper points out, 'Acting alone has never truly been enough for Alan.' And support from Rima, moral and otherwise, was going to prove vital in this new venture.

In July of 2002, Rima had taken early retirement from academia at the age of 55 after a send-off from Kingston University that earned her a herogram tribute on its website. Inevitably, her early retirement meant that Rima and Alan could spend more time together. Friends were wondering whether she might join him in his new producing venture. So far, however, there are no signs of Rima, one of the few experts on applied microeconomics with acting experience, joining her partner in the movie-making business. 'He does have this tendency towards the weaker sex,' says one friend. 'He does like to promote talented women; he's always got a script by some female under his arm. But, although some people say that Rima grounds him, I think they ground each other; it's pretty mutual.'

'He really admires Rima's mind,' says another associate, Theresa Hickey, 'perhaps because, through Rima, he can live a vicarious political life. Actors have multiple identities, not to mention multiple personalities.' With Rima now confining her political ambitions to low-key local-government level, Alan can quietly support her political achievements without the spotlight constantly upon him. If she had been thrust on to the national stage as a Member of Parliament, it would have placed a great strain on a relationship that is based on discretion. And she remains devoted to him. In an interview with the *Daily Mail* in 1991, Alan described their life together without children as 'like a trampoline . . . which gives a certain freedom.'

His playwright friends in particular have strong views about what he should do next. Peter Barnes would like to see him doing more comedy, claiming fretfully that Alan 'shies away from it'. Snoo Wilson thinks that the comic roles immortalise him: 'When you have somebody like that who has great comic timing and can take a whole house of people with him, it's like a good tennis serve. It comes from a fully integrated mind and body; it's like being able to hypnotise. To be able to embody so many qualities and to be funny as well raises the consciousness of audiences; it's a truly great gift, I think. Comedy is a higher art form than tragedy.'

Yet some will assume that he's sold his soul to the devil again and opted to return to villainy if Snoo's screenplay about Aleister Crowley ever gets made with Alan in the lead. 'Alan agreed to lend his name to my script in the early 90s – in other words, he's interested in playing the role,' says Snoo. 'You can then wave that at producers. But I want to do it with Alan because he would understand the comedy of it: the part of Crowley is written as somebody who enjoys being awful and has a wicked sense of humour, who enjoys his role as someone who's vilified in the press as the wickedest man in Britain. I wrote it because Crowley's era is an interesting prism through which to look at us; it was the dawn of psychedelia. I think Alan is a supreme comic actor who can add psychological depth even to Coward, which is quite something.'

Though he can be a curmudgeonly bugger, it says a lot for Rickman that so many of his friends have had such big plans for him: to be a great villain, to be a great comedian, to run a company. Indeed, it's surprising that Alan has not shown any signs of wanting to run another, more manageable theatre than the Riverside arts centre. For someone with such decided opinions on every aspect of his business, he remains remarkably elusive and hard to pin down. It's as if, like Colonel Brandon, he simply aims to be a good influence in the background. One can't help thinking that it's a substitute for a family.

Sir John Gielgud always reacted with a certain amount of giggly horror at the thought of younger actors grovelling at his feet and asking his advice 'as if I were some terrible old Dalai Lama'. Alan Rickman seems to have no such qualms.

'I would hope that one day Alan would be in charge of a company. He's very much a leader of men and women. He has astonishing leadership and spokesman qualities. He has passionate views on subjects and issues: training, the subsidy of theatre, new young actors,' adds Peter James, who asked Alan to address his students at LAMDA in 1995.

Peter wanted a level-headed guide and mentor who would not give them false hopes, but who would still be successful and glamorous enough to be inspirational. 'That's what makes him a great role model: he's a thinking actor. He's being offered parts that take him into the stratosphere, yet he's still asking serious questions.

'He thinks not only about the profession he's in but the political life of the nation. He applies a very strict criterion to what he accepts. His Labour Party commitment is part of a much broader world view; he's concerned with good quality offered to the public. Many actors think "I'd like to do posh work, not pap", but with Alan, there's a moral view about what the public should be sold. It's rather like the Fabian view, although he's not old-fashioned. It's a view about what you offer young people. We share an anxiety about the deregulated free market, whether that can deliver.

'He's anxious about doing quality work,' concludes Peter, who talks about modern standards of 'junk' education and worries that his students haven't read enough classic texts before they arrive at LAMDA. As with all teachers these days, he's even seriously concerned about standards of literacy.

'Someone like Alan, who takes his work seriously, is a person of tremendous value to students. We have similar backgrounds: I came from the working-classes. My father was a casual racist at first, thinking that black people jumped council-house queues and all that stuff. Then he met my black geography teacher who was an absolute charmer. The two of them got on like a house on fire after that.'

Peter believes that Rickman could have been just as successful as a designer. 'He has a wonderful taste in clothes and design. He could equally well have gone in that direction: he has an expertise in all that,' points out Peter.

'He has an elegant, unmistakable face and frame. He is not a chameleon actor, because he is very noticeable. It seemed to me that *Mesmer* was the next step, and I'm very sad it didn't appear to have worked out.'

'He hates to be pigeonholed,' says Blanche Marvin. 'He's much more an Alec Guinness than a Laurence Olivier, and there has been no set pattern to Alec's career.'

As for the charismatic villains, Dusty Hughes never saw them as part of Alan's long-term game-plan. 'He can do the villains standing on his head and probably yours too. Knowing Alan, he'll always try to do the things that aren't easy. His dignity on stage will become an enormous force.

'Perhaps he's too intellectual to be an actor,' hazards Dusty. 'It's terribly hard if you are that. A lot of directors are serious charlatans. Any director who is like that doesn't want to meet Alan, who could eat you for breakfast. But he's never unpleasant. He's always even-tempered: I've never known him lose his temper. Some directors get by on a lot of bullshit. They are all control freaks; I suppose Alan is a bit of a one himself, though he's low down on my list of control freaks. He's a very strong personality and identity, a very likeable one.'

Stephen Poliakoff has argued that he 'needs a part that Mesmer was obviously meant to be. Like Anthony Hopkins with Hannibal Lecter in *Silence of the Lambs*. Alan is the actor closest to Paul Scofield: that worn but urbane and weathered world-weariness. Scofield made it with the role of Sir Thomas More in *A Man for All Seasons*.

'I was surprised that he took *Rasputin* after all; at one stage it had fallen through, and then it was on again. He did say that he wouldn't play any more villains, but it's difficult for actors of his age to get the lead role in films.

'He needs a really good part in the middle of a large film. If he gets that, he could have a career like Anthony Hopkins. Does Alan want that? I don't know. It's unusual for actors to get as successful as late as that.'

It's canny of Poliakoff to question whether Rickman does want all that, because he's still undecided. He has not quite sorted out his attitude towards the fame game.

On the one hand, he's certainly not a self-publicist like the comedienne who was 'on' for the entire length of a Tube train journey I shared with her. On the other hand, no one wants to be ignored, especially if your face is your fortune.

A female friend tells the story of how they were both in a shop, and Alan was not recognised by the staff. He took care to say goodbye with elaborate politeness. That was his usual manner, of course, but she did wonder whether he was just a little piqued at not being spotted and wanted to give them a second chance to realise who he was. That could have been unjust to him, of course . . . he's a kind man.

'Writers don't have the visual currency of actors,' says Stephen Davis. 'I think Alan is ambivalent about publicity. He hasn't yet completely decided what he thinks about it.

'Even I, as a writer, faced a watered-down version of an actor's dilemma: "Shall I live here or shall I go to California and be a stamped-out version of myself?" There's always some price to pay. That's what I mean by the Faustian contract.

'I have known him for years; he's one of my oldest friends. It was Alan Who? in those days. And he said Stephen Who? He walks in his moccasins and I walk in mine.

'We all want to use Hollywood, but it's too big, too relentless and too corrupt for everyone to use it,' warns Stephen.

'Alan was educated in the idea of the virtuoso actor being a chameleon. That versatility that Olivier had, which Antony Sher has. I think Alan recognises that is what acting is all about. As Alan gets more successful, he's threatening to become a cult personality. He could have a tacky career as a Hollywood villain, but he doesn't want that. There are no careers for actors in Hollywood, just careers for stars.

'Tommy Lee Jones is similar to Alan: he gets offered villains because of his strong looks, when he's actually a brilliantly versatile actor. If you play villains all the time, you just get this cheesy repetitiousness.'

If Rickman is wary about publicity, that is because he fears being corrupted by it. No danger of that, say his friends. Unlike some actors, Rickman has not succumbed to the urge to dump his nearest and dearest as soon as he became a serious Hollywood star. 'Alan hasn't changed at all. People do start believing their own publicity, but not him,' says Adrian Noble.

Not that Rickman doesn't feel exhilarated by America every time he goes there. He walks even taller on US soil. 'When you get off the plane in Britain, you've got to shrink a little bit, hug yourself into your coat a bit more,' he told the writer John Lahr in *Woman's Journal* of January 1993.

He likes the place because he feels he is not categorised there by the British class system, by the inferiority complex created by his background. 'I stand straighter in LA. It's something about how the English are brought up and what we're told we can expect. Maybe it's because I drive a car in LA and I don't at home. I feel more in charge of myself. I wouldn't dream of being out there as an actor looking for work. To actually say, OK, I'm going to pitch a tent and wave a flag saying "Employ me" – I couldn't do that. But I enjoy being there. It's disgusting and wonderful. Like going to Dunkin' Donuts every day.'

Rickman's contradictory nature clearly saw the other side of the story with all its pitfalls: 'I like the phrase of David Hare's: "Show business thins the mind!" If you spend any time in Los Angeles, there's only one topic of conversation,' he told *The Times* magazine in 1994.

He calls himself an archetypal Piscean, identifying with the symbol of the two fish who are swimming in different directions. That's another reason why he gets on well with women; few men, frankly, are prepared to discuss their horoscope. Indeed, one friend says that he has the intuition while Rima has the intellect. Rare, indeed, to find a man happy to settle into that role without feeling threatened. 'He really admires Rima's mind,' says another associate, Theresa Hickey. Perhaps because, through Rima, he can live a vicarious political life. Actors have multiple identities, not to mention multiple personalities.

'Alan's quite unique in the intensity of his internal life. He's a shifting, mercurial kind of person – and very, very mesmeric,' his *Mesmer* 'wife' Gillian Barge told *The Times* magazine in 1994.

Which is why, more than most people, he absolutely hates being taken for granted. 'I don't mind seducing as long as at the end of the seduction there's an idea or a shock,' he told John Lahr. 'You can lull the paying customers as long as they get slapped. I like introducing ambiguity. I like the fact that people get confused about my character.

'In every area of my life, complete opposites are at work all the time. I stagger myself sometimes. Who is this person? The "you" who can't organise picking up the laundry – and you know that "you" very well – watches the other one in a rehearsal situation and says "Who is this person who has all these ideas and all this invention?" There's a very, very instinctive person and a very, very practical person. It depends on what time of day it is, I think.'

Some women, of course, would say it depends on their time of the month. Only Alan Rickman would say that it depends on his time of day.

'Most of our lives we function with a huge divide between the head and the body,' he added. He finally felt the gap had closed when he first got to RADA, but he's still trying to be as free as Fred Astaire.

'I like getting ambiguous responses from people. I'm not up there in a glass cage to be admired and for people to be enchanted by me. I like to mix it up. Audiences shouldn't be passive creatures. They come to work.

'I want bigger challenges. I want to touch that unknown part where you know you're not just a collection of other people's preconceptions.' Which is beginning to sound positively transcendental. As ever, Rickman is trying to rise above what he feels are his limitations. 'The typecasting is probably because of the way my face is put together,' he told Jeff Powell in the *Daily Mail* in 1991. 'Each character I play has different dimensions. When people try to stick a label on my life, I think, "It doesn't seem like that to me."'

He became crossly eloquent on the subject in the 1994 *Times* magazine interview with David Nicholson: 'The reason I don't like talking to most journalists is their desire to reduce everything to a one-page article and to make you compare things. You find yourself forced to answer the question, when really what you want to say is: "Nothing is like anything else and I'm not thinking of anything else I've done, just the job in hand." So a slight prison is created.

'I need time to go home and find out who I am,' he added revealingly. 'Most scripts are like junk food, things to keep the cinema full. Some things I'm offered in the States, I can't actually see why anyone's bothering except for the pay cheque. You read the script and think, "Why?" It's a law of diminishing returns because if I don't believe in it, then I won't be any good. You come to see yourself as a chemical component to be injected into something.'

But even that can cause a bad chemical reaction; no wonder Rickman's permanently frustrated, forever chasing some Holy Grail of the perfect performance in the perfect production. He's like the little boy whose mother tells him that he thinks too much.

'You can think, "This is my moment of utter emotional honesty" and then the camera goes another foot lower down and shoots up your nostrils and that's emotional honesty out the window. Suddenly you're being incredibly devious.'

Only the director is in complete control, of course. Which is why Alan Rickman wants to be one as well as everything else.

It strikes me that he enjoyed his villainous parts – while not entirely approving of them, of course – because, fundamentally, they are such wonderful control-merchants.

For Alan Rickman really is the psychopath's psychopath; he would feature strongly in any Good Screen Psycho Guide. In the political satire *Bob Roberts*, the writer, director and star Tim Robbins chose Rickman as the sinister campaign manager Lukas Hart III because, as he told John Lahr in *Woman's Journal*: 'I don't like safe actors. Which is why I chose Alan, who has the courage to make bold choices and chew on the scenery a little bit. He's also got a whimsy to him when he plays evil that's very seductive. I'd like to play opposite him in a movie about competing psychopaths. I'd like to try to out-psychopath Alan Rickman.'

No chance. But Hannibal Lecter was the one great part that got away, of course, and it is tempting to speculate whether Rickman would have added more characteristically dry humour than is seemly to the story of a sophisticated cannibal. For there is a tendency to subvert the genre when he gets up there on the screen. Rickman can be a little too ironic, too knowing, to terrify us thus far.

Kevin Spacey, however, seems to have no scruples about playing completely creepy; neither does Hopkins, of course. 'I've only seen ten minutes of the *Silence of the Lambs* sequel *Hannibal*, and I thought it was cardboard villain stuff,' says Snoo Wilson. 'I could see how an actor of Hopkins' ability would get bored with repeating himself. There's no development there – where do you go beyond cannibalism? What good does making Hannibal do to the planet? Or, indeed, I suspect, Hopkins himself? Apart from his bank balance. So I think Alan is probably very wise to diversify. He's not simply being an actor, a mask for hire; he has a a lot of other things in his life.'

Rickman's irony comes down to the George Sanders/Claude Rains syndrome again, when he can't resist showing off his wit. The *Independent on Sunday*'s Anthony Lane compared him to that select band of thespian brothers – James Mason, Robert Donat and Sanders – who are 'sensual, unhurried, turning everyone else into jitterbugs. Their villains are played like lovers and vice versa; you don't trust them for a minute, but they won't give you a minute to look away.'

Black comedy comes very easily to urbane British actors. Hans Gruber was only scary by flashes, mainly when he showed his teeth; mostly he was a major stylist and ad-lib man who seemed to have strayed in from a menswear catwalk. And the Sheriff, of course, was a wonderfully amusing cartoon who couldn't even claim to be a legend in his own torture-chamber; fine swordsman though he was, this was the kind of sad chump who would always stab himself in the foot.

The Vicomte de Valmont was the absolute heart of darkness for him; and even then, you felt a certain pity for this self-made monster, who had checkmated himself. There's a hint of the psychologist in his approach, though he prefers to think of himself as a pitiless pathologist. He is well aware of the Fascist impulse of which Sylvia Plath wrote. 'People allow the Valmonts of this world,' he told the *Daily Mail* in 1991. 'It was fascinating to watch that kind of evil being so entertaining and erotic. But it was a cruel part to play for a long time. It would take a lot to get me to do that again. I wasn't very pleasant to live with during that period.'

Film allows him to make a quick getaway, from his character as well as the job. Alan Rickman is at heart a theatrical animal because he relishes the control, when the actors take over the play after the director has finished rehearsals. But it also means lingering night after night over every little nuance when it may be driving him mad.

That was why the Sheriff came as such a light relief. 'I thought it important that the Sheriff amused the audience as much as anything else. People should come out of that movie, having had a good time. The characters were up for reinvention.

'With the Sheriff of Nottingham, it's probably okay to be manic and over the top. It was certainly tough shooting my final fight with Kevin Costner. We didn't have any rehearsal for it. We just ran through it sequence by sequence as we put it together, so it had real danger in it.'

Success for him means keeping in touch with reality. 'Being reasonably successful doesn't, God forbid, mean losing touch with what ordinary people are going through. I still suffer because I live here and I step out of my front door and smell the quality of life, the waste, the lack of imagination, the appalling selfishness,' he told GQ magazine indignantly in 1992.

The one thing over which Rickman is never remotely flippant is politics. He will keep the light ironic tone when talking about himself or his perceived difficulties with a certain performance, but he takes his political beliefs seriously. There is also a feeling that he should always be seen to be on his best behaviour, that Rima's work makes the life of an actor seem petty and frivolous. Little wonder, then, that he's so painstakingly analytical, so *academic* about acting.

There is something of the lecturer manqué about Alan Rickman, hence the seraglio, the networking, the feeling of a man on Mount Olympus. As his former schoolmaster Ted Stead says, 'He would have made a very good teacher himself.'

Jenny Topper is very perceptive on his appeal to women in particular. 'Women tend not to be very good at being absolute and sure about things,' she told GQ magazine in the same 1992 feature. 'Alan has this hand-on-heart quality. He is always absolutely sure about his opinions, what is good writing and good theatre, and he has tremendous loyalty to those things.

'Also, in a totally admiring way, I wonder if there isn't a streak of femininity in him, a kind of sweetness that perhaps you expect more from other women than men.' It is still extraordinary in this day and age that a red-blooded man who enjoys the company of women has to justify himself; not that Alan Rickman does any such thing.

He is fortunate to live among that great big family called the British theatre, a substitute for the more traditional nuclear kind. His empathy with the female sex is accepted and respected.

The playful quality that Jules Wright admired, the playmate whom Saskia Reeves teases: all come together in this tall and imposing figure who doesn't need to prove anything. As Elaine Paige once said, small people have to shout 'Look at me, I'm down here.' But showbusiness is full of ambitious midgets. The giants of this world have a more relaxed and almost passive attitude, which brings us back to Alan Rickman's passive aggression.

Friends and colleagues do feel tender about him; despite their criticisms, mostly constructive ones, he is regarded as a force for good. As with Latymer, he cocoons himself within an inner circle of supporters. And, as with all mavericks, he gravitates towards film roles that are sometimes glorified versions of cameos.

In his ideal world, designer, director, writer and actors would come to rehearsals with nothing decided and they would all have a great big glorious nit-picking session. He's taking the academic approach of a tutorial, influenced by his partner Rima.

The acting world knows it as the improvisation process that has been perfected by the idiosyncratic film-maker Mike Leigh. Actors, though they may curse the Method-acting process at times, love the challenge because they feel they have completely created their characters. No longer are they thought to be stupid, empty vessels into which tyrannical directors pour their fatuous fantasies.

'There is a blurring between what I am asked to do as an actor, what I can do and what I'm actually like. It has very little to do with me as a person,' Rickman insisted in a *Drama* magazine interview.

He is a star by instinct on screen. Colonel Brandon was disappointing precisely because there was too little on which to work. Rickman still needs to bring something of himself, to project his own personality with that supreme gift of which his friend Stephen Davis speaks.

Alan Rickman is constantly at odds with himself. Given his eloquence and his status as an actor's adviser, he seems to be strangely inhibited about putting his thoughts down in permanent form. That one essay on Jaques, when he played the old poseur in Adrian Noble's *As You Like It*, is his only published work.

There is another side to him that has never been fully developed: the enticing prospect of an all-singing, all-dancing Alan Rickman to recall his days in *Guys And Dolls* in repertory theatre at Leicester. The longing to be as free as Fred Astaire has not left him.

He won an award at the 1994 Montreal Film Festival for Mesmer, the Evening Standard Best Actor award in 1991, Best Supporting Actor at the 1992 BAFTAS and an Emmy and a Golden Globe for Rasputin. But if he's to be more than the Gossard Wonderbra of acting, Alan Rickman must take control of himself and emerge as a force in his own right – not a flashy foil.

It is relatively easy to hide behind the lead actor, to peer slyly out and be subversive and steal the show. What is harder is to carry the show on your own shoulders; and even he couldn't do that with Mesmer.

One returns to the question raised by Jules Wright, in some ways his fiercest but fondest critic. She saw in him the potential to be a leader, but she had to fight against prejudice from those who thought him merely reactive rather than proactive. For all his insistence on living in the real world and not forgetting his roots, there is something rarefied about Alan Rickman. He tries not to be precious, but there are times when he takes himself just a little too seriously. And friends saying 'He's too intellectual to be an actor' hardly help.

Certainly he feels self-conscious about being one of life's observers as opposed to participators; although he will bridle and insist, as he did with Michael Owen in the London Evening Standard in 1993, that he's always 'got stuck in'.

Well, you can't get stuck in if you don't bang on doors to ask people to vote for your girlfriend because you feel your face is too famous. Wear a pair of glasses or a wig.

Deep down, it's not that he's shallow as the joke goes but that he has an atavistic working-class distrust of anything that is not quite a proper job. One that doesn't leave you with chilblains or ink on your fingers or warts on the palm of your hand. As he once said, acting is 'mostly a great deal of fun'. Hence all the agonising as he endeavours to take everything seriously, tries to analyse what cannot be analysed, especially those strange instincts for performing that take over the body and which cannot be fully articulated.

The only time that Alan Rickman ever got his fingers filthy at work was when he took care to put dirt under his nails in order to play the Vicomte de Valmont. It was, as always with his artist's eye, an inspired detail. The man was, after all, nothing more than a filthy scoundrel, so he might as well look like the kind of rough trade that didn't wash properly.

Rickman is an endearing man, kindly and well intentioned, despite some spectacular sulks that make him seem like a bloody-minded, crotchety human being rather than some effete thespian godhead. Of the kind to be superstitiously touched in awe, as if he imparted some magic power. Alan Rickman made it when he was 42, so there's hope for the rest of us. If he sometimes sounds pompous, that goes with the territory in a looking-glass world.

There is no doubt that he felt damaged by the Riverside débâcle, which thrust him centre-stage in an impossible situation. He may recover and see fit to run his own theatre one day, but it would probably be a tiny studio one such as the Bush, which saved him from the emotional fall-out from the RSC. Meanwhile, he will go on making bigger and bigger movies, always holding something back and luring you further and further into the heart of his darkness or whatever else is on offer. He's a seductive actor.

They rightly call him standoffish, since he's so good at staging stand-offs. But he's also good at seducing, mainly the audience. He's always one step removed, as with all the great stars who play to their fans.

The world awaits Alan Rickman's first real screen love scene: but it will be conducted with the utmost decorum and erotic power, probably with all his and her clothes on. The Japanese would understand such a concept; indeed, they're a Rickman-friendly people. They understand his haughty elegance and delicate sense of style.

There may come a day when Rickman realises that not everything Dennis Potter wrote was wonderful; he may even try to do better himself. And *Mesmer* will disappear into the mists of history, like the man himself.

Whither Alan Rickman? Well, clearly age doesn't wither him nor custom stale his infinite variety of cinematic and theatrical moods. He has produced an impressively diverse portfolio so far, even if the public – being a perverse lot – warm to the criminal element most of all.

'Alan used to get very cross with me at the Bush,' Jenny Topper told *GQ* magazine in 1992, 'when I would suggest an actor for a part and ask his opinion. "Of course he can do it," he would say. "He's an actor, isn't he?" He honestly believes any actor should be able to play any role.' What Clifford Williams calls 'the fat Hamlet syndrome'.

On radio, he certainly did play many different roles: even the trademark voice has been different. On stage and television and film, he most emphatically has done so far. But always flavoured with that pungent aroma, Essence Of Rickman.

The difference between Claude Rains and Alan Rickman – both very feline, subtle actors of great finesse – is the latter's sexy electricity and physicality. There's an incandescence that a million light bulbs can't provide; an intensity, a magnetism that you can't fake. It's easier to simulate sincerity.

What he does with his power next could turn him into a greater star than Anthony Hopkins. It depends on how much Rickman really wants it.

The Faustian contract comes into the frame again as Alan broods about his next step, giving – as Peter Barnes puts it – the decision-making process the full Hamlet treatment. To be a star, or not to be a star? So long as he doesn't have to sell his soul to a damnable film. There have been very few flops in Rickman's movie career; but he's such a workaholic that he makes enough successes to cover up the failures.

If, however, he doesn't make time for more carefully-chosen, prestigious theatre work, then he will become the star turn in movies instead of the star. The man who is brought in to add a touch of class. It's a nice living, but it's a bit frivolous.

Alan Rickman has been the ultimate novelty act so far, a magician of the cinematic senses. There's still a hint of the dilettante about him; could he, like Anthony Hopkins, play Richard Nixon? Or do the crowds simply want him to provide the cabaret, to do one of his dazzling routines that brought the house down at Latymer Upper all those years ago?

Stephen Davis calls him an enigma, not least to his friends. He's also an enigma to himself, an honoured visiting alien in Hollywood who doesn't quite fit into the British theatrical scene either. But that's a problem facing all British actors who try to make it in America, given the embryonic nature of the film industry over here. They become strangers in their own land.

Alan Rickman has become best known for being the Autolycus of the acting trade, the picker and stealer, the grand larcenist *par excellence*.

Now he needs to make his indecision less final in order to march triumphantly on to the next stage.

CHRONOLOGY OF ALAN RICKMAN'S THEATRE, TELEVISION, RADIO AND FILM

THEATRE: Seasons in rep (from 1974–78) at Library Theatre Manchester (1974); Haymarket and Phoenix Theatre Leicester (1975); Crucible Theatre Sheffield (1976–77); Birmingham Rep Theatre and Bristol Old Vic (1976–78).

As actor: *The Devil Is An Ass* and *Measure For Measure* (Birmingham, touring to Edinburgh Festival and National Theatre), 1976–77; *The Tempest, Captain Swing, Love's Labours Lost* and *Antony And Cleopatra* (RSC), 1978–79; *Antonio* (Nottingham Playhouse), 1979; *Fears And Miseries Of The Third Reich* (Glasgow Citizens' Theatre), 1979–80; *The Summer Party* (Crucible Sheffield), 1980; *The Devil Himself* (Lyric Studio Hammersmith), 1980; *Commitments* (Bush Theatre), 1980; *Philadelphia Story* (Oxford Playhouse), 1981; *The Seagull* (Royal Court), 1981; *Brothers Karamazov* (Edinburgh Festival and USSR), 1981; *The Last Elephant* (Bush Theatre), 1981; *Bad Language* (Hampstead Theatre Club), 1983; *The Grass Widow* (Royal Court), 1983; *The Lucky Chance* (Royal Court), 1984; *As You Like It, Troilus And Cressida, Les Liaisons Dangereuses, Mephisto* (RSC), 1985–86; *Les Liaisons Dangereuses* (West End and Broadway), 1986–87; *Tango At The End Of Winter* (Edinburgh and West End), 1991; *Hamlet* (Riverside Studios and British tour), 1992.

As director: *Desperately Yours* (New York), 1980; *Other Worlds* (assistant director, Royal Court), 1983; *Live Wax* (Edinburgh Festival), 1986; *Wax Acts* (West End and tour), 1992; *The Winter Guest* (West Yorkshire Playhouse and Almeida Theatre), 1995; *Antony And Cleopatra* (Royal National Theatre), 1998; *Private Lives* (West End and Broadway), 2001 and 2002.

TELEVISION: *Romeo And Juliet* (BBC), 1978; *Thérèse Raquin* (BBC), 1979; *Barchester Chronicles* (BBC), 1982; *Busted* (BBC), 1982; *Pity In History* (BBC), 1984; *Benefactors* (BBC), 1989; *Revolutionary Witness* (BBC), 1989; *Spirit Of Man* (BBC), 1989; *Fallen*

Angels, 1993; *Rasputin* (HBO), 1995; *Victoria Wood With All The Trimmings* (BBC), 2000; *Play* (Channel 4), 2000.

RADIO: *The Dutch Courtesan, Actors, Polly, Rope, Manchester Enthusiasts, Gridlock, A Trick To Catch The Old One, Billy and Me, A Good Man In Africa, That Man Bracken, Blood Wedding, The Seagull, The Magic Of My Youth.*

FILMS: *Die Hard*, 1988; *The January Man*, 1989; *Quigley Down Under*, 1990; *Truly Madly Deeply*, 1991; *Closetland*, 1991; *Close My Eyes*, 1991; *Robin Hood: Prince Of Thieves*, 1991; *Bob Roberts*, 1992; *Fallen Angels*, 1993; *Mesmer*, 1993; *An Awfully Big Adventure*, 1994; *Sense And Sensibility*, 1995; *Michael Collins*, 1995; *Rasputin*, 1995, *The Winter Guest* (as director), 1997; *Lumière And Company*, 1995; *Dark Harbor*, 1997; *Judas Kiss*, 1997; *Dogma*, 1998; *Galaxy Quest*, 1999; *Blow Dry*, 1999; *The Search For John Gissing*, 2000; *Harry Potter And The Philosopher's Stone*, 2001; *Standing Room Only*, 2002; *Harry Potter And The Chamber Of Secrets*, 2002.

INDEX